FUNDAMENTALS OF THE FAITH

Essays in Christian Apologetics

PETER KREEFT

FUNDAMENTALS OF THE FAITH

Essays in Christian Apologetics

IGNATIUS PRESS   SAN FRANCISCO

Cover by Riz Boncan Marsella

With ecclesiastical approval
(The granting of the *Imprimatur* does not imply
the acceptance of the theological opinions of the author.)
© 1988 Ignatius Press, San Francisco
All rights reserved
ISBN 0-89870-202-X
Library of Congress catalogue number 88–81277
Printed in the United States of America

Contents

II
CODE: FUNDAMENTALS OF CHRISTIAN LIVING

III

CULT: FUNDAMENTALS OF CHRISTIAN COMMUNITY

A. The Church

B. The Churches: Protestant and Catholic

Introduction

This book of bite-sized (or morning-coffee-cup-sized) little essays is not put forth as a complete theological system but as reconnoiterings, forays into key areas of the battlefield in the greatest war ever fought, the war for the minds and souls of human beings, the images of God. They do not intend to be bold, original, creative, groundbreaking landmarks or anything of that kind, but only clear and to-the-point restatements of the ancient and orthodox Faith of the Christian Church. The minds of very many young Christians today have never heard about this Faith, though they think they have. Because their teachers have made Esau's exchange, sold their birthright for a mess of pottage, this old stuff will doubtless appear as radically new and original to many readers. Those are precisely the ones I hope to reach, on both sides of the battlefield: both believers (to arm them with some weapons of the mind) and unbelievers (to engage in a loving duel with them). As Abraham Lincoln said, the only way truly to defeat your enemy is to make him your friend.

Each of these essays except the last is a revision or enlargement of an article that appeared in the *National Catholic Register.* They were written for Catholics by a Catholic. But I believe that nearly everything I say in the first two-thirds of the book will be found by the orthodox Protestant reader to express his faith as well: that solid and substantial core of faith that C. S. Lewis called "mere Christianity".

Like every religion, this faith has three aspects, corresponding to the three parts of the soul and filling the innate needs of all three parts. First, every religion has some *beliefs,* whether expressed in creeds or not, something for the intellect to know. Second, every religion has some *duty* or deed, some practice or program, some moral or ethical code, something for the will to choose. Finally, every religion has some *liturgy,* some worship, some "church",

9

something for the body and the concrete imagination and the aesthetic sense to work at. Creed, code, and cult—words, works, and worship—are useful in outlining any religious faith, including the Catholic Faith of Christians.

Within the first division, creed, we can distinguish those things that can be known by human reason unaided by divine revelation (Aquinas called these the "preambles to faith") and those things that can be known only because God has revealed them to us. Roughly, but not exactly, these correspond to (1) apologetics and natural theology and (2) creeds and revealed theology.

Within the second division, code, we can distinguish religious virtues and religious life, or "spirituality". It is not an exact division, but it corresponds roughly to the three theological virtues on the one hand and the Lord's Prayer on the other (which, as Aquinas pointed out, contains everything we need to know about how to pray, how to commune and communicate with God, i.e., the spiritual life).

Finally, within the third division, cult, we distinguish the four essential marks of the Church and the differences between Protestant and Catholic churches.

PART ONE

CREED: FUNDAMENTALS OF CHRISTIAN BELIEF

A. FUNDAMENTALS
OF CHRISTIAN APOLOGETICS

1

What's the Reason for
Giving Reasons for Faith?

Apologetic about apologetics—that seems to be the prevailing attitude of many professors, priests, ministers, and theologians today. Seldom in the history of Christendom has the very enterprise of apologetics been under attack as it is today. Why?

Apologetics is essentially the enterprise of trying to win men and women for Christ by obeying Scripture's own command to "be ready to give a reason for the hope that is in you" (1 Pet 3:15). Yet the "experts" in religious education sometimes attack this traditional (their code word: outdated) concept more readily than they attack the errors of unbelief. We are living through the incredible situation of teachers in the Church not attacking the errors of the world but attacking the truths of the faith, and attacking the very idea of attacking the errors of the world—as if the only error were the belief that there are errors, and as if the only idea to be refuted were the idea that some ideas are to be refuted.

This is largely the attitude of most of the religious Left, who don't do apologetics because they are too busy giving the Faith away to defend the little they have left. But many of the religious Right, or conservatives, also do not do apologetics anymore, or no longer do it effectively, because many conservatives belong to one or more of three groups. First, there are those who do not argue because they fear that human reason is a Leftist tool, something invented in pagan Athens, or in pagan Boston—the Athens of

America—probably at Harvard. These people are far more prevalent among Protestant fundamentalists than among Catholics. Second, there are those who argue, but for a narrow political agenda. They glue the Faith as tightly to capitalism, militarism, anticommunism, and Americanism as the Left glues it to socialism, pacifism, and anti-Americanism. Thus they buy into the very politicization of the Faith that is the root error of their opponents. Third, there are the pre-Vatican II nostalgia buffs among Catholics and high Anglicans, who secretly hope the whole Council was an elaborate plot of the media that never really happened. These people argue, all right, but they often argue so arrogantly and joylessly that they win no one over, or else so abstractly and scholastically that only a philosopher would be interested.

On the other side of the fence, it's hard to find unbelievers who are willing to argue their case today either. Most ignore rather than try to refute the Faith. Most unbelievers today are relativists, and if you don't believe in objective truth, you won't believe in arguing, except as exercise, like jogging. It won't get you anywhere. That's why you have probably never once in your life heard a real, genuine debate here in freedom-of-thought-loving and freedom-of-speech-loving America. The only thing a debate can be to a relativist is a Ping-Pong match of IQs, or a wild goose chase without the goose of truth.

But when we turn from the teachers to the students, from the small and arrogant oligarchy of opinion molders and "experts" who tell us what we really want, to the ordinary person in the pew, at the desk, or on the street, we find no less interest and no less hunger for reasons today than ever; for the human mind was designed by God, not by John Dewey or Carl Rogers. Jesus the Warm Fuzzy just doesn't have the appeal of Jesus the Eternal Logos. When advertising hype sells mountains of pablum, pablum does not thereby become steak, and people still hunger for "strong meat".

Apologetics is necessary in any age (1) because it is commanded in Scripture and (2) because of the needs of the unchanging human heart. People still want reasons because they still have heads. It is as simple as that. Especially young people need apologetics today, to defend their minds and their faith against the subtle and incessant propaganda with which a secular environment, especially the media establishment, barrages them.

But they are getting none of it, whether in catechism classes or in religious schools (with a few notable exceptions). My own college, the nation's second largest Catholic university—and, I think, in most ways a very fine one—has a theology department that offers about fifty different courses each year; but for over a decade not one of them has been in apologetics.

One reason students are not getting reasons to defend the Faith is that they are not getting the Faith to defend. Fewer than 5 percent of my Catholic-educated students can explain why it is not a contradiction to call God both one and three, or Christ both divine and human. They have never even heard of the distinction between person and nature. Many are astonished at the very idea of giving proofs for the existence of God or for the immortality of the soul. Most shocking of all, well over three-quarters of all the "educated" Catholic college students I have taught do not know, after twelve years of catechism classes, how to get to heaven! Their answer to that question is usually something like "be sincere" or "try your best" or "don't hurt people" or "work for peace" or "have a nice day" or some such trumpet blast. They rarely even mention Jesus when asked that question. Why should they? Warm fuzzies are not stronger than death.

Starved for Reasons

Yet the need remains. They are starved for good reasons. Today's generation needs apologetics more, not less, than previous generations because their faith is constantly challenged by their culture, covertly as well as overtly, and they need to be able to unmask and refute the hidden premises of the covert attacks as well as to defend their faith against the overt attacks. Alas, they have not been taught to do either.

They are victims of our culture's schizoid division between the scientific, empirical mentality and what used to be called the counterculture, the irrational, subjective mentality. On the one hand, they are taught the scientific method when dealing with matters of fact, and, on the other hand, they are taught some form of relativism and subjectivism, such as values clarification, when dealing with moral and religious questions, which they hardly ever dream can also be matters of fact. They do not know that there are other methods of finding the truth, such as honest, straightforward logical reasoning.

They are less aware than previous generations of what good reasons are, for the very word *reason* has drastically shrunk in meaning in modern philosophy. One of the most radical changes in the history of thought can be traced by noting the changes in the meaning of the word *reason* from Aquinas to Ockham, from Ockham to Descartes, from Descartes to Kant, and from Kant to positivism, existentialism, and their heirs. Positivism and existentialism are no longer as popular as they were earlier in this century, but their essential mind-set has taken root securely in our culture, especially the false premise common to both philosophies, namely that reason equals science.

From Socrates through Aquinas, reason meant primarily the understanding of the nature of reality, the knowledge of the essences of things. Ockham denied real universal essences with his nominalism. Descartes narrowed reason to calculation with his new Method. Kant narrowed it further with his "Copernican Revolution" to the mind's subjective imposition of its own categories onto things. Finally, positivism reduced it to clarifying scientific language about things empirically verifiable. The resulting picture of man is that of a computer-equipped animal. A computer-equipped animal does not do apologetics. A computer-equipped animal only balances his checkbook and watches pornographic movies.

A New Apologetic?

Do we need a new apologetic for our new age? Yes and no. Yes, new diseases need new medicines, new ignorances need new remedial courses. But no, the content of the remedial courses is not new, for neither the laws of logic nor the facts about God have changed.

A new apologetic? Yes, because apologetics is a dialogue between two people, and the speaker should always be aware of how his listener's mind has changed if he is to make contact. To shoot a pheasant you must follow it in your rifle sights. But no, because what we say is dictated not by the world but by the truth. We "read not the times but read the eternities" to find that. The target moves, but the bullets remain the same: eternal truth and eternal love.

Do we need a new apologetic? Yes, because apologetics is love, and the lover must chase and pursue the beloved, like the Hound of Heaven, down the labyrinthine ways. No, because truth does not change like underwear or traffic lights or the editorial policies of *Pravda*.

Seven Practical Tools

Here are seven pieces of practical advice for those who do apologetics—which ought to be every Christian, in one way or another. These seven points are probably not the seven most important things one could say on the topic, but they are the things I have learned in my own experience.

First, don't be apologetic. Don't be afraid to be unpopular. You can never make a good impression on other people until you stop worrying about making a good impression. As Mother Teresa says, "God did not call us to be successful but to be faithful." A recent poll of Catholic teenagers revealed that their primary dissatisfaction with priests and nuns was that they tried too hard to be "with it", "relevant", or "cool". The primary thing the teenagers desired but were not receiving from their Church, the thing they asked for most of all, was—get this—"a high and heroic ideal". Teenagers! The Church's future.

Our culture and its "experts" to the contrary notwithstanding, these kids want truth and holiness. They don't want a wimpy Church or a wimpy Christ. Jesus never made it easy to follow him—and thousands flocked to him. Religious educators who claim to be doing his work bend over backward to make it easy to follow him—and the result is empty churches, empty souls, and empty lives. These kids don't want relevance; they want Jesus. They don't want a thirteenth-century Jesus or a sixteenth-century Jesus or a twentieth-century Jesus. They want Jesus. They want his fire, the fire that burned in the hearts of the disciples on the road to Emmaus. They want the gospel of the burning heart. They want the power of God, a power that doesn't have to shout but also doesn't have to shuffle.

A second suggestion is closely connected to the first: don't avoid hard questions. If you do, the message that will come across is that Christianity is a nice, soft thing but not a hard, real thing with a shape of its own, with hard surfaces. You needn't push the hard questions, but don't avoid them either. When they come up, look them squarely in the face.

By the hard questions I do not mean only the hard questions about Christian doctrine, like hell and Jesus' claim to be the only Savior (though these are very important questions too and often stand in the way of someone's conversion and must therefore be squarely addressed). But the hardest questions of all today are, I think, moral questions. Probably they are in any day, for it is always easier to change our minds than to change our lives. And almost every moral question that the world answers today very differently from the Church has to do with sex, the teenager's primary concern. Premarital intercourse, fidelity versus adultery, abortion, contraception, homosexuality, divorce—the most popular objections to Christian morality are all against the Christian view of sex. No one can ignore this; it is not a specialty.

We must tell the young the high and heroic ideal of Christian love, of marriage and chastity, of sex as a beautiful and holy and faithful sacrament of lifelong commitment and total self-giving. But when is the last time you heard a sermon on any of these topics? Perhaps you should gently ask your pastor to pastor you in these perilous places. Perhaps it's time for the sheep to rise up and wake up their shepherds. The wolves have already carried many of them away.

A third suggestion is that much of the work of the apologist in modern culture must be preevangelistic. The ground needs to be cleared and tilled before the seeds of the gospel can take root. The typically modern mind has two enormous rocks in it that prevent the growth of good seed: it does not believe in objective truth and it does not believe in objective values. When the gospel is preached to this mind, its response is likely to be not "What you say is not true", but rather "What you say may be true for you but it is not true for me; what right do you have to impose your personal beliefs on me?" And when you talk about Christian morality, it almost always seems to modern people like a cafeteria choice, like an optional aisle in the supermarket of lifestyles, like a choice of style in clothing or cars. They have never heard the words "thus saith the Lord".

We must say these words, not threateningly or accusingly but not embarrassedly either, for they are the words we have been entrusted with. We are not the writers or rewriters, only the mail carriers. And our master had some rather harsh words for the unfaithful steward who hid his master's wealth in the ground, and even harsher words about those who cause his little ones to stumble—something about millstones.

Remember that the purpose of apologetics is not just to win the head but to win the heart through the head. What is aimed at is not just belief but faith; and, according to the New Testament, repentance must go with faith. Repent and believe—that is the kerygma, the proclamation, the essential formula. But repentance must be to God, not to you; and privately, interiorly. Your work is not to convert but to prepare. When the time is ready, you withdraw, shyly (for love is always shy), and let God take over.

Your work is only to strew your apologetic coat before the humble donkey of repentance and faith, which carries the Lord into the holy city of the student's soul.

Many have never heard the good news that there is such a thing as objective truth and an absolute right and wrong. If only they catch something of the joy and love in us when we tell them this good news, they will see that it is good news indeed. They usually see it neither as good nor as news.

The saints attracted young people. Jesus attracted young people. The pope attracts young people. Mother Teresa attracts young people. The growing movements in the Church today are attracting young people. Biblical orthodoxy is attracting young people. Orthodox Judaism is attracting young people. Even Islamic fundamentalism is attracting young people. The reason is plain: the young heart rejoices when it hears the news that, beyond modern hope, Truth exists. The thing a thousand bland and joyless voices from every corner of our dying culture have abandoned as mere myth, the beloved of the human spirit, Truth with a capital T, really exists!

This brings me to my fourth point: you must be passionately in love with Truth yourself and therefore totally honest. You can't give what you don't have; therefore the love of Truth can never be taught except by a lover of Truth. Not just a respecter of Truth, not even just a believer in Truth, but a lover of Truth is needed for effective apologetics. That is the great secret of every great classic of Christian apologetics: Augustine's *Confessions,* Aquinas' *Summa,* Pascal's *Pensées,* and, in our own day, the writings of a less original philosopher but the most effective apologist of the twentieth century, C. S. Lewis.

A fifth point is the simplest practical tool I have ever found for effective apologetics. It is amazing what a difference it makes. It is simply to listen. Let the teacher listen to the learner. Let him teach you before you teach him. Use this essential ingredient of the Socratic method not as a gimmick but sincerely: exchange places, let the teacher learn from the student first. Be really interested in his opinions, his feelings, his experiences, his ideas, his reasons, his soul. Question him, not accusingly but to help him become clearer to himself.

The reason listening works is twofold. First, truth will out. Upon investigation, upon exposure to the light of day, falsehood will show itself. You don't have to squash the bugs of error with a hammer, just get them out from under the rock where they are hiding, and they will die in the sun.

Second, only listeners are listened to. Only after your student sees that you care about him and his ideas will he really care about yours. Only after you give him two of your life's most precious commodities, attention and time, your life's time, will he give you his attention and his time.

A sixth point is the apologetic equivalent of "fear God and keep your powder dry". It is the answer to the question: How much is up to God and how much is up to us? The answer is that 100 percent is up to God and 100 percent is up to us. As in marriage, it's not a 50-50 proposition but a 100-100 proposition.

Two points must be kept in mind without watering either one down. On the one hand, "unless the Lord build the house, they labor in vain who build it." God does not help us to do it, God does it. We are his arms and legs and feet and mouths. On the other hand, that means activity, not passivity, for although (as Saint Teresa said so simply) "it's all grace", grace redeems nature to be nature, including natural reason. It's a safe bet that no cheap or tacky tables ever came out of a certain carpenter's shop in Nazareth, and no cheap or tacky arguments should come out of our apologetics either. We must pour our whole soul into this job, for apologetics is not a job, it is the courtship of souls.

How much can apologetics do? Much. If both blades of the psychic scissors, head and heart, are sharp, we can cut through tons of modern paper. And if we begin our thinking with loving and our arguing with praying, if we bend our knees before we bend our tongue, then when we tell them of Christ, we will also be showing them Christ.

More specifically, what can logical argument itself do? Though it cannot prove all the truths of the Faith, it can answer all objections to it. If you think this is an exaggerated claim, I will prove it. God is the source of all truth. All truth is God's truth. And God can never contradict himself. Therefore, since nature and natural reason are also God's invention, God's revelation, it necessarily follows that nothing in the Faith revealed by God through Scripture and Church can ever contradict anything in the truths revealed through nature and natural reason. When philosophy or science seem to contradict Christian doctrine, you can be sure there is a fallacy somewhere. You can be sure that is not reason speaking but a misuse of reason. And a rational fallacy can be refuted rationally. Therefore it is possible to answer every single objection anyone ever invents against any of the doctrines of the Faith and to do so by reason alone.

That terribly optimistic-sounding consequence logically follows from the premise that all truth is God's truth. It is not just my idea; it was explicitly taught by Saint Thomas Aquinas in the *Summa Contra Gentiles,* book I, chapter 8. It was the foundation of his whole life's work of showing the synthesis, the compatibility, of reason and faith. Our apologetics is not as effective as his partly because we are not as clear and confident in our belief in that foundation. We should never be afraid to argue with an unbeliever, no matter how much more intelligent or better educated he may be, for we have something on our side far stronger than intelligence and education: the end and point of all intelligence and education, Truth. And where Truth is, God is.

And we can do more than just refute objections. We can, if not prove, at least show, explain, clarify, and present the Faith in its attractive power, clarity, depth, and meaning. We must remember that reason is not merely or even primarily a matter of proving but a means of knowing, or mental seeing. People are often suspicious of proofs, of calculation and cleverness, but if they catch something of the glorious vision, they will fall in love with it. Like the Greeks who came to Philip, their hope—the hope we must fulfill—is this: "We would see Jesus."

My seventh and last point is to be optimistic, not pessimistic; offensive, not defensive. In any age we have reason to be confident but especially in the present age because the tide is turning. Secularism is dying. The modern world is dying. The new Roman Empire is dying. The new world order of secular, scientific humanism is dying. And just as the Church brought us through the earlier Dark Ages, so she will bring us through any new dark age that may loom on our horizon, whether totalitarian, nuclear, or hedonistic brave new world. The Church is no longer the embattled establishment trying desperately to hold on. The Church today is the revolutionaries, the guerillas, enlisting freedom fighters for her wild and wonderful cause. We orthodox Christians are the young today; the Modernists are the old. We are not trying to save a tired, old Church; we are trying to save a tired, old world and make it young with the youth of Christ's Church. Our message is radically new in every age. The present age has not heard it and rejected it; it has not really heard it. That is why we must say anew the old things in this book.

2

Reasons to Believe:
The Argument from Design

Can you prove that God exists? Before we answer this question, we must distinguish five questions that are often confused. First, there is the question of whether something *exists* or not. A thing can exist whether we know it or not.

Second, there is the question of whether we *know* it exists. (To answer this question affirmatively is to presuppose that the first question is answered affirmatively, of course; though a thing can exist without our knowing it, we cannot know it exists unless it exists.)

Third, there is the question of whether we have a *reason* for our knowledge. We can know some things without being able to lead others to that knowledge by reasons. Many Christians think God's existence is like that.

Fourth, there is the question of whether this reason, if it exists, amounts to a *proof*. Most reasons do not. Most of the reasons we give for what we believe amount to probabilities, not proofs. For instance, the building you sit in may collapse in one minute, but the reliability of the contractor and the construction materials is a good reason for thinking that very improbable.

Fifth, if there is a proof, is it a *scientific* proof, a proof by the scientific method, i.e., by experiment, observation, and measurement? Philosophical proofs can be good proofs, but they do not have to be scientific proofs.

I believe we can answer yes to the first four of these questions about the existence of God but not to the fifth. God exists, we can know that, we can give reasons, and those reasons amount to proof, but not scientific proof, except in an unusually broad sense.

There are many arguments for God's existence, but most of them have the same logical structure, which is the basic structure

of any deductive argument. First, there is a major premise, or
general principle. Then, a minor premise states some particular
data in our experience that come under that principle. Finally, the
conclusion follows from applying the general principle to the
particular case.

In each case the conclusion is that God exists, but the premises of
the different arguments are different. The arguments are like
roads, from different starting points, all aiming at the same goal of
God. In subsequent essays we will explore the arguments from
cause and effect, from conscience, from history, and from Pascal's
Wager. This essay explores the argument from design.

The argument starts with the major premise that where there is
design, there must be a designer. The minor premise is the
existence of design throughout the universe. The conclusion is that
there must be a universal designer.

Why must we believe the major premise, that all design implies
a designer? Because everyone admits this principle in practice. For
instance, suppose you came upon a deserted island and found
"S.O.S." written in the sand on the beach. You would not think
the wind or the waves had written it by mere chance but that
someone had been there, someone intelligent enough to design and
write the message. If you found a stone hut on the island with
windows, doors, and a fireplace, you would not think a hurricane
had piled up the stones that way by chance. You immediately infer
a designer when you see design.

When the first moon rocket took off from Cape Canaveral, two
U.S. scientists stood watching it, side by side. One was a believer,
the other an unbeliever. The believer said, "Isn't it wonderful that
our rocket is going to hit the moon by chance?" The unbeliever
objected, "What do you mean, chance? We put millions of man-
hours of design into that rocket." "Oh," said the believer, "you
don't think chance is a good explanation for the rocket? Then why
do you think it's a good explanation for the universe? There's
much more design in a universe than in a rocket. We can design a
rocket, but we couldn't design a whole universe. I wonder who
can?" Later that day the two were strolling down a street and

passed an antique store. The atheist admired a picture in the window and asked, "I wonder who painted that picture?" "No one," joked the believer; "it just happened by chance."

Is it possible that design happens by chance without a designer? There is perhaps one chance in a trillion that "S.O.S." could be written in the sand by the wind. But who would use a one-in-a-trillion explanation? Someone once said that if you sat a million monkeys at a million typewriters for a million years, one of them would eventually type out all of *Hamlet* by chance. But when we find the text of *Hamlet,* we don't wonder whether it came from chance and monkeys. Why then does the atheist use that incredibly improbable explanation for the universe? Clearly, because it is his only chance of remaining an atheist. At this point we need a psychological explanation of the atheist rather than a logical explanation of the universe. We have a logical explanation of the universe, but the atheist does not like it. It's called God.

There is one especially strong version of the argument from design that hits close to home because it's about the design of the very thing we use to think about design: our brains. The human brain is the most complex piece of design in the known universe. In many ways it is like a computer. Now just suppose there were a computer that was programmed only by chance. For instance, suppose you were in a plane and the public-address system announced that there was no pilot, but the plane was being flown by a computer that had been programmed by a random fall of hailstones on its keyboard or by a baseball player in spiked shoes dancing on computer cards. How much confidence would you have in that plane? But if our brain computer has no cosmic intelligence behind the heredity and environment that program it, why should we trust it when it tells us about anything, even about the brain?

Another specially strong aspect of the design argument is the so-called anthropic principle, according to which the universe seems to have been specially designed from the beginning for human life to evolve. If the temperature of the primal fireball that resulted from the Big Bang some fifteen to twenty billion years ago, which was the beginning of our universe, had been a trillionth of a degree colder or hotter, the carbon molecule that is the foundation of all organic life could never have developed. The number of possible universes is trillions of trillions; only one of them could support human life: this one. Sounds suspiciously like a plot. If the cosmic rays had bombarded the primordial slime at a slightly different angle or time or intensity, the hemoglobin molecule, necessary for all warm-blooded animals, could never have evolved. The chance of this molecule's evolving is something like one in a trillion trillion. Add together each of the chances and you have something far more unbelievable than a million monkeys writing *Hamlet*.

There are relatively few atheists among neurologists and brain surgeons and among astrophysicists, but many among psychologists, sociologists, and historians. The reason seems obvious: the first study divine design, the second study human undesign.

But doesn't evolution explain everything without a divine Designer? Just the opposite; evolution is a beautiful example of design, a great clue to God. There is very good scientific evidence for the evolving, ordered appearance of species, from simple to complex. But there is no scientific proof of natural selection as the mechanism of evolution, Natural selection "explains" the emergence of higher forms without intelligent design by the survival-of-the-fittest principle. But this is sheer theory. There is no evidence that abstract, theoretical thinking or altruistic love make it easier for man to survive. How did they evolve then?

Furthermore, could the design that obviously now exists in man and in the human brain come from something with less or no design? Such an explanation violates the principle of causality, which states that you can't get more in the effect than you had in the cause. If there is intelligence in the effect (man), there must be intelligence in the cause. But a universe ruled by blind chance has no intelligence. Therefore there must be a cause for human intelligence that transcends the universe: a mind behind the physical universe. (Most great scientists have believed in such a mind, by the way, even those who did not accept any revealed religion.)

How much does this argument prove? Not all that the Christian means by God, of course—no argument can do that. But it proves a pretty thick slice of God: some designing intelligence great enough to account for all the design in the universe and the human mind. If that's not God, what is it? Steven Spielberg?

3
Reasons to Believe:
The First-Cause Argument

The most famous of all arguments for the existence of God are the "five ways" of Saint Thomas Aquinas. One of the five ways, the fifth, is the argument from design, which we looked at in the last essay. The other four are versions of the first-cause argument, which we explore here.

The argument is basically very simple, natural, intuitive, and commonsensical. We have to become complex and clever in order to doubt or dispute it. It is based on an instinct of mind that we all share: the instinct that says everything needs an explanation. Nothing just is without a reason why it is. Everything that is has some adequate or sufficient reason why it is.

Philosophers call this the Principle of Sufficient Reason. We use it every day, in common sense and in science as well as in philosophy and theology. If we saw a rabbit suddenly appear on an empty table, we would not blandly say, "Hi, rabbit. You came from nowhere, didn't you?" No, we would look for a cause, assuming there has to be one. Did the rabbit fall from the ceiling? Did a magician put it there when we weren't looking? If there seems to be no physical cause, we look for a psychological cause: perhaps someone hypnotized us. As a last resort, we look for a supernatural cause, a miracle. But there must be some cause. We never deny the Principle of Sufficient Reason itself. No one believes the Pop Theory: that things just pop into existence for no reason at all. Perhaps we will never *find* the cause, but there must *be* a cause for everything that comes into existence.

Now the whole universe is a vast, interlocking chain of things that come into existence. Each of these things must therefore have a cause. My parents caused me, my grandparents caused them, et cetera. But it is not that simple. I would not be here without billions of causes, from the Big Bang through the cooling of the galaxies and the evolution of the protein molecule to the marriages of my ancestors. The universe is a vast and complex chain of causes.

But does the universe as a whole have a cause? Is there a first cause, an uncaused cause, a transcendent cause of the whole chain of causes? If not, then there is an infinite regress of causes, with no first link in the great cosmic chain. If so, then there is an eternal, necessary, independent, self-explanatory being with nothing above it, before it, or supporting it. It would have to explain itself as well as everything else, for if it needed something else as its explanation, its reason, its cause, then it would not be the first and uncaused cause. Such a being would have to be God, of course. If we can prove there is such a first cause, we will have proved there is a God.

Why must there be a first cause? Because if there isn't, then the whole universe is unexplained, and we have violated our Principle of Sufficient Reason for everything. If there is no first cause, each particular thing in the universe is explained in the short run, or proximately, by some other thing, but nothing is explained in the long run, or ultimately, and the universe as a whole is not explained. Everyone and everything says in turn, "Don't look to me for the final explanation. I'm just an instrument. Something else caused me." If that's all there is, then we have an endless passing of the buck. God is the one who says, "The buck stops here."

If there is no first cause, then the universe is like a great chain with many links; each link is held up by the link above it, but the whole chain is held up by nothing. If there is no first cause, then the universe is like a railroad train moving without an engine. Each car's motion is explained proximately by the motion of the car in front of it: the caboose moves because the boxcar pulls it, the boxcar moves because the cattle car pulls it, et cetera. But there is no engine to pull the first car and the whole train. That would be impossible, of course. But that is what the universe is like if there is no first cause: impossible.

Here is one more analogy. Suppose I tell you there is a book that explains everything you want explained. You want that book very much. You ask me whether I have it. I say no, I have to get it from my wife. Does she have it? No, she has to get it from a neighbor. Does he have it? No, he has to get it from his teacher, who has to get it . . . et cetera, et cetera, ad infinitum. No one actually has the book. In that case, you will never get it. However long or short the chain of book borrowers may be, you will get the book only if someone actually has it and does not have to borrow it. Well, existence is like that book. Existence is handed down the chain of causes, from cause to effect. If there is no first cause, no being who is eternal and self-sufficient, no being who has existence by his own nature and does not have to borrow it from someone else, then the gift of existence can never be passed down the chain to others, and no one will ever get it. But we did get it. We exist. We got the gift of existence from our causes, down the chain, and so did every actual being in the universe, from atoms to archangels. Therefore there must be a first cause of existence, a God.

In more abstract philosophical language, the proof goes this way. Every being that exists either exists by itself, by its own essence or nature, or it does not exist by itself. If it exists by its own essence, then it exists necessarily and eternally, and explains itself. It cannot not exist, as a triangle cannot not have three sides. If, on the other hand, a being exists but not by its own essence, then it needs a cause, a reason outside itself for its existence. Because it does not explain itself, something else must explain it. Beings whose essence does not contain the reason for their existence, beings that need causes, are called contingent, or dependent, beings. A being whose essence is to exist is called a necessary being. The universe contains only contingent beings. God would be the only necessary being—if God existed. Does he? Does a necessary being exist? Here is the proof that it does. Dependent beings cannot cause themselves. They are dependent on their causes. If there is no independent being, then the whole chain of dependent beings is dependent on nothing and could not exist. But they do exist. Therefore there is an independent being.

Saint Thomas has four versions of this basic argument. First, he argues that the chain of movers must have a first mover because nothing can move itself. (Moving here refers to any kind of change, not just change of place.) If the whole chain of moving things had no first mover, it could not now be moving, as it is. If there were an infinite regress of movers with no first mover, no motion could ever begin, and if it never began, it could not go on and exist now. But it does go on, it does exist now. Therefore it began, and therefore there is a first mover.

Second, he expands the proof from proving a cause of motion to proving a cause of existence, or efficient cause. He argues that if there were no first efficient cause, or cause of the universe's coming into being, then there could be no second causes because second causes (i.e., caused causes) are dependent on (i.e., caused by) a first cause (i.e., an uncaused cause). But there are second causes all around us. Therefore there must be a first cause.

Third, he argues that if there were no eternal, necessary, and immortal being, if everything had a possibility of not being, of ceasing to be, then eventually this possibility of ceasing to be would be realized for everything. In other words, if everything could die, then, given infinite time, everything would eventually die. But in that case nothing could start up again. We would have universal death, for a being that has ceased to exist cannot cause itself or anything else to begin to exist again. And if there is no God, then there must have been infinite time, the universe must have been here always, with no beginning, no first cause. But this universal death has not happened; things do exist! Therefore there must be a necessary being that cannot not be, cannot possibly cease to be. That is a description of God.

Fourth, there must also be a first cause of perfection or goodness or value. We rank things as more or less perfect or good or valuable. Unless this ranking is false and meaningless, unless souls don't really have any more perfection than slugs, there must be a real standard of perfection to make such a hierarchy possible, for a thing is ranked higher on the hierarchy of perfection only insofar as it is closer to the standard, the ideal, the most perfect. Unless there is a most-perfect being to be that real standard of perfection, all our value judgments are meaningless and impossible. Such a most-perfect being, or real ideal standard of perfection, is another description of God.

There is a single common logical structure to all four proofs. Instead of proving God directly, they prove him indirectly, by refuting atheism. Either there is a first cause or not. The proofs look at "not" and refute it, leaving the only other possibility, that God is.

Each of the four ways makes the same point for four different kinds of cause: first, cause of motion; second, cause of a beginning to existence; third, cause of present existence; and fourth, cause of goodness or value. The common point is that if there were no first cause, there could be no second causes, and there are second causes (moved movers, caused causers, dependent and mortal beings, and less-than-wholly-perfect beings). Therefore there must be a first cause of motion, beginning, existence, and perfection.

How can anyone squirm out of this tight logic? Here are four ways in which different philosophers try. First, many say the proofs don't prove God but only some vague first cause or other. "God of Abraham, Isaac, and Jacob, not the God of philosophers and scholars", cries Pascal, who was a passionate Christian but did not believe you could logically prove God's existence. It is true that the proofs do not prove everything the Christian means by God, but they do prove a transcendent, eternal, uncaused, immortal, self-existing, independent, all-perfect being. That certainly sounds more like God than like Superman! It's a pretty thick slice of God, at any rate—much too much for any atheist to digest.

Second, some philosophers, like Hume, say that the concept of cause is ambiguous and not applicable beyond the physical universe to God. How dare we use the same term for what clouds do to rain, what parents do to children, what authors do to books, and what God does to the universe? The answer is that the concept of cause is analogical—that is, it differs somewhat but not completely from one example to another. Human fatherhood is *like* divine fatherhood, and physical causality is like divine causality. The way an author conceives a book in his mind is not exactly the same as the way a woman conceives a baby in her body either, but we call both causes. (In fact, we also call both conceptions.) The objection is right to point out that we do not fully understand how God causes the universe, as we understand how parents cause children or clouds cause rain. But the term remains meaningful. A cause is the sine qua non for an effect: if no cause, no effect. If no creator, no creation; if no God, no universe.

Third, it is sometimes argued (e.g., by Bertrand Russell) that there is a self-contradiction in the argument, for one of the premises is that everything needs a cause, but the conclusion is that there is something (God) which does not need a cause. The child who asks "Who made God?" is really thinking of this objection. The answer is very simple: the argument does not use the premise that everything needs a cause. Everything in motion needs a cause, everything dependent needs a cause, everything imperfect needs a cause.

Fourth, it is often asked why there can't be infinite regress, with no first being. Infinite regress is perfectly acceptable in mathematics: negative numbers go on to infinity just as positive numbers do. So why can't time be like the number series, with no highest number either negatively (no first in the past) or positively (no last in the future)? The answer is that real beings are not like numbers: they need causes, for the chain of real beings moves in one direction only, from past to future, and the future is caused by the past. Positive numbers are not caused by negative numbers. There is, in fact, a parallel in the number series for a first cause: the number one. If there were no first positive integer, no unit one, there could be no subsequent addition of units. Two is two ones, three is three ones, and so on. If there were no first, there could be no second or third.

If this argument is getting too tricky, the thing to do is to return to what is sure and clear: the intuitive point we began with. Not everyone can understand all the abstract details of the first-cause argument, but anyone can understand its basic point: as C. S. Lewis put it, "I felt in my bones that this universe does not explain itself."

4

Reasons to Believe:
The Argument from Conscience

The argument from conscience is one of the only two arguments for the existence of God alluded to in Scripture, the other being the argument from design (both in Romans). Both arguments are essentially simple natural intuitions. Only when complex, artificial objections are made do these arguments begin to take on a complex appearance.

The simple, intuitive point of the argument from conscience is that everyone in the world knows, deep down, that he is absolutely obligated to be and do good, and this absolute obligation could come only from God. Thus everyone knows God, however obscurely, by this moral intuition, which we usually call conscience. Conscience is the voice of God in the soul.

Like all arguments for the existence of God, this one proves only a small part of what we know God to be by divine revelation. But this part is significantly more than the arguments from nature reveal about God because this argument has richer data, a richer starting point. Here we have inside information, so to speak: the very will of God speaking, however obscurely and whisperingly, however poorly heard, admitted, and heeded, in the depths of our souls. The arguments from nature begin with data that are like an author's books; the argument from conscience begins with data that are more like talking with the author directly, live.

Before beginning, we should define and clarify the key term *conscience*. The modern meaning tends to indicate a mere feeling that I did something wrong or am about to do something wrong. The traditional meaning in Catholic theology is the knowledge of what is right and wrong: intellect applied to morality. The meaning of conscience in the argument is knowledge and not just a feeling; but it is intuitive knowledge rather than rational or analytical knowledge, and it is first of all the knowledge that I must always do right and never wrong, the knowledge of my absolute obligation to goodness, all goodness: justice and charity and virtue and holiness; only in the second place is it the knowledge of which things are right and which things are wrong. This second-place knowledge is a knowledge of moral facts, while the first-place knowledge is a knowledge of my personal moral obligation, a knowledge of the moral law itself and its binding authority over my life. That knowledge forms the basis for the argument from conscience.

If anyone claims he simply does not have that knowledge, if anyone says he simply doesn't see it, then the argument will not work for him. The question remains, however, whether he honestly doesn't see it and really has no conscience (or a radically defective conscience) or whether he is repressing the knowledge he really has. Divine revelation tells us that he is repressing the knowledge (Rom 1:18b; 2:15). In that case, what is needed before the rational, philosophical argument is some honest introspection to see the data. The data, conscience, is like a bag of gold buried in my backyard. If someone tells me it is there and that this proves some rich man buried it, I must first dig and find the treasure before I can infer anything more about the cause of the treasure's existence. Before conscience can prove God to anyone, that person must admit the presence of the treasure of conscience in the backyard of his soul.

Nearly everyone will admit the premise, though. They will often explain it differently, interpret it differently, insist it has nothing to do with God. But that is exactly what the argument tries to show: that once you admit the premise of the authority of conscience, you must admit the conclusion of God. How does that work?

Nearly everyone will admit not only the existence of conscience but also its authority. In this age of rebellion against and doubt about nearly every authority, in this age in which the very word *authority* has changed from a word of respect to a word of scorn, one authority remains: an individual's conscience. Almost no one will say that one ought to sin against one's conscience, disobey one's conscience. Disobey the church, the state, parents, authority figures, but do not disobey your conscience. Thus people usually admit, though not usually in these words, the absolute moral authority and binding obligation of conscience.

Such people are usually surprised and pleased to find out that Saint Thomas Aquinas, of all people, agrees with them to such an extent that he says if a Catholic comes to believe the Church is in error in some essential, officially defined doctrine, it is a mortal sin against conscience, a sin of hypocrisy, for him to remain in the Church and call himself a Catholic, but only a venial sin against knowledge for him to leave the Church in honest but partly culpable error.

So one of the two premises of the argument is established: conscience has an absolute authority over me. The second premise is that the only possible source of absolute authority is an absolutely perfect will, a divine being. The conclusion follows that such a being exists.

How would someone disagree with the second premise? By finding an alternative basis for conscience besides God. There are four such possibilities: (1) something abstract and impersonal, like an idea; (2) something concrete but less than human, something on the level of animal instinct; (3) something on the human level but not divine; and (4) something higher than the human level but not yet divine. In other words, we cover all the possibilities by looking at the abstract, the concrete-less-than-human, the concrete-human, and the concrete-more-than-human.

The first possibility means that the basis of conscience is a law without a lawgiver. We are obligated absolutely to an abstract ideal, a pattern of behavior. The question then comes up, where does this pattern exist? If it does not exist anywhere, how can a real person be under the authority of something unreal? How can "more" be subject to "less"? If, however, this pattern or idea exists in the minds of people, then what authority do they have to impose this idea of theirs on me? If the idea is only an idea, it has no personal will behind it; if it is only someone's idea, it has only that someone behind it. In neither case do we have a sufficient basis for absolute, infallible, no-exceptions authority. But we already admitted that conscience has that authority, that no one should ever disobey his conscience.

The second possibility means that we trace conscience to a biological instinct. "We must love one another or die", writes the poet W. H. Auden. We unconsciously know this, says the believer in this second possibility, just as animals unconsciously know that unless they behave in certain ways the species will not survive. That's why animal mothers sacrifice for their children, and that's a sufficient explanation for human altruism too. It's the herd instinct.

The problem with that explanation is that it, like the first, does not account for the absoluteness of conscience's authority. We believe we ought to disobey an instinct—any instinct—on some occasions. But we do not believe we ought ever to disobey our conscience. You should usually obey instincts like mother love, but not if it means keeping your son back from risking his life to save his country in a just and necessary defensive war, or if it means injustice and lack of charity to other mothers' sons. There is no instinct that should always be obeyed. The instincts are like the keys on a piano (the illustration comes from C. S. Lewis); the moral law is like sheet music. Different notes are right at different times.

Furthermore, instinct fails to account not only for what we ought to do but also for what we do do. We don't always follow instinct. Sometimes we follow the weaker instinct, as when we go to the aid of a victim even though we fear for our own safety. The herd instinct here is weaker than the instinct for self-preservation, but our conscience, like sheet music, tells us to play the weak note here rather than the strong one.

Honest introspection will reveal to anyone that conscience is not an instinct. When the alarm wakes you up early and you realize that you promised to help your friend this morning, your instincts pull you back to bed, but something quite different from your instincts tells you you should get out. Even if you feel two instincts pulling you (e.g., you are both hungry and tired), the conflict between those two instincts is quite different, and can be felt and known to be quite different, from the conflict between conscience and either or both of the instincts. Quite simply, conscience tells you that you ought to do or not do something, while instincts simply drive you to do or not do something. Instincts make something attractive or repulsive to your appetites, but conscience makes something obligatory to your choice, no matter how your appetites feel about it. Most people will admit this piece of obvious introspective data if they are honest. If they try to wriggle out of the argument at this point, leave them alone with the question, and if they are honest, they will confront the data when they are alone.

A third possibility is that other human beings (or society) are the source of the authority of conscience. That is the most popular belief, but it is also the weakest of all the four possibilities. For society does not mean something over and above other human beings, something like God, although many people treat society exactly like God, even in speech, almost lowering the voice to a whisper when the sacred name is mentioned. Society is simply other people like myself. What authority do they have over me? Are they always right? Must I never disobey them? What kind of blind status quo conservatism is this? Should a German have obeyed society in the Nazi era? To say society is the source of conscience is to say that when one prisoner becomes a thousand prisoners, they become the judge. It is to say that mere quantity gives absolute authority; that what the individual has in his soul is nothing, no authoritative conscience, but that what society (i.e., many individuals) has is. That is simply a logical impossibility, like thinking stones can think if only you have enough of them. (Some proponents of artificial intelligence believe exactly that kind of logical fallacy, by the way: that electrons and chips and chunks of metal can think if only you have enough of them in the right geometrical arrangements.)

The fourth possibility remains, that the source of conscience's authority is something above me but not God. What could this be? Society is not above me, nor is instinct. An ideal? That is the first possibility we discussed. It looks as though there are simply no candidates in this area.

And that leaves us with God. Not just some sort of God, but the moral God of the Bible, the God at least of Judaism. Among all the ancient peoples, the Jews were the only ones who identified their God with the source of moral obligation. The gods of the pagans demanded ritual worship, inspired fear, designed the universe, or ruled over the events in human life, but none of them ever gave a Ten Commandments or said, "Be ye holy for I the Lord your God am holy." The Jews saw the origin of nature and the origin of conscience as one, and Christians (and Muslims) have inherited this insight. The Jews' claim to be God's chosen people interprets the insight in the humblest possible way: as divine revelation, not human cleverness. But once revealed, the claim can be seen to be utterly logical.

To sum up the argument most simply and essentially, conscience has absolute, exceptionless, binding moral authority over us, demanding unqualified obedience. But only a perfectly good, righteous divine will has this authority and a right to absolute, exceptionless obedience. Therefore conscience is the voice of the will of God.

Of course, we do not always hear that voice aright. Our consciences can err. That is why the first obligation we have, in conscience, is to form our conscience by seeking the truth, especially the truth about whether this God has revealed to us clear moral maps (Scripture and Church). If so, whenever our conscience seems to tell us to disobey those maps, it is not working properly, and we can know that by conscience itself if only we remember that conscience is more than just immediate feeling. If our immediate feelings were the voice of God, we would have to be polytheists or else God would have to be schizophrenic.

5
Reasons to Believe:
The Argument from History

This argument is both stronger and weaker than the other arguments for the existence of God. It is stronger because its data (its evidence) are some facts of history, things that have happened on this planet, rather than principles or ideas. People are more convinced by facts than by principles. But it is weaker because the historical data amount only to strong clues, not to deductive proofs.

The argument from history is the strongest psychologically with most people, but it is not the logically strongest argument. It is like footprints in the sands of time, footprints made by someone great enough to be God.

There are at least eight different arguments from history, not just one. First, we could argue from the meaningfulness of history itself. History, both human and prehuman, has a story line. It is not just random. The atheist Jean-Paul Sartre has his alter ego Roquentin say something like this about history in the novel *Nausea:* "I have never had adventures. Things have happened to me, that's all." If atheism is true, there are no adventures, nothing has intrinsic significance, life is "a tale told by an idiot, full of sound and fury, signifying nothing". But life is not that. Life is a story. Stories are not told by idiots.

In J. R. R. Tolkien's great epic *The Lord of the Rings,* Frodo and Sam are crawling through the slag heaps of Mordor desperately attempting to fulfill their perilous quest when Sam stops to ask, "I wonder what kind of story we're in, Mr. Frodo?" It is a great question, a concrete way of asking the abstract question, "What is the meaning of life?" That the question is asked at all shows that we are in a story, not a jumble, and a story points to a storyteller.

Thus the general argument from history is a version of the argument from design.

A second argument concentrates more specifically on the moral design in history. Thus it can be seen as similar to the argument from conscience in that it uses the same evidence, morality. But in this case the premise is the justice revealed in history rather than the obligation imposed by individual conscience. The historical books of the Old Testament constitute an extended argument for the existence of God based on the history of the Jewish people. The argument is implicit, not explicit, of course; the Bible is not a book of philosophical arguments. It is not so much an argument as an invitation to look and see the hand of God in history. Whenever God's laws are followed, the people prosper. When they are violated, the people perish. History shows that moral laws are as inescapable as physical laws. Just as you can flout gravity only temporarily before you fall, so you can flout the moral laws of God only temporarily before you fall. Great tyrants like Adolf Hitler flourish for a day, like the mayfly, and perish. Great saints experience apparent failure, and emerge into triumph and joy. The same is true of nations as well as individuals. The lesson is scorned not because it is unknown or obscure but because it so well known; it is what our mothers and nurses told us as children. And however "square" it may be, it is true. History proves you can't cut the corners of the moral square. In geometry, you can't square the circle, and in history you can't circle the square. Now is this moral design (which the East calls karma) mere chance or the product of a wise moral will, a lawgiver? But no human lawgiver invented history itself. The only adequate cause for such an effect is God.

A third argument from history looks at providential "coincidences", like the Red Sea's parting (moved by an east wind, according to Exodus) at just the right time for the Jews to escape Pharaoh. Our own individual histories usually have some similar bits of incredible timing. Insightful and unprejudiced examination of these "coincidences" will bring us at least to the suspicion, if not to the conviction, that an unseen divine hand is at work here. The writers of the Bible often shortcut the argument and simply ascribe such natural events to God. Indeed, another passage in Exodus says simply that God parted the sea. This may not be miracle; God may have worked here, as he continues to work, through the second causes of natural agents. But it is God who works, and the hand of the Worker is visible through the work, if we only look. The argument is not a logical compulsion but an invitation to look, like Christ's "come and see."

A fourth argument from history, the strongest one of all, is the argument from miracles. Miracles directly and inescapably show the presence of God, for a miracle, in the ordinary sense of the word, is a deed done by supernatural, not natural, power. Neither nature nor chance nor human power can perform a miracle. If miracles happen, they show God's existence as clearly as reproduction shows the existence of organic life or rational speech shows the existence of thought.

If I were an atheist, I think I would save my money to buy a plane ticket to Italy to see whether the blood of Saint Januarius really did liquefy and congeal miraculously, as it is supposed to do annually. I would go to Medjugorge. I would study all published interviews of any of the seventy thousand who saw the miracle of the sun at Fatima. I would ransack hospital records for documented "impossible", miraculous cures. Yet, strangely, almost all atheists argue against miracles philosophically rather than historically. They are convinced a priori, by argument, that miracles can't happen. So they don't waste their time or money on such an empirical investigation. Those who do soon cease to be atheists—like the sceptical scientists who investigated the Shroud of Turin, or like Frank Morrison, who investigated the evidence for the "myth" of Christ's Resurrection with the careful scientific eye of the historian—and became a believer. (His book *Who Moved the Stone?* is still a classic and still in print after more than sixty years.)

The evidence is there for those who have eyes to see or, rather, the will to look. God provided just enough evidence of himself: enough for any honest and open-minded seeker whose heart really cares about the truth of the matter but not so much that dull and hardened hearts are convinced by force. Even Christ did not convince everyone by his miracles. He could have remained on earth, offered to walk into any scientific laboratory of the twentieth century, and invited scientists to perform experiments on him. He could have come down from the Cross, and then the doubters would have believed. But he did not. Even the Resurrection was kept semiprivate. The New Testament speaks of five hundred who saw him. Why did he not reveal himself to all?

He will, on the last day, when it will be too late to change sides. His mercy gives us time to choose and freedom to choose. The evidence for him, especially his miracles, is clear enough throughout history so that anyone with an honest, trusting, and seeking heart will find him: "All who seek find." But those who do not seek will not find. He leaves us free. He is like a lover with a marriage proposal, not like a soldier with a gun or a policeman with a warrant.

A fifth argument from history is Christ himself. Here is a man who lived among us and claimed to be God. If Christ was God, then, of course, there is a God. But if Christ was not God, he was a madman or a devil—a madman if he really thought he was God but was not, and a devil if he knew he was not God and yet tempted men to worship him as God. Which is he—Lord, lunatic, or liar?

Part of the data of history are the Gospel records of his life and his character. Reading the Gospels is like reading Plato's accounts of Socrates, or Boswell's account of Dr. Johnson: an absolutely unforgettable character emerges, on a human level. His personality is distinctive and compelling to every reader of the Gospels, even unbelievers, even his enemies, like Nietzsche. And the character revealed there is utterly unlike that of a lunatic or a liar. If it is impossible that a lunatic could be that wise or a liar that loving, then he must be the Lord; he must be the one he claims to be.

This is the progress of the argument in Scripture: you meet God through Christ, and (as the next argument will show) you meet Christ through Christians, through the Church. The logical order is: first prove the existence of God, then prove the divinity of

Christ, then prove the authority of Christ's Church. But the actual order in which an individual confronts these things is the reverse: he meets Christ through Christians (first, the apostles and writers of the Gospels; then the saints, past and present) and God through Christ. Once again, the "argument" is more like an invitation to "come and see."

A sixth argument is the saints, especially their joy. G. K. Chesterton once said that the only unanswerable argument against Christianity was Christians. (He meant bad and sad Christians.) Similarly, the only unanswerable argument for Christianity is Christians—saintly Christians. You can argue against Mother Teresa's theology if you are sceptical of mind, but you cannot argue against Mother Teresa unless you are hopelessly hard of heart. If there is no God, how can life's most fundamental illusion cause life's greatest joy? If God didn't do it, who put smiles on the lips of martyrs? "By their fruits you shall know them." Illusions do not have the staying power that the Faith has.

And that brings us to our seventh argument from history: the conversion of the world. How explain the success of the Faith in winning the hearts of men? Hard-hearted Romans give up worldly pleasures and ambitions, and often life itself. Worldly men pin their hopes on otherworldly goals and do it consistently, en masse, century after century. If Christianity is not true and there are no miracles, then the conversion of the world is an even greater miracle. Greek philosophy won converts through rational proofs, and Mohammed through force of arms in the jihad, or holy war, but Christ won the hearts of men by the miracle of "amazing grace, how sweet the sound, that saved a wretch like me." (I almost believe it is our high and holy duty to sing loudly the original "wretch" line that our liturgical experts have bowdlerized out of that great old song whenever the congregation sings the bland version instead. God in his wisdom saw that the American Church lacked persecutions and so sent her liturgists.)

The eighth and last argument from history is from our own individual history and life's experiences. The Christian faith is verifiable in a laboratory, but it is a subtle and complex laboratory:

the laboratory of one's life. If God exists, he wants to get in touch with us and reveal himself to us, and he has promised that all who seek him will find him. Well, then, all the agnostic has to do is to seek, sincerely, honestly, and with an open mind, and he will find, in God's way and in God's time. That is part of the hypothesis, part of the promise.

How to seek? Not just by arguing but by praying, not just by talking about God, as Job's three friends did and did not find him, but by talking to God, as Job did, and found him. I always tell a sceptic to pray the prayer of the sceptic if he really wants to know whether God exists. This is the scientific thing to do, to test a hypothesis by performing the relevant experiment. I tell him to go out into his backyard some night when no one can see and hear him and make him feel foolish, and say to the empty universe above him, "God, I don't know whether you exist or not. Maybe I'm praying to nobody, but maybe I'm praying to you. So if you are really there, please let me know somehow, because I do want to know. I want only the Truth, whatever it is. If you are the Truth, here I am, ready and willing to follow you wherever you lead." If our faith is not a pack of lies, then whoever sincerely prays that prayer will find God in his own life, no matter how hard, how long, or how complex the road, as Augustine's was in the *Confessions*. "All roads lead to Rome" if only we follow them.

6
Reasons to Believe:
The Argument from Pascal's Wager

Most philosophers think Pascal's Wager is the weakest of all arguments for believing in the existence of God. Pascal thought it was the strongest. After finishing the argument in his *Pensées,* he wrote, "This is conclusive, and if men are capable of any truth, this is it." That is the only time Pascal ever wrote a sentence like that, for he was one of the most sceptical philosophers who ever wrote.

Suppose someone terribly precious to you lay dying, and the doctor offered to try a new "miracle drug" that he could not guarantee but that seemed to have a 50-50 chance of saving your beloved friend's life. Would it be reasonable to try it, even if it cost a little money? And suppose it were free—wouldn't it be utterly reasonable to try it and unreasonable not to?

Suppose you hear reports that your house is on fire and your children are inside. You do not know whether the reports are true or false. What is the reasonable thing to do—to ignore them or to take the time to run home or at least phone home just in case the reports are true?

Suppose a winning sweepstakes ticket is worth a million dollars, and there are only two tickets left. You know that one of them is the winning ticket, while the other is worth nothing, and you are allowed to buy only one of the two tickets, at random. Would it be a good investment to spend a dollar on the good chance of winning a million?

No reasonable person can be or ever is in doubt in such cases. But deciding whether to believe in God is a case like these, argues Pascal. It is therefore the height of folly not to "bet" on God, even if you have no certainty, no proof, no guarantee that your bet will win.

To understand Pascal's Wager you have to understand the background of the argument. Pascal lived in a time of great scepticism. Medieval philosophy was dead, and medieval theology was being ignored or sneered at by the new intellectuals of the scientific revolution of the seventeenth century. Montaigne, the great sceptical essayist, was the most popular writer of the day. The classic arguments for the existence of God were no longer popularly believed. What could the Christian apologist say to the sceptical mind of this age? Suppose such a typical mind lacked both the gift of faith and the confidence in reason to prove God's existence; could there be a third ladder out of the pit of unbelief into the light of belief?

Pascal's Wager claims to be that third ladder. Pascal well knew that it was a low ladder. If you believe in God only as a bet, that is certainly not a deep, mature, or adequate faith. But it is something, it is a start, it is enough to dam the tide of atheism. The Wager appeals not to a high ideal, like faith, hope, love, or proof, but to a low one: the instinct for self-preservation, the desire to be happy and not unhappy. But on that low natural level, it has tremendous force. Thus Pascal prefaces his argument with the words, "Let us now speak according to our natural lights."

Imagine you are playing a game for two prizes. You wager blue chips to win blue prizes and red chips to win red prizes. The blue chips are your mind, your reason, and the blue prize is the truth about God's existence. The red chips are your will, your desires, and the red prize is heavenly happiness. Everyone wants both prizes, truth and happiness. Now suppose there is no way of calculating how to play the blue chips. Suppose your reason cannot win you the truth. In that case, you can still calculate how to play the red chips. Believe in God not because your reason can prove with certainty that it is true that God exists but because your will seeks happiness, and God is your only chance of attaining happiness eternally.

Pascal says, "Either God is, or he is not. But to which view shall we be inclined? Reason cannot decide this question. [Remember that Pascal's Wager is an argument for sceptics.] Infinite chaos separates us. At the far end of this infinite distance [death] a coin is being spun that will come down heads [God] or tails [no God]. How will you wager?"

The most powerful part of Pascal's argument comes next. It is not his refutation of atheism as a foolish wager (that comes last) but his refutation of agnosticism as impossible. Agnosticism, not-knowing, maintaining a sceptical, uncommitted attitude, seems to be the most reasonable option. The agnostic says, "The right thing is not to wager at all." Pascal replies, "But you must wager. There is no choice. You are already committed [embarked]." We are not outside observers of life, but participants. We are like ships that need to get home, sailing past a port that has signs on it proclaiming that it is our true home and our true happiness. The ships are our own lives and the signs on the port say "God". The agnostic says he will neither put in at that port (believe) nor turn away from it (disbelieve) but stay anchored a reasonable distance away until the weather clears and he can see better whether this is the true port or a fake (for there are a lot of fakes around). Why is this attitude unreasonable, even impossible? Because we are moving. The ship of life is moving along the waters of time, and there comes a point of no return, when our fuel runs out, when it is too late. The Wager works because of the fact of death.

Suppose Romeo proposes to Juliet and Juliet says, "Give me some time to make up my mind." Suppose Romeo keeps coming back day after day, and Juliet keeps saying the same thing day after day: "Perhaps tomorrow." In the words of a small, female, red-haired American philosopher, "Tomorrow is always a day away." And there comes a time when there are no more tomorrows. Then "maybe" becomes "no". Romeo will die. Corpses do not marry. Christianity is God's marriage proposal to the soul. Saying "maybe" and "perhaps tomorrow" cannot continue indefinitely because life does not continue indefinitely. The weather will never clear enough for the agnostic navigator to be sure whether the port is true home or false just by looking at it through binoculars from a distance. He has to take a chance, on this port or some other, or he will never get home.

Once it is decided that we must wager; once it is decided that there are only two options, theism and atheism, not three, theism, atheism, and agnosticism; then the rest of the argument is simple. Atheism is a terrible bet. It gives you no chance of winning the red prize. Pascal states the argument this way:

> You have two things to lose: the true and the good; and two things to stake: your reason and your will, your knowledge and your happiness; and your nature has two things to avoid: error and wretchedness. Since you must necessarily choose, your reason is no more affronted by choosing one rather than the other. That is one point cleared up. But your happiness? Let us weigh up the gain and the loss involved in calling heads that God exists. Let us assess the two cases: if you win, you win everything: if you lose, you lose nothing. Do not hesitate then: wager that he does exist.

If God does not exist, it does not matter how you wager, for there is nothing to win after death and nothing to lose after death. But if God does exist, your only chance of winning eternal happiness is to believe, and your only chance of losing it is to refuse to believe. As Pascal says, "I should be much more afraid of being mistaken and then finding out that Christianity is true than of being mistaken in believing it to be true." If you believe too much, you neither win nor lose eternal happiness. But if you believe too little, you risk losing everything.

But is it worth the price? What must be given up to wager that God exists? Whatever it is, it is only finite, and it is most reasonable to wager something finite on the chance of winning an infinite prize. Perhaps you must give up autonomy or illicit pleasures, but you will gain infinite happiness in eternity, and "I tell you that you will gain even in this life"—purpose, peace, hope, joy, the things that put smiles on the lips of martyrs.

Lest we take this argument with less seriousness than Pascal meant it, he concludes: "If my words please you and seem cogent, you must know that they come from a man who went down upon his knees before and after."

To the high-minded objector who refuses to believe for the low motive of saving the eternal skin of his own soul, we may reply that the Wager works quite as well if we change the motive. Let us say we want to give God his due if there is a God. Now if there is a God, justice demands total faith, hope, love, obedience, and worship. If there is a God and we refuse to give him these things, we sin maximally against the truth. But the only chance of doing infinite justice is if God exists and we believe, while the only chance of doing infinite injustice is if God exists and we do not believe. If God does not exist, there is no one there to do infinite justice or infinite injustice to. So the motive of doing justice moves the Wager just as well as the motive of seeking happiness. Pascal used the more selfish motive because we all have that all the time, while only some are motivated by justice, and only some of the time.

Because the whole argument moves on the practical rather than the theoretical level, it is fitting that Pascal next imagines the listener offering the practical objection that he just cannot bring himself to believe. Pascal then answers the objection with stunningly practical psychology, with the suggestion that the prospective convert "act into" his belief if he cannot yet "act out" of it.

> If you are unable to believe, it is because of your passions since reason impels you to believe and yet you cannot do so. Concentrate then not on convincing yourself by multiplying proofs of God's existence but by diminishing your passions. You want to find faith, and you do not know the road. You want to be cured of unbelief, and you ask for the remedy: learn from those who were once bound like you and who now wager all they have. . . . They behaved just as if they did believe.

This is the same advice Dostoevsky's guru, Father Zossima, gives to the "woman of little faith" in *The Brothers Karamazov*. The behavior Pascal mentions is "taking holy water, having Masses said, and so on". The behavior Father Zossima counsels to the same end is "active and indefatigable love of your neighbor." In both cases, living the Faith can be a way of getting the Faith. As Pascal says: "That will make you believe quite naturally and will make you more docile." "But that is what I am afraid of." "But why? What have you to lose?"

An atheist visited the great rabbi and philosopher Martin Buber and demanded that Buber prove the existence of God to him. Buber refused, and the atheist got up to leave in anger. As he left, Buber called after him, "But can you be *sure* there is no God?" That atheist wrote, forty years later, "I am still an atheist. But Buber's question has haunted me every day of my life." The Wager has just that haunting power.

7
The Problem of Evil

The problem of evil is the most serious problem in the world. It is also the one serious objection to the existence of God.

When Saint Thomas Aquinas wrote his great *Summa Theologica,* he could find only two objections to the existence of God, even though he tried to list at least three objections to every one of the thousands of theses he tried to prove in that great work. One of the two objections is the apparent ability of natural science to explain everything in our experience without God; and the other is the problem of evil.

More people have abandoned their faith because of the problem of evil than for any other reason. It is certainly the greatest test of faith, the greatest temptation to unbelief. And it's not just an intellectual objection. We feel it. We live it. That's why the Book of Job is so arresting.

The problem can be stated very simply: If God is so good, why is his world so bad? If an all-good, all-wise, all-loving, all-just, and all-powerful God is running the show, why does he seem to be doing such a miserable job of it? Why do bad things happen to good people?

The unbeliever who asks that question is usually feeling resentment toward and rebellion against God, not just lacking evidence for his existence. C. S. Lewis recalls that as an atheist he "did not believe God existed. I was also very angry with him for not existing. I was also angry with him for having created the world."

When you talk to such a person, remember that it is more like talking to a divorcée than to a sceptical scientist. The reason for unbelief is an unfaithful lover, not an inadequate hypothesis. The unbeliever's problem is not just a soft head but a hard heart. And the good apologist knows how to let the heart lead the head as well as vice versa.

There are four parts to the solution to the problem of evil. First, evil is not a *thing,* an entity, a being. All beings are either the Creator or creatures created by the Creator. But every thing God created is good, according to Genesis. We naturally tend to picture evil as a thing—a black cloud, or a dangerous storm, or a grimacing face, or dirt. But these pictures mislead us. If God is the Creator of all things and evil is a thing, then God is the Creator of evil, and he is to blame for its existence. No, evil is not a thing but a wrong choice, or the damage done by a wrong choice. Evil is no more a positive thing than blindness is. But it is just as real. It is not a thing, but it is not an illusion.

Second, the origin of evil is not the Creator but the creature's freely choosing sin and selfishness. Take away all sin and selfishness and you would have heaven on earth. Even the remaining physical evils would no longer rankle and embitter us. Saints endure and even embrace suffering and death as lovers embrace heroic challenges. But they do not embrace sin.

Furthermore, the cause of physical evil is spiritual evil. The cause of suffering is sin. After Genesis tells the story of the good God creating a good world, it next answers the obvious question "Where did evil come from then?" by the story of the fall of mankind. How are we to understand this? How can spiritual evil (sin) cause physical evil (suffering and death)?

God is the source of all life and joy. Therefore, when the human soul rebels against God, it loses its life and joy. Now a human being is body as well as soul. We are single creatures, not double: we are not even body *and* soul as much as we are embodied soul, or ensouled body. So the body must share in the soul's inevitable punishment—a punishment as natural and unavoidable as broken bones from jumping off a cliff or a sick stomach from eating rotten food rather than a punishment as artificial and external as a grade for a course or a slap on the hands for taking the cookies.

Whether this consequence of sin was a physical change in the world or only a spiritual change in human consciousness—whether the "thorns and thistles" grew in the garden only after the fall or whether they were always there but were only felt as painful by the newly fallen consciousness—is another question. But in either case the connection between spiritual evil and physical evil has to be as close as the connection between the two things they affect, the human soul and the human body.

If the origin of evil is free will, and God is the origin of free will, isn't God then the origin of evil? Only as parents are the origin of the misdeeds their children commit by being the origin of their children. The all-powerful God gave us a share in his power to choose freely. Would we prefer he had not and had made us robots rather than human beings?

A third part of the solution to the problem of evil is the most important part: how to resolve the problem in practice, not just in theory; in life, not just in thought. Although evil is a serious problem for thought (for it seems to disprove the existence of God), it is even more of a problem in life (for it is the real exclusion of God). But even if you think the solution in thought is obscure and uncertain, the solution in practice is as strong and clear as the sun: it is the Son. God's solution to the problem of evil is his Son Jesus Christ. The Father's love sent his Son to die for us to defeat the power of evil in human nature: that's the heart of the Christian story. We do not worship a deistic God, an absentee landlord who ignores his slum; we worship a garbageman God who came right down into our worst garbage to clean it up. How do we get God off the hook for allowing evil? God is not off the hook; God is the hook. That's the point of a crucifix.

The Cross is God's part of the practical solution to evil. Our part, according to the same Gospel, is to repent, to believe, and to work with God in fighting evil by the power of love. The King has invaded; we are finishing the mop-up operation.

Finally, what about the philosophical problem? It is not logically contradictory to say an all-powerful and all-loving God tolerates so much evil when he could eradicate it? Why do bad things happen to good people? The question makes three questionable assumptions.

First, who's to say we are good people? The question should be not "Why do bad things happen to good people?" but "Why do good things happen to bad people?" If the fairy godmother tells Cinderella that she can wear her magic gown until midnight, the question should be not "Why not after midnight?" but "Why did I get to wear it at all?" The question is not why the glass of water is half empty but why it is half full, for all goodness is gift. The best people are the ones who are most reluctant to call themselves good people. Sinners think they are saints, but saints know they are sinners. The best man who ever lived once said, "No one is good but God alone."

Second, who's to say suffering is all bad? Life without it would produce spoiled brats and tyrants, not joyful saints. Rabbi Abraham Heschel says simply, "The man who has not suffered, what can he possibly know, anyway?" Suffering can work for the greater good of wisdom. It is not true that all things are good, but it is true that "all things work together for good to those who love God."

Third, who's to say we have to know all God's reasons? Who ever promised us all the answers? Animals can't understand much about us; why should we be able to understand everything about God? The obvious point of the Book of Job, the world's greatest exploration of the problem of evil, is that we just don't know what God is up to. What a hard lesson to learn: Lesson One, that we are ignorant, that we are infants! No wonder Socrates was declared by the Delphic oracle to be the wisest man in the world. He interpreted that declaration to mean that he alone knew that he did not have wisdom, and that was true wisdom for man.

A child on the tenth story of a burning building cannot see the firefighters with their safety net on the street. They call up, "Jump! We'll catch you. Trust us." The child objects, "But I can't see you." The firefighter replies, "That's all right. I can see you." We are like that child, evil is like the fire, our ignorance is like the smoke, God is like the firefighter, and Christ is like the safety net. If there are situations like this where we must trust even fallible human beings with our lives, where we must trust what we hear, not what we see, then it is reasonable that we must trust the infallible, all-seeing God when we hear from his word but do not see from our reason or experience. We cannot know all God's reasons, but we can know why we cannot know.

God has let us know a lot. He has lifted the curtain on the problem of evil with Christ. There, the greatest evil that ever happened, both the greatest spiritual evil and the greatest physical evil, both the greatest sin (deicide) and the greatest suffering (perfect love hated and crucified), is revealed as his wise and loving plan to bring about the greatest good, the salvation of the world from sin and suffering eternally. There, the greatest injustice of all time is integrated into the plan of salvation that Saint Paul calls "the righteousness (justice) of God". Love finds a way. Love is very tricky. But love needs to be trusted.

The worst aspect of the problem of evil is eternal evil, hell. Does hell not contradict a loving and omnipotent God? No, for hell is the consequence of free will. We freely choose hell for ourselves; God does not cast anyone into hell against his will. If a creature is really free to say yes or no to the Creator's offer of love and spiritual marriage, then it must be possible for the creature to say no. And that is what hell is, essentially. Free will, in turn, was created out of God's love. Therefore hell is a result of God's love. Everything is.

No sane person wants hell to exist. No sane person wants evil to exist. But hell is just evil eternalized. If there is evil and if there is eternity, there can be hell. If it is intellectually dishonest to disbelieve in evil just because it is shocking and uncomfortable, it is the same with hell. Reality has hard corners, surprises, and terrible dangers in it. We desperately need a true road map, not nice feelings, if we are to get home. It is true, as people often say, that "hell just feels unreal, impossible." Yes. So does Auschwitz. So does Calvary.

8
The Divinity of Christ

The doctrine of Christ's divinity is the central Christian doctrine, for it is like a skeleton key that opens all the others. Christians have not independently reasoned out and tested each of the teachings of Christ, received via Bible and Church, but believe them all on his authority. For if Christ is divine, he can be trusted to be infallible in everything he said, even hard things like exalting suffering and poverty, forbidding divorce, giving his Church the authority to teach and forgive sins in his name, warning about hell (very often and very seriously), instituting the scandalous sacrament of eating his flesh—we often forget how many "hard sayings" he taught!

When the first Christian apologists began to give a reason for the faith that was in them to unbelievers, this doctrine of Christ's divinity naturally came under attack, for it was almost as incredible to Gentiles as it was scandalous to Jews. That a man who was born out of a woman's womb and died on a cross, a man who got tired and hungry and angry and agitated and wept at his friend's tomb, that this man who got dirt under his fingernails should be God was, quite simply, the most astonishing, incredible, crazy-sounding idea that had ever entered the mind of man in all human history.

The argument the early apologists used to defend this apparently indefensible doctrine has become a classic one. C. S. Lewis used it often, e.g., in *Mere Christianity,* the book that convinced Chuck Colson (and thousands of others). I once spent half a book (*Between Heaven and Hell*) on this one argument alone. It is the most important argument in Christian apologetics, for once an unbeliever accepts the conclusion of this argument (that Christ is divine), everything else in the Faith follows, not only intellectually (Christ's teachings must all then be true) but also personally (if Christ is God, he is also your total Lord and Savior).

The argument, like all effective arguments, is extremely simple: Christ was either God or a bad man.

Unbelievers almost always say he was a good man, not a bad man; that he was a great moral teacher, a sage, a philosopher, a moralist, and a prophet, not a criminal, not a man who deserved to be crucified. But a good man is the one thing he could not possibly have been according to simple common sense and logic. For he *claimed* to be God. He said, "Before Abraham was, I Am", thus speaking the word no Jew dares to speak because it is God's own private name, spoken by God himself to Moses at the burning bush. Jesus wanted everyone to believe that he was God. He wanted people to worship him. He claimed to forgive everyone's sins against everyone. (Who can do that but God, the One offended in every sin?)

Now what would we think of a person who went around making these claims today? Certainly not that he was a good man or a sage. There are only two possibilities: he either speaks the truth or not. If he speaks the truth, he is God and the case is closed. We must believe him and worship him. If he does not speak the truth, then he is not God but a mere man. But a mere man who wants you to worship him as God is not a good man. He is a very bad man indeed, either morally or intellectually. If he knows that he is not God, then he is morally bad, a liar trying deliberately to deceive you into blasphemy. If he does not know that he is not God, if he sincerely thinks he is God, then he is intellectually bad—in fact, insane.

A measure of your insanity is the size of the gap between what you think you are and what you really are. If I think I am the greatest philosopher in America, I am only an arrogant fool; if I think I am Napoleon, I am probably over the edge; if I think I am a butterfly, I am fully embarked from the sunny shores of sanity. But if I think I am God, I am even more insane because the gap between anything finite and the infinite God is even greater than the gap between any two finite things, even a man and a butterfly.

Josh McDowell summarized the argument simply and memorably in the trilemma "Lord, liar, or lunatic?" Those are the only options. Well, then, why not liar or lunatic? But almost no one who has read the Gospels can honestly and seriously consider that option. The savviness, the canniness, the human wisdom, the attractiveness of Jesus emerge from the Gospels with unavoidable force to any but the most hardened and prejudiced reader. Compare Jesus with liars like the Reverend Sun Myung Moon or lunatics like the dying Nietzsche. Jesus has in abundance precisely those three qualities that liars and lunatics most conspicuously lack: (1) his practical wisdom, his ability to read human hearts, to understand people and the real, unspoken question behind their words, his ability to heal people's spirits as well as their bodies; (2) his deep and winning love, his passionate compassion, his ability to attract people and make them feel at home and forgiven, his authority, "not as the scribes"; and above all (3) his ability to astonish, his unpredictability, his creativity. Liars and lunatics are all so dull and predictable! No one who knows both the Gospels and human beings can seriously entertain the possibility that Jesus was a liar or a lunatic, a bad man.

No, the unbeliever almost always believes that Jesus was a good man, a prophet, a sage. Well then, if he was a sage, you can trust him and believe the essential things he says. And the essential thing he says is that he is the divine Savior of the world and that you must come to him for salvation. If he is a sage, you must accept his essential teaching as true. If his teaching is false, then he is not a sage.

The strength of this argument is that it is not merely a logical argument about concepts; it is about Jesus. It invites people to read the Gospels and get to know this man. The premise of the argument is the character of Jesus, the human nature of Jesus. The argument has its feet on the earth. But it takes you to heaven, like Jacob's ladder (which Jesus said meant him: Gen 28:12; Jn 1:51). Each rung follows and holds together. The argument is logically airtight; there is simply no way out.

What, then, do people say when confronted with this argument? Often, they simply confess their prejudices: "Oh, I just can't believe that!" (But if it has been proved to be true, you must believe it if you really seek the truth!)

Sometimes, they go away, like many of Jesus' contemporaries, wondering and shaking their heads and thinking. That is perhaps the very best result you can hope for. The ground has been softened up and plowed. The seed has been sown. God will give the increase.

But if they know some modern theology, they have one of two escapes, Theology has an escape; common sense does not. Common sense is easily convertible. It is the theologians, now as then, who are the hardest to convert.

The first escape is the attack of the Scripture "scholars" on the historical reliability of the Gospels. Perhaps Jesus never claimed to be divine. Perhaps all the embarrassing passages were inventions of the early Church (say "Christian community"—it sounds nicer).

In that case, who invented traditional Christianity if not Christ? A lie, like a truth, must originate somewhere. Peter? The twelve? The next generation? What was the motive of whoever first invented the myth (euphemism for lie)? What did they get out of this elaborate, blasphemous hoax? For it must have been a deliberate lie, not a sincere confusion. No Jew confuses Creator with creature, God with man. And no man confuses a dead body with a resurrected, living one.

Here is what they got out of their hoax. Their friends and families scorned them. Their social standing, possessions, and political privileges were stolen from them by both Jews and Romans. They were persecuted, imprisoned, whipped, tortured, exiled, crucified, eaten by lions, and cut to pieces by gladiators. So some silly Jews invented the whole elaborate, incredible lie of Chrisitanity for absolutely no reason, and millions of Gentiles believed it, devoted their lives to it, and died for it—for no reason. It was only a fantastic practical joke, a hoax. Yes, there is a hoax indeed, but the perpetrators of it are the twentieth-century theologians, not the Gospel writers.

The second escape (notice how eager we are to squirm out of the arms of God like a greased pig) is to Orientalize Jesus, to interpret him not as the unique God-man but as one of many mystics or "adepts" who realized his own inner divinity just as a typical Hindu mystic does. This theory takes the teeth out of his claim to divinity, for he only realized that everyone is divine. The problem with that theory is simply that Jesus was not a Hindu but a Jew! When he said "God", neither he nor his hearers meant Brahman, the impersonal, pantheistic, immanent all; he meant Yahweh, the personal, theistic, transcendent Creator. It is utterly unhistorical to see Jesus as a mystic, a Jewish guru. He taught prayer, not meditation. His God is a person, not a pudding. He said he was God but not that everyone was. He taught sin and forgiveness, as no guru does. He said nothing about the "illusion" of individuality, as the mystics do.

Attack each of these evasions—Jesus as the good man, Jesus as the lunatic, Jesus as the liar, Jesus as the man who never claimed divinity, Jesus as the mystic—take away these flight squares, and there is only one square left for the unbeliever's king to move to. And on that square waits checkmate. And a joyous mating it is. The whole argument is really a wedding invitation.

9
Miracles

In the *Summa,* Saint Thomas could find only two objections to belief in God. One of them is the problem of evil. The other is, essentially, the problem of the miraculous, the supernatural. (God and miracles go together as supernatural actor and supernatural acts.) Can't everything we experience be explained by the sciences without any supernatural agency, any God, any miracles? Here are twelve common forms this objection takes in our day.

1. "Science has disproved miracles. Belief in miracles was possible in prescientific eras, but not today, in the era of science."

Which science has disproved miracles? How? By what proof? What discovery? Who proved it? When? No one can answer these specific questions. Instead, the objector appeals to a vague, dreamy abstraction called Science with a capital S. That is not science; that is religion—bad religion.

2. "People used to believe in miracles only because they didn't know the scientific explanations for events. For instance, they thought an angry god, Zeus, hurled thunderbolts down from heaven only because they didn't know about electrical energy. Once they knew that, Zeus disappeared."

Yes, modern science has explained away some of the things some of the ancients thought miraculous, like thunderbolts. But it has not explained away any of the miracles in the New Testament. Science has not made the Virgin Birth or the Resurrection or the feeding of the five thousand one bit less miraculous.

3. "But the science of the future will do just that. Just as modern science has explained away some of what the ancients thought miraculous, future science will explain away all of what we think miraculous."

This objection is a religious faith, not science. What science will do tomorrow, no one knows today, and we cannot argue scientifically from what is not known.

64

4. "The true meaning of a miracle is anything that excites wonder and joy and love. Human love is the real miracle, in the only important sense of the word."

Nature and human acts are miracles only in the same sense that everyone is a Christian—an empty and meaningless sense. You can empty any word of meaning by stretching it so thin that it covers everything. Sunsets and babies and acts of love are wonderful and beautiful, but they are not miracles. Miracle means supernatural wonder, not natural wonder.

5. "The world has its own laws and stands on its own. Once we stopped seeing the world as a mere stage set moved about at will by arbitrary gods, we stopped believing in miracles."

Exactly the opposite is true! Only if you believe in a world that stands on its own, a world with natural laws inherent in it, can you believe in miracles. The two presuppositions of miracles are a transcendent God and a distinct world of nature with inherent laws. If there are no natural laws, there are no supernatural exceptions to them. Atheists, pagans, and pantheists cannot believe in miracles: atheists because they have no supernatural God to perform them; pagans because their gods are parts of nature; pantheists because their God is the whole of nature. Atheists and pagans have no God outside nature; pantheists have no nature outside God.

6. "Belief in miracles contradicts the laws of science, which tell us that things like virgin births simply do not happen."

Science does not tell us what always happens. It certainly does not tell us what can or cannot happen. Science's laws are only generalizations from our observations of how nature usually works. They do not forbid exceptions.

Miracles do not contradict the laws of science any more than a gift of extra money contradicts a bank balance. It is an addition, not a subtraction. Dropping food into a goldfish bowl does not contradict the ecology of the fishbowl. A presidential pardon does not contradict the usual laws of the courts. Supernatural events do not contradict natural events. Science tells us what agencies operate in nature, not what agencies, if any, operate outside it.

7. "Belief in miracles demeans nature and the integrity and identity of nature."

Miracles no more demean nature than a husband demeans a wife. A miracle is like Father God impregnating Mother Nature. It fulfills, not demeans, her. In fact, only supernaturalists can appreciate nature for the same reason that only those who know a foreign language can appreciate their own, and only those who face death can appreciate life: you appreciate a thing only by contrast. If *nature* means simply everything—well, everything is not a topic about which we can feel very passionate. Everything has no character, only every *thing* does. Only if nature is a thing does she have character—and she is a thing only to a supernaturalist.

8. "The issue of miracles is not really important; the essence of religion is not at stake here."

That depends on which religion you mean. No other religion but Christianity absolutely demands belief in miracles. Disbelieve in miracles and you have not lost anything essential to Islam, Hinduism, Buddhism, Confucianism, or modern Judaism (as distinct from Biblical Judaism); but disbelieve in miracles and you are, quite simply, not a Christian. Christianity is essentially the good news of the Incarnation, Atonement, and Resurrection, not an abstract set of timeless ethical truths.

9. "The miracle stories were added to the Bible later."

There is absolutely no textual or historical evidence whatever for this common assumption, only guesswork or prejudice. However, miracles stories *were* added later to many other religions, and even contradict the original idea. For instance, the story of Mohammed flying to the moon on his horse contradicts Mohammed's insistence that the Koran be his only miracle. And Buddha taught that anyone who performed a miracle was not teaching his dharma (doctrine) because a miracle would encourage belief in the illusion of the separate, objective material world.

10. "Ah, but we must interpret the Bible in light of our own sincerely held, honest beliefs. If we do not believe in miracles, the

most charitable interpretation of the Bible's miracle stories is to accept them as myth and symbol, not to reject them as lies."

Perhaps that is charitable, but it is not clearheaded or even honest—and therefore it is not charitable either. We must *not* interpret the Bible (or any other book) in light of our own beliefs but in light of the author's beliefs. The objector is confusing *interpretation* with *belief.* You may believe in capitalism, but please do not interpret Marx' *Das Kapital* as procapitalist. That would be imposing your views on the author, assuming that he must believe the same things you do. That is not charitable; that is arrogant. Yet it is amazing how common this arrogant mistake is when "scholars" interpret the Bible.

11. "Jesus' Resurrection is the central miracle claimed by traditional Christians. But isn't it crass, crude, vulgar, and materialistic to insist on the literal, physical meaning of the Resurrection, on the biological reunification of Jesus' molecules? Isn't it the resurrection of Easter faith in the disciples' (and our) hearts that really matters?"

Easter faith in what if Easter did not really happen? Faith in faith? That is a hall of mirrors. If there is no Resurrection, there is no faith, for there is no object for faith to believe in. "If Christ is not raised from the dead, your faith is vain", insists Saint Paul.

Death is a crass, crude, vulgar, and materialistic problem. It needs a crass, crude, vulgar, and materialistic solution, like the resurrection of the body. What set the ancient world on fire was not faith in faith, a psychology, a philosophy, or an ethic, but the astonishing news that God became man, died, and rose from death to save us from sin and death.

12. "A nonmiraculous explanation of the Resurrection (and of any other miracle) is more likely, more reasonable."

Which explanation? None of the alternatives suggested works. If Jesus did not really rise from the dead, three questions are unanswerable: Who moved the stone? Who got the body? and Who started the Resurrection myth and why? What profit did the liars get out of their lie?

I will tell you what they got out of it. They got mocked, hated, sneered and jeered at, exiled, deprived of property and reputation and rights, imprisoned, whipped, tortured, clubbed to a pulp, beheaded, crucified, boiled in oil, sawed in pieces, fed to lions, and cut to ribbons by gladiators. If the miracle of the Resurrection did not really happen, then an even more incredible miracle happened: twelve Jewish fishermen invented the world's biggest lie for no reason at all and died for it with joy, as did millions of others. This myth, this lie, this elaborate practical joke transformed lives, gave despairing souls a reason to live and selfish souls a reason to die, gave cynics joy and libertines conscience, put martyrs in the hymns and hymns in the martyrs—all for no reason. A fantastic con job, a myth, a joke.

A myth indeed. That idea is the myth. The miracle is the sober fact.

10
Life after Death

Pie in the sky bye and bye—that's what you Christians believe.

C. S. Lewis in *The Problem of Pain* answers:

> We are afraid of the jeer about "pie in the sky". . . . But either there is "pie in the sky" or there is not. If there is not, then Christianity is false, for this doctrine is woven into its whole fabric. If there is, then this truth, like any other, must be faced, whether it is useful at political meetings or not.

But isn't it true that the essence of Christ's teachings is about how to live in this world? Can't you drop your concern for the next world and still be Christians?

That's like saying you can drop hope for a communist revolution and a classless society and still be a communist.

But hope for heaven diverts you from making earth a better place to live in. You Christians are really traitors to the earth.

No. Throughout history it has been precisely those who believed most strongly in the next world who did the most to improve this one. That's what you would expect. If you believe the road you're on goes nowhere, you don't take it too seriously. If you believe it goes to somewhere important, you keep it up. If a pregnant woman thinks her baby will be born dead, she does not take much care of it. If she hopes it will have life after birth, she takes care of her pregnancy.

But concern for the next world is escapism.

Who talk the most against "escapism"? Jailers. Think about it.

But heaven is just wishful thinking. Belief in life after death can be explained away so easily that way.

Is belief in hell wishful thinking too? We believe in both because Christ taught them, and we believe in him. Long ago, Lucretius, the ancient Roman materialist philosopher, let the cat out of the bag when he said that we should stop believing in life after death because then we don't have to be afraid of hell. *That's* wishful thinking.

Then why is it that mainly the poor believe? Isn't it a suspicious coincidence that those who have the hardest time in this world believe most readily in the next?

It isn't the poor but the rich who have the hardest time being happy in this world, as is evidenced by comparing suicide rates. The poor believe not because they are blinded by their poverty but because they are not blinded by riches. (Jesus said some shockingly strong things about the dangers of riches, you remember.)

But the motive for believing in life after death is the same kind of thing as the deceptive desire for riches. It's mercenary. If I'm good now, I'll get the goods later. That's not honesty and love and a true heart. Life after death corrupts your motive. You should love God and your neighbor for their sakes, not for your sake or the sake of your heavenly reward, to pile up Brownie points. It's a bribe.

Our motive for believing it is that Jesus taught it. Would he hold out a bribe to us? No selfish soul really wants heaven because what you do in heaven is give yourself away in self-forgetful love forever. Heaven is not the external reward tacked onto a life of love and selflessness; it is that life itself, consummated. Heaven is no more a bribe or a mercenary reward than marriage is.

But aren't the pictures we have in our minds of heaven suspiciously earthly? Doesn't it look like wish fulfillment—meeting the dear departed dead on the other shore and all that?

Those are only our pictures. In reality, "eye has not seen, ear has not heard, nor has it entered into the heart of man, the things God has prepared for those who love him."

Then it's too unearthly. I wouldn't feel comfortable with angels.

Jesus assures us he is preparing our apartments ("mansions") for us in heaven. He's got to be better than any earthly hotel manager.

The one who designed us can certainly arrange a heaven that fits us.

You've answered my objections but you haven't given any proof of your belief. Prove life after death.

How? Scientifically? If that could be done, no one would disbelieve, and there would be no free choice and no merit in trusting and believing.

Then it's blind faith? A leap in the dark?

No, a leap in the light. There are reasons for believing. Here are seven. The word of God, for one: both Jesus and Scripture are called that, and both teach about heaven. The nature of God as all-loving and all-powerful, for another thing. If even *your* love wants to save your loved ones from death, does God love us any less? But he can do whatever he wills. A third reason is long-range justice, which is not accomplished in this life. "Nice guys finish last", and the meek do not yet inherit the earth. If death ends all, "all" is a pretty bad story. Here's a fourth reason: the intrinsic value and indispensability of a person, which is a truth seen by the eyes of unselfish love. If death ends everything, then the indispensable is dispensed with like diapers: then persons are treated like things. Then God does exactly what he commands us not to do. And a fifth reason: the image of God in us, the soul, the self, the I—that's not a thing or object or *it*. That's not a bodily organ. It's not a thing that can be killed by a bullet or a cancer. It's my soul, my personhood. I am not just a body because I *have* my body. The possessor is more than the possessed. Sixth, there is the testimony of seers, saints, mystics, and resuscitated patients who have touched the next world in near-death experiences. They know. But my solidest reason for believing in life after death is the Resurrection of Jesus. The Church has been witnessing to that for twenty centuries. It's no theory; it's fact.

The Church teaches that there's a hell too, though. That's a barbaric doctrine, a horrible stick to hit people over the head with. Hell shows that the Church is based on fear.

We believe in hell because Jesus taught it, and Jesus was not one to use fear instead of love when he didn't have to. Hell *is* horrible. Some things on earth are horrible too; that doesn't mean they aren't real.

Didn't Jesus preach a simple gospel of love and compassion? Wasn't hell the later emphasis of the Church or Saint Paul?

Almost the opposite. No one talked more about hell than Jesus. If anything, Saint Paul softened his message. In a few texts he seems to hold out a dim hope that all may be saved.

But hell absolutely contradicts God's love.

No it doesn't. It manifests God's love. God's love created us free, not robots, and our free choice of evil is the only thing that makes hell.

But if God is all-powerful, why can't he arrange for no one to go to hell?

Against their will? Freedom, once again. What if they insist on saying no?

But is it just to punish people eternally for sins committed in time? Isn't infinite punishment for finite sins unjust?

It's not math; it's love. Decline a lover's invitation, and you remain loveless; it's as simple as that. Decline infinite love and you experience infinite lovelessness. The God-shaped hole in our heart is already infinite, in a sense: it can be filled only by infinite love. If we refuse, it remains unfilled infinitely.

How could a sane person prefer hell to heaven? And if it takes insanity to make that choice, how can anyone be blamed for it?

The same argument "proves" there's no sin on earth either. All sin is insanity: preferring self without God to God. All sin is a little souvenir from hell. It is crazy. But it's real.

How could God accept you into heaven if your only motive is fear of hell? Isn't that low and mercenary?

Love stoops to conquer. And it's not mercenary because hell is not only punishment for sin but sin itself, brought to consummation; just as heaven is not just reward for goodness, it's goodness itself consummated. If you don't like goodness, you wouldn't like heaven.

Are you saying hell and heaven are right here in life?

Their seeds are. Wheat and tares grow up together here (see Mt 13). That's what every choice in life is: to help the heavenly wheat grow or the hellish tares. That's the relevance of this "escapist" doctrine to everyday life. We're in a great battle. We walk on a razor edge.

And your eyes are glued to the fires of hell in fear?

No, to the eyes of God in love.

11
Comparative Religions: The Uniqueness of Christianity

Ronald Knox once quipped that "the study of comparative religions is the best way to become comparatively religious." The reason, as G. K. Chesterton says, is that, according to most "scholars" of comparative religion, "Christianity and Buddhism are very much alike, especially Buddhism."

But any Christian who does apologetics must think about comparative religions because the most popular of all objections against the claims of Christianity today comes from this field. The objection is not that Christianity is not true but that it is not the truth; not that it is a false religion but that it is only *a* religion. The world is a big place, the objector reasons; "different strokes for different folks". How insufferably narrow-minded to claim that Christianity is the one true religion! God just has to be more open-minded than that.

This is the single most common objection to the Faith today, for "today" worships not God but equality. It fears being right where others are wrong more than it fears being wrong. It worships democracy and resents the fact that God is an absolute monarch. It has changed the meaning of the word *honor* from being respected because you are superior in some way to being accepted because you are not superior in any way but just like us. The one unanswerable insult, the absolutely worst name you can possibly call a person in today's society, is "fanatic", especially "religious fanatic". If you confess at a fashionable cocktail party that you are plotting to overthrow the government, or that you are a PLO terrorist or a KGB spy, or that you molest porcupines or bite bats' heads off, you will soon attract a buzzing, fascinated, sympathetic circle of listeners. But if you confess that you believe that Jesus is the Christ, the Son of the living God, you will find yourself suddenly alone, with a distinct chill in the air.

Here are twelve of the commonest forms of this objection, the odium of elitism, with answers to each.

1. *"All religions are the same, deep down."*

That is simply factually untrue. No one ever makes this claim unless he is (1) abysmally ignorant of what the different religions of the world actually teach or (2) intellectually irresponsible in understanding these teachings in the vaguest and woolliest way or (3) morally irresponsible in being indifferent to them. The objector's implicit assumption is that the distinctive teachings of the world's religions are unimportant, that the essential business of religion is not truth but something else: transformation of consciousness or sharing and caring or culture and comfort or something of that sort—not conversion but conversation. Christianity teaches many things no other religion teaches, and some of them directly contradict those others. If Christianity isn't true, why be a Christian?

By Catholic standards, the religions of the world can be ranked by how much truth they teach. Catholicism is first, with Orthodoxy equal except for the one issue of papal authority. Then comes Protestantism and any "separated brethren" who keep the Christian essentials as found in Scripture. Third comes traditional Judaism, which worships the same God but not via Christ. Fourth is Islam, greatest of the theistic heresies; fifth, Hinduism, a mystical pantheism; sixth, Buddhism, a pantheism without a *theos;* seventh, modern Judaism, Unitarianism, Confucianism, Modernism, and secular humanism, none of which have either mysticism or supernatural religion but only ethics; eighth, idolatry; and ninth, Satanism. To collapse these nine levels is like thinking the earth is flat.

2. *"But the essence of religion is the same at any rate: all religions agree at least in being religious."*

What is this essence of religion anyway? I challenge anyone to define it broadly enough to include Confucianism, Buddhism, and modern Reform Judaism but narrowly enough to exclude Platonism, atheistic Marxism, and Nazism.

The unproved and unprovable assumption of this second objection is that the essence of religion is a kind of lowest common denominator or common factor. Perhaps the common factor is a weak and watery thing rather than an essential thing. Perhaps it does not exist at all. No one has ever produced it.

3. *"But if you compare the Sermon on the Mount, Buddha's* Dhammap-ada, *Lao-tzu's* Tao-te-ching, *Confucius'* Analects, *the* Bhagavad-Gita, *the Proverbs of Solomon, and the* Dialogues of Plato, *you will find it: a real, profound, and strong agreement."*

Yes, but this is ethics, not religion. The objector is assuming that the essence of religion is ethics. It is not. Everyone has an ethic, not everyone has a religion. Tell an atheist that ethics equals religion. He will be rightly insulted, for you would be calling him either religious if he is ethical, or unethical because he is nonreligious. Ethics may be the first step in religion but it is not the last. As C. S. Lewis says, "The road to the Promised Land runs past Mount Sinai."

4. *"Speaking of mountains reminds me of my favorite analogy. Many roads lead up the single mountain of religion to God at the top. It is provincial, narrow-minded, and blind to deny the validity of other roads than yours."*

The unproved assumption of this very common mountain analogy is that the roads go up, not down; that man makes the roads, not God; that religion is man's search for God, not God's search for man. C. S. Lewis says this sounds like "the mouse's search for the cat".

Christianity is not a system of man's search for God but a story of God's search for man. True religion is not like a cloud of incense wafting up from special spirits into the nostrils of a waiting God, but like a Father's hand thrust downward to rescue the fallen. Throughout the Bible, man-made religion fails. There is no human way up the mountain, only a divine way down. "No man has seen

God at any time. The only begotten Son who is in the bosom of the Father, he has made him known."

If we made the roads, it would indeed be arrogant to claim that any one road is the only valid one, for all human things are equal, at least in all being human, finite, and mixtures of good and bad. If we made the roads, it would be as stupid to absolutize one of them as to absolutize one art form, one political system, or one way of skinning a cat. But if God made the road, we must find out whether he made many or one. If he made only one, then the shoe is on the other foot: it is humility, not arrogance, to accept this one road from God, and it is arrogance, not humility, to insist that our man-made roads are as good as God's God-made one.

But which assumption is true? Even if the pluralistic one is true, not all religions are equal, for then one religion is worse and more arrogant than all others, for it centers on one who claimed, "I am the Way, the Truth, and the Life; no man can come to the Father but by me."

5. *"Still, it fosters religious imperialism to insist that your way is the only way. You're on a power trip."*

No, we believe it not because we want to, because we are imperialistic, or because we invented it, but because Christ taught it. It isn't our way, it's his way, that's the only way. We're just being faithful to him and to what he said. The objector's assumption is that we can make religion whatever we want it to be.

6. *"If the one-way doctrine comes from Christ, not from you, then he must have been arrogant."*

How ironic to think Jesus is arrogant! No sin excited his anger more than the arrogance and bigotry of religious leaders. No man was ever more merciful, meek, loving, and compassionate.

The objector is always assuming the thing to be proved: that Christ is just one among many religious founders, human teachers. But he claimed to be the Way, the Truth, and the Life; if that claim is not true, he is not one among many religious sages but one among many lunatics. If the claim is true, then again he is not one among many religious sages, but the Way, the Truth, and the Life.

7. *"Do you want to revive the Inquisition? Don't you value religious tolerance? Do you object to giving other religions equal rights?"*

The Inquisition failed to distinguish the heresy from the heretic and tried to eliminate both by force or fire. The objector makes the same mistake in reverse: he refuses to condemn either. The state has no business defining and condemning heresy, of course, but the believer must do it—if not through the Church, then by himself. For to believe *x* is to condemn non-*x* as false. If you don't believe non-*x* is false, then you don't really believe *x* is true.

8. *"I'm surprised at this intolerance. I thought Christianity was the religion of love."*

It is. It is also the religion of truth. The objector is separating two divine attributes. We are not. We are "speaking the truth in love".

9. *"But all God expects of us is sincerity."*

How do you know what God expects of us? Have you listened to God's revelation? Isn't it dangerous to assume without question or doubt that God must do exactly what you would do if you were God? Suppose sincerity were not enough; suppose truth was needed too. Is that unthinkable? In every other area of life we need truth. Is sincerity enough for a surgeon? An explorer? Don't we need accurate road maps of reality?

The objector's implicit assumption here is that there is no objective truth in religion, only subjective sincerity, so that no one can ever be both sincere and wrong; that the spirit does not have objective roads like the body and the mind, which lead to distinct destinations: the body's physical roads lead to different cities and the mind's logical roads lead to different conclusions. True sincerity wants to know the truth.

10. *"Are non-Christians all damned then?"*

No. Father Feeny was excommunicated by the Catholic Church for teaching that "outside the Church, no salvation" meant outside the visible Church.

God does not punish pagans unjustly. He does not punish them for not believing in a Jesus they never heard of, through no fault of their own (invincible ignorance). But God, who is just, punishes them for sinning against the God they do know through nature and conscience (see Rom 1–2). There are no innocent pagans, and there are no innocent Christians either. All have sinned against God and against conscience. All need a Savior. Christ is the Savior.

11. *"But surely there's a little good in the worst of us and a little bad in the best of us. There's good and bad everywhere, inside the Church and outside."*

True. What follows from that fact? That we need no Savior? That there are many Saviors? That contradictory religions can all be true? That none is true? None of these implied conclusions has the remotest logical connection with the admitted premise.

There is a little good in the worst of us, but there's also a little bad in the best of us; more, there's sin, separation from God, in all of us; and the best of us, the saints, are the first to admit it. The universal sin Saint Paul pinpoints in Romans 1:18 is to suppress the truth. We all sin against the truth we know and refuse it when it condemns us or threatens our self-sufficiency or complacency. We all rationalize. Our duty is plain to us—to be totally honest—and none of us does his duty perfectly. We have no excuse of invincible ignorance.

12. *"But isn't God unjust to judge the whole world by Christian standards?"*

God judges justly. "All who sinned without [knowing] the [Mosaic] law will also perish without the law, and all who have sinned under the law will be judged by the law" (Rom 2:12). Even pagans show "that what the law requires is written on their hearts" (Rom 2:15). If we honestly consult our hearts, we will find two truths: that we know what we ought to do and be, and that we fail to do and be that.

Fundamentalists, faithful to the clear one-way teaching of Christ, often conclude from this that pagans, Buddhists, et cetera, cannot be saved. Liberals, who emphasize God's mercy, cannot bring themselves to believe that the mass of men are doomed to hell, and they ignore, deny, nuance, or water down Christ's own claims to uniqueness. The Church has found a third way, implied in the New Testament texts. On the one hand, no one can be saved except through Christ. On the other hand, Christ is not only the incarnate Jewish man but also the eternal, preexistent word of God, "which enlightens every man who comes into the world" (Jn 1:9). So Socrates was able to know Christ as word of God, as eternal Truth; and if the fundamental option of his deepest heart was to reach out to him as Truth, in faith and hope and love, however imperfectly known this Christ was to Socrates, Socrates could have been saved by Christ too. We are not saved by knowledge but by faith. Scripture nowhere says how explicit the intellectual content of faith has to be. But it does clearly say who the one Savior is.

The Second Vatican Council took a position on comparative religions that distinguished Catholicism from both Modernist relativism and Fundamentalist exclusivism. It taught that on the one hand there is much deep wisdom and value in other religions and that the Christian should respect them and learn from them. But, on the other hand, the claims of Christ and his Church can never be lessened, compromised, or relativized. We may add to our religious education by studying other religions but never subtract from it.

12

Comparative Religions: Christianity and Judaism

If Jesus returned to earth today, which church would he attend? A Catholic church, of course, replies the Catholic. No, a Protestant church, protests the Protestant. Perhaps both are wrong. If he did now what he did then, he would begin in a Jewish synagogue.

There is only one other religion in the world that Christianity totally agrees with and affirms as divine revelation. It is, of course, Judaism.

The long history of Christian anti-Semitism, in thought and deed, is perhaps the blackest scandal in all the Church's history. It is the Oedipus complex because Judaism is Christianity's father. All Christians are spiritually Jews, said Vatican II, echoing Saint Paul. Christianity subtracts nothing from Judaism but only fulfills it. This is the point of the "Jews for Jesus", who insist that a Jew who becomes a Christian does not lose anything Jewish but rather completes it. When a Hindu or a pagan becomes a Christian, he is converted. When a Jew becomes a Christian, he is completed.

This was surely Jesus' point of view too, for he said he came "not to destroy the law and the prophets but fulfill them". From this point of view, Christianity is more Jewish than modern Judaism. Pre-Christian Judaism is like a virgin; post-Christian Judaism is like a spinster. In Christ, God consummates the marriage to his people and through them to the whole world.

What have Christians inherited from the Jews? Everything in the Old Testament: the knowledge of the true God. Comparing that knowledge with the knowledge of all the other religions of the world is like comparing sunlight with fog. Six crucial and distinctive concepts stand out: monotheism, creation, law, redemption, sin, and faith.

1. Only rarely and obscurely did a few Gentiles like Socrates and Akhenaton ever reach to the heights and simplicity of monotheism. A world of many forces seemed to most pagans to point to many gods. A world of good and evil seemed to indicate good and evil gods. Polytheism seems eminently reasonable. In fact, I wonder that it is not much more popular today than it is.

There are only two possible explanations for the Jews' unique idea of a single, all-powerful, and all-good God. Either they were the most brilliant philosophers in the world, or else they were the chosen people, i.e., God told them. The latter explanation, which is their traditional claim, is just the opposite of elitist. It is the humblest possible interpretation of the data.

2. Along with a unique idea of God came the unique idea of the creation of the universe out of nothing. The so-called creation myths of other religions are only formation myths, for their gods always fashion the world out of some preexisting stuff, some primal glop the gods were stuck with and on which one can blame evil: matter, darkness, fate, et cetera. But a Jew can't blame evil on matter, for God created it; nor on God, since he is all-good. The idea of free will, therefore, as the only possible origin of evil is a corollary of the idea of creation.

The Hebrew word *to create* (*bara'*) is used only three times in the Genesis account: for the creation of the universe (1:1), life (1:21), and man (1:27). Everything else was not created (out of nothing) but was formed (evolved?) out of something else.

The consequences of this idea of creation are revolutionary. A world created by God is real, not a dream either of God or of man. And that world is rational. Finally, it is good. Christianity is a realistic, rational, and world-affirming religion rather than a mystical, mythical, or world-denying religion because of its Jewish source. It is no accident that a disproportionate number of the world's great scientists have been Jewish.

3. The essence of Judaism, which is above all a practical religion, is the divine law. The law binds the human will to the divine will, for the God of the Jews is not just a being, or a force, or even just a mind, but a will, a person. His will is that our will

should conform to his: "Be ye holy for I the Lord your God am holy" (Lev 19:2).

The law has levels of intimacy and depth ranging from the multitudinous civil and ceremonial laws through the Ten Commandments of the moral law to the single heart of the law. This heart is expressed in the central prayer of Judaism, the *sh'ma* (from its first word, *hear*): "Hear, O Israel: the Lord, the Lord our God is one Lord; and you shall love the Lord your God with all your heart and with all your soul and with all your might" (Dt 6:4–5).

Thus the essence of Judaism is the same as the essence of Christianity: the love of God. But the way of fulfilling that essence is different. Judaism knows the Truth and the Life, but not the Way. As the song says, half-seriously, "Two out of three ain't bad."

4. Even the Way is foreshadowed in Judaism, of course, by the prophets and by the priesthood. The act that was dramatically brought before the Jews each time they worshipped in the temple was an act of sacrifice, the blood of bulls and goats and lambs foretelling forgiveness by Christ's shed blood. The Christian can see each detail of Old Testament Judaism as a line or dot in the portrait of Christ. That is why it is so ironic and tragic that "he came unto his own and his own received him not" (Jn 1:11). Scripture is his picture, but most Jews preferred the picture to the person. Thus the irony of his saying, "You search the scriptures because you think that in them you have eternal life; and it is they that bear witness to me; yet you refuse to come to me that you may have life" (Jn 5:39–40).

5., 6. No religion outside Judaism and Christianity posits such an intimate relationship with God as faith. Faith means not just belief but fidelity, fidelity to the covenant, like a marriage covenant. Sin is the opposite of faith, for sin means not just vice but divorce, breaking the covenant bond. Thus "whatsoever does not proceed from faith is sin" (Rom 14:23). In Judaism, as in Christianity, sin is not just a moral thing and faith is not just an intellectual thing. Both are spiritual, i.e., from the heart, the center, the I. Rabbi Martin Buber's little classic *I and Thou* lays bare the essence of Judaism and its deep likeness to Christianity in this respect.

Christians are often asked by Jews not to prosyletize. They cannot comply, of course, because their Lord and God has solemnly commanded them otherwise (Mt 28:18–20). But the request is understandable, for Judaism does not prosyletize. Originally Jews believed that only when the Messiah came was the Jewish revelation to spread to the Gentiles. Orthodox Jews still believe this, but modern Judaism is nonprosyletizing for other reasons, often relativistic ones.

Christianity and Judaism are both closer and farther apart than any two other religions in the world. On the one hand, Christians are completed Jews; but, on the other hand, while dialogue between any two other religions may always fall back on the idea that they may not really contradict each other because they are talking different languages and about different things, Jews and Christians both know who Jesus is and simply differ about who he is. He is the rock of stumbling (Is 8:14), and we dare not reduce him to a pebble.

13
Comparative Religions: Christianity and Islam

There are two disturbing aspects in the relationship between Christianity and Islam: (1) Dialogue between the two is almost nonexistent. Islam resists ecumenical dialogue more than any other religion. To prosyletize in any way in a Muslim country is to go to prison. (2) Islam once nearly conquered the world, in the early Middle Ages, when its empire stretched from Spain to Indonesia, and it looks as if it is on that road again. Islamic growth rates in Africa, France, and America are phenomenal. (Islam is especially popular among blacks because of its strong stand on racial equality and its freedom from a history of racism and colonialism.) In other words, Muslims have the world's lowest rate of being converted and one of the world's highest rates of converting.

What accounts for this success? What makes Islam such an attractive creed? In a word, simplicity. Islam reflects the stark, strong simplicity of the Arabian desert, where it was born. A Muslim knows exactly where he stands. To a world more and more confused, befuddled, foggy, gray, relativistic, and wimpy, Islam comes with a sword that cuts the Gordian knot of modern malaise at a single sharp stroke. The stroke, the striking simplicity of Islam's creed, is summed up in the formula that shatters the silence daily from every mosque and minaret: *La illaha illa Allah!*— "There is no God but Allah!"

Allah, of course, is God—the same God Jews and Christians know and worship. Islam is not only a Western, theistic religion rather than an Oriental, pantheistic religion, but it bases itself explicitly on the historical revelation of the God of the Jews, tracing itself to Ishmael, Isaac's brother, to whom God also promised special blessings, according to Genesis. Isaac and

Ishmael, Jews and Muslims, have been engaged in sibling rivalry ever since.

The older name that "infidels" gave this religion, Mohammed-anism, is inaccurate, for neither Mohammed nor any of his followers ever claimed Mohammed was anything more than a man, a prophet. "There is no God but Allah and Mohammed is his prophet" is the complete Muslim creed.

The code is almost as simple as the creed. The "five pillars" of Islam define the duties of every Muslim. They include a pilgrimage to Mecca at least once in a lifetime if possible, to commemorate Islam's initial event in 622 A.D., the hegira, Mohammed's flight from Mecca; fasting; almsgiving; ritual prayer five times a day; and professing the creed "there is no God but Allah and Mohammed is his prophet."

In one sense Islam is a simplification of Christianity, as Buddhism is a simplification of Hinduism. In another sense Islam adds to Christianity, for where Jews have only our Old Testament scriptures and Christians add the New Testament, Muslims also add the Koran. They accept the claims of the Jewish prophets to be sent by God. They believe Jesus deepened this revelation and that Mohammed completed it. Mohammed is the "seal" of the prophets. He tells how to live Jesus' ethic (Jesus is seen only as a man, an ethical teacher).

Actually, Islam neither simply simplifies Christianity nor simply adds to it, but reinterprets it, somewhat as Christianity reinterprets Judaism. As the Christian interpretation of the Old Testament is not the same as the Jewish one, the Muslim interpretation of the New Testament is not the same as the Christian one; for a Muslim the Koran authoritatively interprets the New Testament as the New interprets the Old.

The Koran itself is the only miracle Mohammed claimed—though perhaps equally miraculous is the fact that Mohammed's wife became his first convert. An illiterate peasant, Mohammed received the Koran through word-for-word dictation from Allah, according to orthodox Islam. When Muslims read the Koran, they become ecstatic with admiration. They say no outsider can appreciate it nor can it be adequately translated from Arabic. In this sense, Islam is a bit esoteric, though it is a religion with a public revelation in a book.

Islam believes in a single, all-just, all-perfect, all-powerful God who created the world and man, insists on obedience to his will, and promises salvation and immortality to believers and obeyers. In all these ways Islam is like Judaism and Christianity (Western) rather than like Hinduism and Buddhism (Eastern). Allah is not a force but a person; not merely being or even merely consciousness but also moral will. From the will of Allah come both the existence of the world by creation and the rule over it—over nature and history by providence and over human free choice by moral law.

The three major Christian doctrines Islam denies are the Trinity, the Incarnation, and the Resurrection. Like Judaism, Islam denies Christ's claim to divinity. Allah is one; how could he be three? Jesus is human; how could he be divine? "It is unfitting for Allah to have a son", wrote Mohammed, apparently interpreting sonship biologically.

The Koran teaches Christ's Virgin Birth but not his Resurrection; his prophetic function (teaching) but not his priestly function (salvation) or his kingly function (ruling); his moral authority but not his supernatural authority. To Muslims, as to Jews, Christ is the stumbling block. The theology of God the Father and the ethics of human living are essentially the same for Jews, Christians, and Muslims. What then is missing? Aren't these the two essentials? No. What is missing is the link between the two, the "missing link", Christ the mediator between God and man. Mohammed and the Koran are essentially another Moses (lawgiver) and another law. Missing are grace, salvation, redemption: precisely the essential things.

There are two kinds of Muslims today as there were in the Middle Ages: modernists and orthodox, liberals and fundamentalists, Mutazilites (rationalists) and Mutikalimoun. In the thirteenth century Thomas Aquinas confronted Latin Averroism, the European version of the Muslim philosopher Averroës' way of reconciling the Koran with the philosophy of Aristotle by reducing much of the Koran to myth and giving Aristotle's views the authority of pure reason. Averroës taught that a literal interpretation of the Koran (which the vast majority of Muslims accept) is proper for the masses, who cannot rise to the level of philosophical abstraction, but, for those who can, Aristotle's arguments must prevail over belief in divine providence, creation of the world, and individual immortality (all of which Aristotle denied). Things have not changed much, it seems.

We have not yet mentioned the most important thing about Islam: What is it to be a Muslim? How do Muslims exist religiously? Here too, as in Muslim theology and ethics, there is a striking simplicity, summarized in the very title of the religion. *Islam* means both *peace* (etymologically connected with the Hebrew *shalom*) and *submission,* or surrender; it is the peace that comes from submission to Allah's will. Muslims would applaud T. S. Eliot's choice of Dante's line "in his [God's] will, our peace" as "the profoundest line in all of human literature".

Muslims' famous fatalism ("it is the will of Allah"), like the Calvinistic doctrine of predestination, makes them work harder, not less hard. Muslims, like Christians, believe in man's free will as well as God's sovereignty. Theirs is not the modern fatalism from below, Freudian or Skinnerian determinism, but fatalism from above. It is in practice energizing and liberating, not squashing. Islam, like Judaism and Christianity, has produced a rich crop of saints and mystics, especially in the Sufi tradition, which is similar in many ways to the Jewish Hasidic tradition.

Can Muslims be saved? They reject Christ as Savior, yet they seek and love God. Islam means essentially the fundamental option of a wholehearted Yes to God. Most Muslims, like most Jews, see Christ only through broken lenses. If God-seeking and God-loving Jews, both before and after Christ's Incarnation, can find God, then surely God-seeking Muslims can too, according to Christ's own promise that "all who seek, find"—whether in this life or the next. Yet Christ also insists that "no one can come to the Father but by me." Whatever truth Mohammed taught Muslims about God is present in Christ the Logos, the full revelation of God. If

Muslims are saved, they are saved by Christ. Christians should hope and pray that their separated Islamic brothers and sisters will be reunited with our common Father by finding Christ the Way. We cannot stop prosyletizing, for prosyletizing means leading our brothers to the Way home.

14
Comparative Religions: Christianity and Hinduism

There are two essential kinds of religions in the world: Eastern (Oriental) and Western (Occidental). The main differences between Hinduism and Christianity are typical of the differences between Eastern and Western religions in general. There are at least ten such general differences.

1. Hindusim is pantheistic, not theistic. The doctrine that God created the world out of nothing rather than emanating it out of his own substance or merely shaping some preexisting material is an idea that simply did not ever occur to anyone but the Jews and those who learned it from them. Everyone else either thought of the gods as part of the world (paganism) or thought of the world as part of God (pantheism).

2. If God is in everything, God is in what we call good and evil. Then there is no absolute morality, no divine law, no divine will discriminating good and evil. Morality is only a means to purify the soul from desires so that it can attain mystical consciousness. Again, the Jews are unique in identifying the source of morality with the object of religion. Everyone has two innate senses: the religious sense of worship and the moral sense of conscience; but only the Jewish God is the focus of both. Only the God of the Bible is absolutely righteous.

3. Eastern religions come from private mystical experiences; Western religions come from public revelations recorded in a book or summarized in a creed. In the East, human experience validates the scriptures; in the West, Scripture judges experience. (For this reason Eastern religions are naturally more popular with secular psychologists.)

4. Therefore Eastern religions are esoteric, elitist, fully understandable only from within by the few who share the

experience. Western religions are exoteric, public, democratic, open to all. In Hinduism there are many levels of truth: polytheism, sacred cows, and reincarnation for the masses; monotheism (or monism) for the mystics, who declare the individual soul one with Brahman (God) and beyond reincarnation ("Brahman is the only reincarnator"). Truth is thus relative to level of experience.

When C. S. Lewis was converted from atheism, he sort of shopped around in the world's religious supermarket and narrowed his choice to Hinduism or Christianity as the only two religions that were both "thick" and "thin". Religions are like soups, he said. Some, like consomme, are thin and clear (Unitarianism, Confucianism, modern Judaism); others, like minestrone, are thick and dark (paganism, "mystery religions"). Only Hinduism and Christianity are both thin (philosophical) and thick (sacramental, mysterious). But Hinduism is really two religions: thick for the masses, thin for the sages. Only Christianity is both together for everyone.

5. Individuality is illusion according to Eastern mysticism. Not that we are not real but that we are not distinct from God or each other. Christianity tells you to love your neighbors; Hinduism tells you you are your neighbors. The word spoken by God himself as his own essential name, the word *I,* is the ultimate illusion, not the ultimate reality, according to the East. There is no separate ego; all is one.

6. Because individuality is illusion, so is free will.

7. If free will is illusion, so is sin. And if sin is illusion, so is hell. Perhaps the strongest attraction of Eastern religions is in their denial of sin, guilt, and hell.

8. Thus the two essential points of Christianity (as summarized by Saint Paul in Romans, the first systematic Christian theology), sin and salvation, are both missing in the East. If there is no sin, no salvation is needed, only enlightenment. We need not be born again, only to wake up to our innate divinity. If I am part of God, I can never be really alienated from God by sin.

9. Body, matter, history, and time itself are not independently

real according to Hinduism. Mystical experience lifts the spirit out of time and the world. Judaism and Christianity are essentially news, events in time: creation, providence, prophets, Messiah, death and Resurrection, ascension, Second Coming. Incarnation and new birth are eternity dramatically entering time. Eastern religions are not dramatic. (Demythologizers are Eastern in this way, seeing miraculous events as mere mythic parables, the point of which is some eternal, abstract truth.)

10. The ultimate ideal is not sanctity but mysticism. Sanctity is fundamentally a matter of the will: willing God's will, loving God and neighbor. Mysticism is fundamentally a matter of intellect, intuition, consciousness which fits the Eastern picture of God as consciousness, not will, not lawgiver.

Hinduism claims that all other religions are yogas: ways, deeds, paths. Christianity is a form of bhakti yoga (yoga for emotional types and lovers). There is also jnana yoga (yoga for intellectuals), raja yoga (yoga for experimenters), karma yoga (yoga for workers, practical people), and hatha yoga, the physical preliminary to the other four. For Hindus, religions are human roads up the divine mountain to enlightenment, "different strokes for different folks". Religion is relative to human need; there is no one way, no one objective truth.

There is, however, a universal subjective truth about human nature: that it has "four wants"—pleasure, power, altruism, and enlightenment. Hinduism encourages us to try all four paths, confident that only the fourth brings complete fulfillment. If there is reincarnation and if there is no hell, Hindus can afford to be patient and let us learn the long hard way: by experience rather than by faith and revelation. Hindus are hard to have a dialogue with for the opposite reason Muslims are: Muslims are very intolerant, Hindus are very tolerant. Nothing is false; everything is true in a way. Islam is like a cold iron spike; Hinduism is like a warm fog.

The point and summit of Hinduism is the mystical experience called mukti, or moksha: "liberation" from the illusion of finitude, realization that *tat tvam asi,* "thou art That [Brahman]". At the center of your being is not individual ego but atman, universal self, which is identical with Brahman, "the great one", the All, the One. This sounds like the most absurd and blasphemous thing one could say: that I am God. But it is not that I, John Smith, am God the Father Almighty. Atman is not ego and Brahman is not God the Father. Hinduism identifies not the immanent human self with the transcendent divine self but the transcendent human self with the immanent divine self. It is not Christianity. It is even a Christian heresy. But it is not idiocy.

It may even be skewed profundity. Martin Buber, in *I and Thou,* suggests that mukti is the profound experience of the "original prebiographical unity" of the self, beneath all forms and contents brought to it by experience, but confused with God. Even Aristotle said that "the soul is in a way all things". Hinduism construes this way as identity, or inclusion, rather than knowing: being all things substantially rather than mentally. The soul is in truth a mirror for the whole world. But it is also an object in God's mirror. Hinduism sees that the soul is like a God to the world but forgets that it is like a thing in the world to God.

Such pantheism is very popular today. Most of my Catholic college students believe we are parts of God and that God is in everyone. Thus we need not be "born again" but need only recognize our intrinsic value and accept ourselves as we are. They have been educated by pop psychologists masquerading as theologians. Pop psychology is basically nonreligious Hinduism, humanistic pantheism.

In one sense Hinduism and Christianity are as far apart as two religions can be. Compare the crucifix with the meditating guru. Christ has his eyes open, his arms outstretched, and his body torn. The Cross is what happens when good meets evil. The guru has his eyes closed, turned inward. His arms and whole body are self-contained, like a sphere. His is not torn; he is one, all conflict transcended. Sin is not solved but dissolved.

In another sense, however, Hinduism and Christianity may be less far apart than Judaism and Christianity, for they speak quite different languages. Hindus have not rejected Christ; they just do now know him. Or perhaps they do. Perhaps, as Raymond Pannikar suggests, there is a "hidden Christ of Hinduism" in Isvara, "the Lord", the manifestation, or theophany, of Brahman. Krishna in the *Bhagavad-Gita* is also something like Christ, almost an incarnation—a Docetic Christ, an appearance in human form of Brahman. Hinduism also has something a little like a Trinity in *Sat-cit-ananda,* the three things Brahman is: infinite being, infinite consciousness, and infinite bliss.

But "something like" is not the real thing, the substance. It is a shadow, a hint, a guess, an intuition, a dream, a myth, glimpsed from afar, "through a glass, darkly". C. S. Lewis calls myths "good dreams". We need more than dreams; we need wakefulness. Hinduism says we are dreaming now and when we realize in mystical experience our divine identity, we wake up. Perhaps it is the reverse.

Practical Hinduism is also like a dream. Dostoevsky says, "Love in action is a harsh and dreadful thing compared with love in dreams." Hinduism teaches compassion, but not love in action, the demanding, willful, personal, moral love of Jesus. Some orthodox Hindus saw Mother Teresa as an alien interference, imposing Christian values of active personal charity on a Hindu society where people are left to die lest one interfere with their karma (fate). But most Hindus love her and recognize her as a saint.

Hinduism classifies Christianity as bhakti yoga, but Christians might classify Hinduism as a possible means to prayer. If we are to meditate when we pray and if Hindus have a long and rich tradition of methods of meditation, we should use whatever is good and useful there, just as we have used many intellectual techniques and insights from pagan Greek philosophy, but with discernment and transformed by a Christian consciousness. Many Christians are trying to do just that today. We must avoid uncritical syncretism and equally uncritical blanket condemnation with equal resolution—far from an easy task. That is why Modernism and Fundamentalism are popular—they are two quick and easy answers to a complex question. The Church will probably take centuries to define a middle way with Hinduism.

15
Comparative Religions:
Christianity and Buddhism

The great German Catholic theologian Romano Guardini says, in his profoundly insightful and profoundly orthodox meditation on the life of Christ, *The Lord,* that no man in human history ever came closer to rivaling the enormity of Christ's claim to transform human nature itself at its roots than did Buddha (though in a radically different way). Huston Smith says in *The Religions of Man* that there have been only two people in history who so astonished people that they asked not "Who are you?" but "What are you? A man or a god?" They were Jesus and Buddha.

Buddha's clear answer to this question was: "I am a man, not a god"; Christ's clear answer was: "I am both son of Man and Son of God." Buddha said, "Look not to me, look to my dharma [doctrine]"; Christ said, "Come unto me." Buddha said, "Be ye lamps unto yourselves"; Christ said, "I am the light of the world." Yet contrary to the original intentions of both men, some later Buddhists (the Pure Land sect) divinized Buddha, and some later Christians (Arians and Modernists) dedivinized Christ.

The claims of Buddha and Christ are in fact so different that we may well wonder whether Buddhism should be called a religion at all. It does not speak of God, or Brahman, as does the Hinduism from which it emerged. Nor does it speak of atman, or soul. In fact, it teaches the doctrine of *an-atta,* no-soul—the doctrine that we are made of strands (*skandhas*) of impersonal consciousness woven together by causal necessity without any underlying substance, self, or soul.

Buddhism does not deny God. It is silent about God. It is agnostic, not atheistic. But it is not silent about soul. Its denial of soul has practical importance: it teaches us not to be "attached", not to send our soul out in desire, not to love. Instead of personal, individual, free-willed *agape* (active love), Buddhism teaches an impersonal, universal feeling of compassion (*karuna*). Compassion is something we often hear more about than *agape* in the modern West.

Karuna and *agape* lead the disciple to do similar strikingly selfless deeds but in strikingly different spirits. This difference is illustrated by the Buddhist story of a saint who, like Saint Martin of Tours, gave his cloak to a beggar, in fact a robber. But the Buddhist's explanation was not "because I love you" or "because Christ loves you" but rather that "this is the enlightened thing to do, for if you were freezing and you had two gloves on one hand and none on the other hand, would it not be the enlightened thing to do to give one of the gloves to the bare hand?"

The point of charity for a Buddhist is not the welfare of the recipient but the liberation of the giver from the burden of self. The same end could be achieved without a recipient. Consider, for instance, the following Buddhist story: A man, fleeing a man-eating tiger, came to the edge of a cliff. The only way was down. He found a vine and climbed down it; but there, at the foot of the cliff, was a second man-eating tiger. Then he saw two mice, one black and one white (yin and yang), chewing the vine in two above him. Just before it broke, he saw a wild strawberry on the face of the cliff. He plucked it and ate it. It was delicious! The "unenlightened" will wonder what the point is, or why he didn't distract the tiger with the strawberry. But the "enlightened" will explain the parable thus: The man tasted to the tiger exactly as the strawberry did to the man. In other words, the man, the tiger, and the strawberry are all one self. The "illusion" of individuality is seen through. There is no soul. So there is no fear—no fear of death because there is no one there to die.

According to Buddhism, egotism (selfish desire) causes the illusion of an ego. According to the West, secular as well as religious, a real ego is the cause and egotism is the effect. *Agape* is a different effect coming from the same cause: altruism from the ego instead of egotism from the ego. To the Buddhist, *agape* is impossible; there can be no ego without egotism, no self without

West:

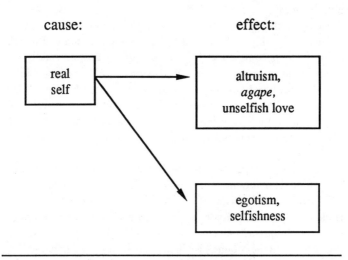

cause: effect:

real self → altruism, *agape*, unselfish love

real self → egotism, selfishness

Buddhism:

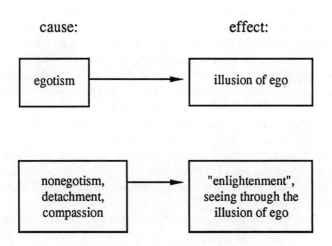

cause: effect:

egotism → illusion of ego

nonegotism, detachment, compassion → "enlightenment", seeing through the illusion of ego

selfishness, because the self is not a real cause that might conceivably change its effect. Rather, the self is the illusion caused by selfishness.

How can this apparent nihilism, this philosophy of nothingness, seem so liberating to Buddhists? The answer is found in Buddha himself: his personality and the events of his life, especially his "great enlightenment". Like Jesus, Buddha taught a very shocking lesson. And, like Jesus, Buddha was believed only because of his personality. "Holy to his fingertips" is how he is described. If you or I said what Buddha or Jesus said, we would be laughed at. There was something deep and moving there that made the incredible credible.

The events of Buddha's life are dramatic and offer a clue to this something. It is not, however, Buddha's life or his personality that is central to Buddhism; there could be a Buddhism without Buddha. (There could not, of course, be a Christianity without Christ, except to a Modernist, for whom Christianity is essentially the Sermon on the Mount.) Buddha is a title, not a given name—as is Christ (Messiah). It is his essential claim; for it means the enlightened one or the one who woke up. Buddha claims we are all spiritually asleep until the experience of enlightenment, or awakening. Here is the story of how Buddha became Buddha, of how a man woke up.

Born Siddhartha Gautama, son of a king who hoped his heir would become the most successful king in India's history, he was protected in a palace of earthly delights to make kingship irresistibly attractive to him. But curiosity led him to sneak away into the forbidden world outside, where he saw the "four distressing sights". The first three were a sick man, an old man, and a dead man. Siddhartha puzzled deeply over these newly discovered mysteries of sickness, old age, and death, but to no avail. Then came the fourth sight: a begging ascetic who had renounced the world to seek enlightenment. Siddhartha decided to do the same.

He spent years meditating on life's deepest mystery: Why is man unhappy? After years of torturing his body to free his soul, all in vain, he decided on the "middle way" between his earlier self-indulgence and his later self-torture. After eating a decent meal for the first time in years, he sat in full lotus position under the sacred bodhi tree in Benares and resolved not to rise until he was enlightened. When he rose he proclaimed that he was Buddha. He had broken through the great mystery of life.

The breakthrough had to be experienced, not just verbalized. Buddhism is not essentially a doctrine but an experience. Yet Buddha also verbalized a doctrine (dharma): the "four noble truths" summarized everything he taught. Whenever he was pressed by his disciples to go beyond the four noble truths, he refused. Everything else was "questions not tending to edification".

The first noble truth is that all of life is dukkha, suffering. The word means out-of-joint-ness or separation—something similar to sin but without the personal, relational dimension: not a broken relationship but a broken consciousness. Inner brokenness is Buddhism's "bad news", which precedes its gospel, or "good news".

The second noble truth is that the cause of suffering is tanha, grasping, selfish desire. We suffer because of the gap between what we want and what we have. This gap is created by our dissatisfaction, our wanting to get what we do not have or want-ing to keep what we do have (e.g., life, which causes fear of death). Thus desire is the villain for Buddha, the cause of all suffering.

This second truth explains the no-soul doctrine. Desire creates the illusion of a desirer alienated from the desired object, the illusion of twoness. Enlightenment is the extinction of this illusion. "I want that" creates the illusion of an "I" distinct from the "that"; and this distinction is the cause of suffering. Desire is thus the fuel of suffering's fire.

The third noble truth follows inevitably. To remove the cause is to remove the effect; therefore suffering can be extinguished (nirvana) by extinguishing its cause, desire. Remove the fuel and you put out the fire.

The fourth noble truth tells you how to extinguish desire: by the "noble eightfold path" of ego reduction in each of life's eight defined areas, inward and outward (e.g., "right thought", "right association").

The content of the four noble truths is specifically Buddhist, but the form is universal. Every religion, every practical philosophy, every therapy, spiritual or physical, has its four noble truths: the symptom, the diagnosis, the prognosis, and the prescription. They are the bad effect, the bad cause, the good effect, and the good cause, respectively. For instance, Platonism's four noble truths are vice, ignorance, virtue, and knowledge. Marxism's four noble truths are class conflict, capitalism, communism, and revolution. Christianity's four noble truths are death, sin, Christ, and salvation. Romans 6:23 sums up all four: "The wages of sin is death, but the gift of God is eternal life in Christ Jesus our Lord."

The crucial one of the four steps is the second. The patient knows his own symptoms, but only a trained doctor can diagnose the hidden cause, the disease. Once diagnosed, most diseases have a standard prognosis and prescription that can be looked up in a medical textbook. On this crucial issue, the diagnosis of the human problem, Christianity and Buddhism seem about as far apart as possible, for where Buddha finds our desires too strong, Christ finds them too weak. Christ wants us to love more, not less: to love God with our whole heart, soul, mind, and strength. Buddha "solves" the problem of pain by a spiritual euthanasia: curing the disease of egotism and the suffering it brings by killing the patient, the ego, self, soul, or I-image of God (I AM) in man.

Yet perhaps things are not quite as contradictory as that, for the desire Buddha speaks of is only selfish desire. He does not distinguish unselfish love (*agape*) from selfish love (*eros*); he simply does not know of *agape* at all. He profoundly knows and condemns the desire to possess something less than ourselves, like money, sex, or power; but he does not know the desire to be possessed by something more than ourselves. Buddha knows greed but not God. And surely we Westerners, whose lives and economic systems are often based on greed, need to hear Buddha when he speaks about what he knows and we have forgotten. But Buddhists even more desperately need to hear what they do not know: the good news about God and his love.

16

Comparative Religions: Christianity and the New Paganism

The most serious threat to Christianity today is not any one of the other great religions of the world such as Islam or Buddhism. Nor is it simple atheism, which has no depth, no mass appeal, and no roots, tradition, or staying power. Rather, it is a religion most of us think is dead. The religion is paganism, and it is very much alive.

There is an Old Paganism and a New Paganism. What holds both together under the same name is a vague folk religion, a popular religious alternative to Christianity without a supernaturally revealed creed, code, or cult. Paganism is simply the natural gravity of the human spirit, the religious line of least resistance, religion in its natural, fallen state.

The Old Paganism came from the countryside. Indeed, the very word *paganism* comes from the Latin *pagani,* which means those from the fields or country dwellers. Country people were the last to be converted to Christianity during the Roman Empire, the last to abandon their ancestral roots in pre-Christian paganism. Today, country people in the Western world are the last to abandon Christianity for the New Paganism, which flourishes in the cities.

The Old Paganism was a far greater thing than the New. In fact, G. K. Chesterton brilliantly summarizes the entire spiritual history of the world in these three statements: "Paganism was the biggest thing in the world, and Christianity was bigger, and everything since has been comparatively small."

There were at least three elements in the Old Paganism that made it great. All three are missing in the New Paganism. The first is the sense of piety (*pietas*), the natural religious instinct to respect something greater than yourself, the humility that instinctively realizes man's subordinate place in the great scheme of things. Moderation or temperance (*sophrosune* in Greek) went along with piety, especially in classical civilization. The motto "nothing too much" was inscribed over every temple to Apollo, along with "know thyself".

This natural modesty and respect contrast sharply with the brash and arrogant attitude of the New Pagan in the modern West. Today it is mainly Oriental societies that still preserve the traditional reverence and reticence. The West (especially America) does not understand this reverence, and thinks it quaint at best and hypocritical at worst.

The New Paganism is the virtual divinization of man, the religion of man as the new God. One of its popular slogans, often repeated unthinkingly by Christians, is "the infinite value of the human person". Its aim is building a heaven on earth, a secular salvation. Another word for the New Paganism is humanism, the religion that will not lift up its head to the heavens but stuffs the heavens into its head.

A second ingredient of the Old Paganism that is missing in the new is an objective and absolute morality, what C. S. Lewis called "the Tao" in his prophetic little classic *The Abolition of Man*. To premodern man, pagan as well as Christian, moral laws were absolute: unyielding, nonnegotiable, and unquestionable. They were also objective: discovered rather than created; given, in the nature of things.

The New Paganism is relativistic, subjectivistic, and pragmatic. It says we are makers of moral values. It finds the moral law written not only in the human heart but also *by* the human heart. It acknowledges no divine revelation, nothing to contradict human values, no inconvenient corners out there to puncture our smooth bubbles of self-generated ideals. No one's values can be judged to be wrong. The New Paganism's favorite Scripture is "judge not." The only judgment is the judgment against judging. The only thing wrong is the idea that there is a real wrong. The only absolute is that there are absolutely no absolutes. The only thing to feel guilty about is feeling guilty. And because man rather than God is the origin of values, please don't impose your values on me! (Another favorite line.)

This is really polytheism: many gods, many goods, many moralities. No one believes in Zeus and Apollo and Neptune anymore. (I wonder why; has science really refuted them? Or is it due to total conformity to fashion, supine submission to newspapers?) But moral relativism is the new equivalent of the old polytheism. Each of us has become a god or goddess, a sacred absolute, a giver of law rather than a receiver.

A third ingredient of the Old Paganism but not of the New is awe at something transcendent and supernatural, the sense of worship and wonder and mystery. What the Old Pagan worshipped differed widely—almost anything from Zeus to cows— but he worshipped something. In the modern world the very sense of worship is dying, even in our own new liturgies which sound as if they were invented by a Central State Committee for the Abolition of Poetry meeting in a suburban ranch house.

Even in modern *religion,* the religious sense has dried up. Modern religion is demythologized, demiracalized, dedivinized. God is not the Lord but "the force", not transcendent but immanent, not supernatural but natural. The New Paganism is a vague form of pantheism, the religion of the Blob God. It scorns traditional theism as the worship of the Snob God; in other words it confuses theism with deism. (Pantheism denies transcendence; deism denies immanence; Christianity affirms both, especially by the Incarnation.)

Pantheism is comfortable, and comfort is the modern *summum bonum.* Whenever I want to trick my students on multiple-choice exams, all I have to do is mention the magic words *comfort* or *peace of mind,* and they check it like salivating Pavlovian dogs. "The force" of *Star Wars* is a pantheistic god, and he (or rather it) is immensely popular because it is "like a book on the shelf", as C. S. Lewis put it in *Miracles:* available whenever you want it, but not bothersome when you don't want it. How convenient to think we are bubbles in a divine froth rather than rebellious children of a righteous divine Father! Pantheism has no sense of sin, for sin means separation, and no one can ever be separated from the All. Thus the third feature, no transcendence, is connected with the second, no absolute morality.

The New Paganism is a great triumph of wishful thinking. Without losing the thrill and glow of religion, the terror of religion is removed. The New Paganism stoutly rejects "the fear of God". Nearly all self-styled experts in religious education today are agreed that the thing the Bible calls "the beginning of wisdom" is instead the thing we must above all eradicate from the minds of the young with all the softly destructive power of the weapons of modern pop psychology—namely the fear of the Lord. "Perfect love casts out fear", says Saint John (1Jn 4:18); but when God has become the Pillsbury Dough Boy, there is no fear left to cast out, and when there is no fear to cast out, perfect love lacks its strong roots and seedbed. It becomes instead mere compassion: something good but weak, or even wimpy, precisely the idea people have today of religion. The shock is gone. That the God of the Bible should love us is a thunderbolt; that the God of the New Paganism should love us is a self-evident platitude.

The New Paganism is winning not by opposing but by infiltrating the Church. It is cleverer than the Old. It knows that any opposition from without, even by vastly superior force, has never worked, for "the blood of the martyrs is the seed of the Church." When China welcomed Western missionaries, there were two million conversions in sixty years; when Mao Zedong and Communism persecuted the Church there were twenty million conversions in twenty years. The Church in East Germany is immensely stronger than the Church in West Germany for the same reason. The New Paganism understands this paradox, so it uses the soft, suggestive strategy of the serpent. It whispers, through the mouths of Scripture scholars, the very words of the serpent: "Has God really said . . . ?" (Gen 3:1).

The New Paganism is a joining of forces by three of the enemies of theism: humanism, polytheism, and pantheism. The only five possibilities for ultimate meaning and values are atheism (no God); humanism (man as God); polytheism (many gods); pantheism (one immanent God); and theism (one transcendent God). The battle of the five Kings in the Valley of Armageddon seems to be beginning. Predictions are always rash, but the signs of the times seem, to nearly all thoughtful observers, to be pointing to a fundamental turning point, the end of an age, perhaps of all ages.

The so-called new-age movement combines all the features I have described under the rubric of the New Paganism. It is a loosely organized movement, basically a reflowering of sixties hippiedom, rather than a centralized conspiracy. But strategies are concocted in three places. There may be no conspiracy on *earth* to unify the enemies of the Church, but the strategy of hell is more than the strategy of earth. Only one thing is more than the strategy of hell: the strategy of heaven. The gates of hell cannot prevail against the Church; in fact, God uses the devil to defeat the devil, just as he did on Calvary, when the forces of the Hebrew, Greek, and Roman world united to crucify Christ, as symbolized by the three languages on the accusation sign over the Cross. The very triumph of the devil, the death of God, was the defeat of the devil, the redemption of mankind, *Good* Friday. God, who spoke the first word, always gets the last word. The New Paganism will one day be as dead as the Old.

17
What's the Point of Creeds?

I remember vividly how deeply moved I was as a young Protestant to hear how one of the Catholic martyrs died: scratching in the sand with his own blood the words of the creed, "Credo . . . " ("I believe").

My heart was moved, but my head did not yet understand. What do these Catholics see in their creeds anyway? How can a set of words be worth dying for? Why have wars been fought over a word? What's the point of creeds?

Then I read Dorothy Sayers' little masterpiece *Creed or Chaos?*, and I was answered.

The question can be answered by remembering another question, the one Pilate asked Christ in another life-or-death situation: "What is truth?"

And that is the point of the creeds: truth. In fact, Primal Truth, the truth about God. That is why the words of the Creed are sacred words. Just as God's material houses are sacred, so are his verbal houses. Of course God is no more confined to words, even the sacred words of creeds, than he is confined to the sacred buildings of tent or temple, church or cathedral. But both are holy, set apart, sacred. "Thou shalt not take the *name* of the Lord thy God in vain."

Faith has two dimensions: the objective and the subjective. Creeds express these two dimensions: "I believe in God." There is an I, a believing subject, and there is God, the object of belief. There is the psychology of believing, which is something in us, and there is the theology of belief, which is the Truth believed. There is the eye, and there is the light. And woe to him who mistakes the one for the other.

When the Church formulated her creeds, humanity was more interested in the light than in the eye. God providentially arranged for the great creeds of the Church to be formulated in ages that cared passionately about objective truth. By modern standards, they ignored the subjective, psychological dimension of faith.

But we moderns fall into the opposite and far worse extreme: we are so interested in the subject that we often forget or even scorn the object. Psychology has become our new religion, as Paul Vitz and Kirk Kilpatrick have both so brilliantly shown.

Yet it's the object, not the subjective act, of faith that makes the creeds sacred. They are sacred because Truth is sacred, not because believing is sacred. Creeds do not say merely what *we believe,* but what *is*. Creeds wake us from our dreams and prejudices into objective reality. Creeds do not confine us in little cages, as the modern world thinks; creeds free us into the outdoors, into the real world where the winds of heaven whip around our heads.

What is the object, the Truth? Saint Thomas says that the primary object of faith is not words and statements but God himself. "We believe in God." Further, as Christians we know God most fully in Christ, God incarnate, and as Catholics we know Christ through Holy Mother Church and her creeds.

When human reason raved, in the Arian heresy, that Christ could not possibly be both fully human and fully divine, Athanasius stood against the world; today we know Christ as he really is because of Athanasius and his creed.

When contemporary forms of the same heresy water down the "strong meat" of Christ, the Church again braves the media, the mouth of the world, and calmly thunders the full truth about Christ. True, it is Christ rather than words that is the primary object of the Christian's faith, but *what* Christ? Here words are crucial.

Two extremes must be avoided: intellectualism and anti-intellectualism, worshipping the words and scorning the words. If the ancient mind tended to the former extreme, the modern mind certainly tends to the latter. Both errors are deadly.

Intellectualism misses the core of faith, both objectively and subjectively. Objectively, the core of faith is God, who is a Person, not a concept. Subjectively, the core of faith is the will, not the intellect. Though informed by the intellect, it is the will that freely chooses to believe.

Faith is not the relation between an intellect and an idea, but the relation between an I and a Thou. That is why faith makes the difference between heaven and hell. God does not send you to hell for flunking his theology exam but for willingly divorcing from him.

Anti-intellectualism also misses the core of faith, both objectively and subjectively. Objectively, because its faith has no object. It calls faith an experience ("the faith experience")—a term *never* used by our Lord, Scripture, the creeds, or the popes. Modern people are constantly saying, "Have faith!" But faith in what or whom? They often mean "have faith in faith." But faith in faith in what?

Anti-intellectualism is a modern reaction against the modern narrowing of reason to scientific reason. When the ancients and medievals called man a "rational animal", they did not mean a computerized camera mounted in an ape. They meant by "reason" understanding, wisdom, insight, and conscience as well as logical calculation.

Modern thinkers often forget this dimension of man and think only of reasoning (as in calculating) and feeling. And because they see that faith is not a matter of reasoning, they conclude that it must be a matter of feeling. Thus "I believe" comes to mean "I feel", and creeds simply have no place. Faith becomes a "leap" in the dark instead of a leap in the light.

Many of the Church's greatest saints have been doctors of the Church, theologians, philosophers, intellectuals: Augustine, Anselm, Aquinas, Bonaventure. Anti-intellectuals like Tatian and Tertullian and Luther (who called reason "the devil's whore") often die excommunicated, as heretics.

The Church—repeating what Saint Paul said in Romans 1:19–20—even teaches as a matter of faith that God's existence can be known by reason, independent of faith!

The Catholic ideal is the complete person, with a cool head *and* a warm heart, a hard head and a soft heart. The mere intellectual has a cool heart; the anti-intellectual has a hot head. The intellectual has a hard heart, the anti-intellectual has a soft head. The Church puts the severed parts in the right order because the Church has the blueprint: Christ (Eph 4:13). The Church has always had a conservative head and a liberal heart, and the world has never understood her, just as it never understood Christ.

Creeds are to the head what good works are to the heart: creeds express truth, the head's food, as good works express love, the heart's food. Both are sacred.

If there is any doubt about the need for creeds, it can be settled by fact: the fact that the Church established by Christ, the Church Christ promised to "guide into all truth", has in fact formulated and taught creeds.

The first bishops, the apostles, formulated the Church's first, shortest, and most important creed, the Apostles' Creed. Whether the apostles literally wrote it, as tradition says, or whether it was written by their disciples to preserve the apostles' teaching, in either case it is the teaching of the apostles. When we recite this creed we speak in unison with them.

There is a strange notion abroad that creeds oppress, repress, or suppress people. That is like saying that light or food is repressive. The practical purpose of the creeds is truth, and truth is light and food for the soul.

Each of the Church's creeds was written in response to a heresy, to combat it not by force but by truth, as light combats darkness. Creeds are "truth in labeling". Those who disbelieve in truth or scorn it, or who disbelieve in our ability to know it, see creeds as power plays.

The media's hysterical rhetoric about the pope's labeling Hans Kung's theology as non-Catholic theology is a good example of the world's utter confusion here. The media conjured up visions of the return of the Inquisition simply because the pope said, in effect, that Kung's teachings about Christ should not be confused with the Church's teachings about Christ. But this reaction should be expected if we remember the words of Christ himself (read Jn 3:17–21 prayerfully).

The most important creeds were those formulated by the Church's ecumenical (universal) councils in response to the most important heresies, the heresies about Christ; and of these the two most important were Chalcedon and Nicaea. (The Nicene Creed is the one we recite each Sunday at Mass.) The Church's most recent council, Vatican II, formulated no new creeds and no new doctrines but applied the old ones to new needs and situations.

The pope called an extraordinary synod of bishops in 1985 in part to clarify Catholic confusion concerning Vatican II. Anyone who would take the trouble to read the actual documents (which are much, much longer than creeds) would see how traditional they are. The "spirit of Vatican II" conjured by the media and some theologians is a phantom, a ghostlike half-person, with the fatal split between head and heart, creed and deed, theology and social action, love of God and love of man, eternal principles and updated applications.

But the pope is a bridge builder, a pontifex; he will patch what the world has torn. And the blueprint he will follow in doing this will be the historic, never-abandoned creeds of the Church of Christ.

18
Defining the Church's Twin Mysteries: The Athanasian Creed

The Text of the Athanasian Creed

Whoever desires to be saved must above all things hold the Catholic faith. Unless a man keeps it in its entirety inviolate, he will assuredly perish eternally.

Now this is the Catholic faith, that we worship one God in Trinity and Trinity in unity, without either confusing the persons or dividing the substance. For the Father's person is one, the Son's another; but the Godhead of the Father, the Son, and the Holy Spirit is one, their glory is equal, their majesty coeternal.

Such as the Father is, such is the Son, such also the Holy Spirit. The Father is uncreated, the Son uncreated, the Holy Spirit uncreated. The Father is infinite, the Son infinite, the Holy Spirit infinite. The Father is eternal, the Son eternal, the Holy Spirit eternal. Yet there are not three eternals, but one eternal; just as there are not three uncreateds of three infinities, but one uncreated and one infinite. In the same way the Father is almighty, the Son almighty, the Holy Spirit almighty; yet there are not three almighties but one almighty.

Thus the Father is God, the Son God, the Holy Spirit God; and yet there are not three Gods, but there is one God. Thus the Father is Lord, the Son Lord, the Holy Spirit Lord; and yet there are not three Lords, but there is one Lord. Because just as we are obliged by Christian truth to acknowledge each Person separately both God and Lord, so we are forbidden by the Catholic religion to speak of three Gods or Lords.

The Father is from none, not made nor created nor begotten. The Son is from the Father alone, not made nor created but begotten. The Holy Spirit is from the Father and the Son, not made nor created nor begotten but proceeding. So there is one Father, not three Fathers; one Son, not three Sons; one Holy Spirit, not three Holy Spirits. And in this Trinity there is nothing before or after, nothing greater or less, but all three persons are coeternal with each other and coequal. Thus in all things, as has been stated above, both Trinity in unity and unity in Trinity must be worshipped. So he who desires to be saved should think thus of the Trinity.

It is necessary, however, to eternal salvation that he would also faithfully believe in the Incarnation of our Lord Jesus Christ. Now the right faith is that we should believe and confess that our Lord Jesus Christ, the Son of God, is equally both God and man. He is God from the Father's substance, begotten before time; and he is man from his mother's substance, born in time. Perfect God, perfect man composed of a rational soul and human flesh, equal to the Father in respect of his divinity, less than the Father in respect of his humanity.

Who, although he is God and man, is nevertheless not two but one Christ. He is one, however, not by the transformation of his divinity into flesh, but by the taking up of his humanity into God; one certainly not by confusion of substance, but by oneness of person. For just as rational soul and flesh are a single man, so God and man are a single Christ.

Who suffered for our salvation, descended to hell, rose from the dead, ascended to heaven, sat down at the Father's right hand, whence he will come to judge living and dead; at whose coming all men will rise again with their bodies, and will render an account of their deeds; and those who have behaved well will go to eternal life, those who have behaved badly to eternal fire. This is the Catholic faith. Unless a man believes it faithfully and steadfastly, he will not be able to be saved.

It is said that the only two things that are certain about the origin of the Athanasian Creed are that it was not written by Athanasius and that it was not written as a creed.

Yet it is Athanasian theology, and it looks very much like a creed. It probably dates from 434 or 440 A.D. No one knows its author. Medieval scholastic theologians put it on a par with the Apostles' and Nicene creeds. Protestant reformers accepted it. Anglicans still use it in their liturgy. But it is used only once a year in the Roman Catholic Church: in the Divine Office on the Feast of the Most Blessed Trinity.

Those who are familiar with it—mainly Anglicans and older Roman Catholics—often find it devotionally as well as intellectually profound and magnificent. Its style is high and beautiful, like God himself. Its rhythmic cadences are sonorous and awesomely formal. It is eminently chantable.

Its outline is the same as that of the Apostles' and Nicene creeds.

It goes beyond them in defining the two major doctrines of the Christian faith, the Trinity and the Incarnation, both of which center on the identity of Christ.

Trinity and Incarnation are "mysteries of the faith" in the technical theological sense. A *mystery* is a divine revelation of a truth previously hidden and otherwise inaccessible to human reason. A mystery is neither sheer light nor sheer darkness to our mind, but like a bright spot of light surrounded by darkness. We are invited to extend the circle of light more and more, exploring its inexhaustible recesses without ever coming to an end and exhausting the darkness.

There is a black or white, either/or aspect to a revealed mystery: we know that it is true because God, who can neither deceive nor be deceived, has revealed it. But we do not know what it means simply or fully, only partially and imperfectly.

Mainly because they misunderstand the Catholic notion of mystery, many moderns are turned off by creeds, especially by the Athanasian, which goes deeper into both the mystery and the definition of Trinity and Incarnation than any previous creed. Such critics (1) find it unintelligible because they are impatient with mystery and have a narrow, controlled little concept of intelligibility in mind, or even an arrogant assumption that what is not intelligible to them at first reading must be in itself unintelligible and unworthy of attention; or (2) they find it too rationalistic, too specific, too full of definitions; finally, at times, (3) these two opposite criticisms can be heard from the same critic! Such critics do not understand (1) mystery, (2) rationality, or (3) the possibility of both occurring together.

They *can* occur together. A mystery is not illogical; it is more than logical, but not less. For instance, the mystery of the Trinity means that there is one God in three Persons—not three Gods or one Person—"without either confusing the persons or dividing the substance". This answers the objection that Christians believe a logical contradiction when they believe God is both one and three. The same distinction between nature (or substance or essence) and person answers the similar objection against believing Christ to be both God and man: it is no contradiction, for he is one person (not two) with two natures (not one). It is mystery, but not contradiction.

Such creedal definitions do not seek to prove, only to specify, what is believed. Faith is not proof. But neither is it confusion or vagueness. Critics who scorn the clarifications of creeds often actually prefer vagueness; it is certainly more convenient and comfortable to have a foggy faith because in a fog you can never be sure you have lost your way.

The Athanasian Creed asserts that all three Persons of the Trinity are unmade and uncreated, but differentiates them in that the Father is sourceless, the Son begotten by the Father, and the Holy Spirit proceeds from the Father and the Son. The Eastern Church rejects the *filioque* ("and the Son") clause, first specified in the Nicene Creed, and believes that the Spirit proceeds from the Father only. (But this theological difference did not cause the great schism, which happened not at Nicaea in the fourth century but seven centuries later, in 1054. There is, therefore, hope that the schism can be healed without either side compromising on the *filioque*.)

The creed says that Christ is one "not by the transformation of his divinity into flesh but by the taking up of his humanity into God". It is gain, not loss; the same for us, at the Resurrection and in the beatific vision. The creeds specify our destiny as well as the nature of God because God is our destiny.

Also remarkable and worthy of much meditation is the creed's analogy of Christ's hypostatic union of divinity and humanity to our own union of soul and body: "For just as the rational soul and flesh are a single man, so God and man are a single Christ." There are more kinds of unity than the simple ones we usually think about.

For contemporary man the most problematic and offensive statements in this creed are certainly its opening words, from which its gets its traditional name, the *quicumque vult.* "Whoever desires to be saved must above all things hold the Catholic faith. Unless man keeps it in its entirety inviolate, he will assuredly perish eternally." The last words of the creed reiterate this point: "This is the Catholic faith. Unless a man believes it faithfully and steadfastly, he will not be able to be saved." Does this mean that not only all good pagans, Hindus, Buddhists, and Jews but also all theologically defective Christians are doomed to hell?

If that is what it means, then it is simply not true. For Scripture, the Fathers of the Church, and the dogmatic statements of one of the Church's ecumenical councils (Vatican II) contradict that terrible thought. No one can read the New Testament without agreeing with Saint Thomas Aquinas that "the primary object of our faith is not a proposition but a Person." It is *Christ* who saves us, not the correctness of our theology.

But it is not necessary to interpret these "damnation clauses" of the Athanasian Creed thus. The creed's purpose is not to save but accurately to specify the propositional content of what is believed, to answer the question: Who and what is the Christ who alone saves? The creed answers correctly that he is the uncreated second Person of the eternal Trinity, who was incarnated and became a man without losing his divinity. It's a legitimate question: Who and what is the Savior? And it's a "straight" and legitimate answer: "This is the Catholic faith." The "damnation clauses" do not state that Socrates and Ghandi are in hell, but that unless one believes in *this* Savior, who in fact is all that the creed says he is, one cannot be saved. But how explicit the intellectual content of one's faith in Christ must be in order to be saved is another question.

The answer to that question can be very liberal. Fathers of the Church like Saint Justin and Saint Clement of Alexandria explicitly make room for the salvation of the good pagan like Socrates without compromising Christ's assertion that "I am the Way . . . no one can come to the Father but through Me." They noted that Scripture calls Christ "the real light which gives light to every man" (Jn 1:9).

Everyone gets a chance to know Christ and to love him. Precisely because Christ is the uncreated, eternal, preincarnate, divine Person specified by the creeds, there is hope for Socrates; for if the creeds speak the Truth, then the light of Truth that

Socrates or anyone else sought with his deepest heart and soul was in fact Christ, who promised that "all who seek find."

Christ is the only Savior, but Christ is very large. The creed does not confine him, it only refines our knowledge of him. But even unrefined flour can bake living bread. I think that when truth seekers meet the one who is the Truth after death, they may hear from his lips such words as these: "Inasmuch as you loved and lived one of the least of these, my traces of truth, in my world, you did so unto me." I would be very surprised not to find Socrates in heaven. But I would be far more surprised not to find him chanting the Athanasian Creed there.

19
The Apostles' Creed: God the Father

"I believe in God the Father Almighty, maker of heaven and earth."

If we are to be honest and sane, our beliefs should follow reality. Trying to follow reality is what honesty means, and following reality is what sanity means. Our creeds, which are the summaries of our beliefs, should do the same. That is why the first creed, the Apostles' Creed, begins where all reality begins, in the place where the most realistic book ever written begins: "In the beginning, God." For the creed is a map of reality.

Both the biblical beginning, in Genesis 1, and the creed's beginning are remarkable in their simplicity. (So is God: he is absolutely simple!) They are so astoundingly simple that only a child or a genius could have invented them. But behind this simplicity there is profundity that makes a difference to everything we think. Beginning with God means that we think not just theistically but also theocentrically.

Many people are theistic but not theocentric because their God, their *theos*, is something less than the absolute center and point of all reality and all of life. He (or she or it) is a God out there (deism) or a God down here (naturalism) or a God who is an ingredient in reality (paganism) or a God in which we are ingredients (pantheism) or a God of the gaps, who comes in only to explain whatever we can't, or a God in whom there are gaps—in short, *a* God.

But the creed does not speak of a God, only of God. The God of Abraham, Isaac, and Jacob, the God of Jesus Christ, is the absolute, the Alpha and Omega, the point and pinnacle of all reality. He is not an it or object; his name is I AM, the absolute subject. He is not our object, we are his. He is the I and we are his Thou, not vice versa.

Theocentrism is not just theory but also practice. The practical difference it makes is a total one: because God is God, we can live utterly relative to him, immersed in the God relationship, surrounded and confronted by God through all things. As the Psalmist says, "Thou hast beset me behind and before." Everything in the universe is between God and us. We are characters in his story, not he in ours. "In him we live and move and have our being." We are in him not as a sardine is in a can or as wood is in a house—that is pantheism—but as Hamlet is in Shakespeare or Scrooge is in Dickens. He invented us, created us.

Pagans did not know this. They were not theocentric but cosmocentric: their gods found their place in the cosmos, the ordered and fated whole that was their absolute. Everything had to have a place, even the gods.

The modern mind also does not know the theocentric God, for the modern mind is anthropocentric, not theocentric. God and the cosmos are thought of in relation to man and their effect in human life. Modernity prefers a "realistic" religion. But this anthropocentrism is precisely the opposite of realism, i.e., living in reality, conforming to reality. For God really is the center, not man. The medieval Christian mind was most realistic; the modern mind takes refuge in superstition and fantasy. Anthropocentrism is like Hamlet thinking that Shakespeare exists for him and is to be judged by him. As C. S. Lewis puts it, for modern man, man is the judge and God is "in the dock", like a prisoner on trial.

But the biblical idea of God is the greatest idea that has ever entered into the mind of man. It is the idea of the absolutely perfect being, "that than which nothing greater can be conceived", as Saint Anselm put it: omnipotent, omniscient, omnipresent, all-good, all-just, all-loving, all-holy, all-merciful, and "whatever it is better to be than not to be".

What difference does this idea of God make to our lives? A total difference. For either God is less than this, and then he is an ingredient surrounded by us or our lives or our minds or the universe; or else we and the whole universe are surrounded by him. If God is God, then our whole lives, with all the spots of darkness in them, are surrounded by light. If God is not God, then our lives, with all the spots of light in them, are surrounded by darkness. God is light and goodness; if God is not absolute, then light and goodness are not absolute.

Lady Julian of Norwich saw the whole universe, in a God-given vision, as a tiny hazelnut held in God's palm. ("He's got the whole world in his hands.") What difference does that make? The greatest difference imaginable, I think, for as I write these words my twenty-three-year-old cousin is dying. Is he dying into the darkness or into the light? What has the last word?

Trinity

The creed tells us who God is. That is the hardest question in the world. Tradition says that Thomas Aquinas at the age of four asked his mother that question: "Who is God?" Because his mother could not answer his question satisfactorily, he became Saint Thomas Aquinas.

But students today usually do not read Aquinas or any other premodern theologians. Nineteen out of twenty of my students at one of the best Catholic colleges in America cannot answer the simple question: "Isn't the doctrine of the Trinity a logical contradiction? Is God three persons or one person?" They have simply never been taught the creed's distinction between person and nature—or the formulas for which so much blood, sweat, and tears were shed—that God is one nature in three persons, not one person and not three natures. (Actually, I think most of them are really Unitarians: they believe in "the fatherhood of God, the brotherhood of man, and the neighborhood of Boston".)

So it is necessary to begin at the beginning. What does the Trinity mean? Where did the idea come from? It did not come from the philosophical cogitations of white-bearded medieval monks and bishops fussing about words to confuse the laity, as many people seem to think. It came from the Bible. The ecumenical councils of the catholic (ecumenical, universal)

Church that officially and solemnly defined the doctrine (note: defined *the doctrine,* not defined *God*) in the first six centuries A.D. were just interpreting Scripture. That is the essential teaching (magisterial) function of the Church. Creeds do not add to Scripture but summarize it and resist subtractions from it, i.e., heresies. Mother Church is the living interpreter of the Father's letters to us.

We believe the Trinity because God has told us; it is as simple as that. Though the content of the doctrine is infinitely mysterious and not at all simple, the motive for believing it is not at all mysterious, but as realistic and simple as the good sense of Moses. No one in the world had ever guessed God's own essential name, and then Moses had the good sense to ask him, and God told Moses his name (Ex 3:14). Why only Moses? Because only he had the good sense to ask, while everyone else was trying to figure it out for himself!

Why do we need to be told? When we want to know something less than ourselves, like a stone, we are active and it is passive. When we want to know something equal to ourselves, another human being, we must both act. If the other person does not want to reveal himself, I cannot force him. Finally, when we want to know something greater than ourselves, when it comes to knowing God, the initiative must be his. He must tell us. That is the reasonable basis for revelation, and it is the reason why revelation is always beyond reason and mysterious. It is also why it is usually surprising: it is not something we could have guessed or understood by ourselves—like the Trinity.

What does the doctrine mean, essentially? That God, without compromising his unity, is (or contains, or is expressed in) three Persons, three I's, three knowing and willing selves. These are not like triplets, who are not one *being* but three beings. Nor are they like water, which is three potential *states* (liquid, solid, and gas) of the same stuff. Nor are they three *parts* of God, like the three petals of a clover. (St. Patrick's legendary explanation of the Trinity to the Irish was a bad one.)

People often think the idea of the Trinity is irrelevant. But no one thinks the idea that "God is love" is irrelevant. Yet if God is not a Trinity, God is not love, for you need more than one person for unselfish love. If God were only one person he could only be selfish love. At best, he could be a lover of human persons, but not Love Itself. And then he would be dependent on those human persons; without them he could not be unselfish love. Only the Trinity allows God to be unselfish love in his own essential, independent being. The Father loves the Son, not himself; the Son loves the Father, not himself; the Spirit is the love between the Father and the Son, a love so real that it is a third Person. (The same thing happens to that image of the Trinity in time, the human family, but only with the aid of biology.)

The Trinity is no less one than the non-Trinitarian God of Unitarians, Jews, or Moslems, for love is a closer union than arithmetic. The lover feels more one with the beloved than with himself. He "identifies" more with her than with himself. The love among the three Persons of the Trinity is a stronger glue than the arithmetical oneness within any one person. God is more one by being three than by just being one. Nothing is more one than God, and God is Trinity, therefore nothing is more one than Trinity.

The Trinity means that relationship is the fundamental category of reality. Relationship goes all the way up into ultimate reality, into God. God is a society, an I-Thou relationship; God is love. Because we are made in the image of the Trinity, love and family and community and friendship are not peripheral but central, not accidental but essential to us, at the very core of human existence.

Thus it is trinitarian dogma that grounds the social emphasis in Christianity. The quarrel between liberals, who emphasize this social aspect but usually ignore or scorn dogma, and conservatives, who emphasize dogma but usually ignore the social, is like a quarrel between the two sides of a coin.

What can human reason say about the doctrine of the Trinity?

1. It can't prove it true, but it can't prove it false either, and it can answer objections to it, disprove attempts to disprove it.

2. Reason also can't discover it by itself—no one in the world

ever did—but once it has been revealed, it can be known by faith. (Faith is simply our response to divine revelation.)

3. Reason also cannot adequately understand it, but it can understand what is isn't (contra heresies) and what is is like, by analogies (for we are his images, his analogies). Thus, e.g., Saint Augustine sees an image of the Trinity in the soul's three powers of memory (which transcends time, like the Father), understanding (which is like the Logos, the inner word of God), and will (which is like the Spirit, the love between Father and Son, for love is the work of the will). We can even see a dim and distorted reflection of the Trinity in the Freudian picture of the psyche as superego, ego, and id, or in Plato's common-sense psychology of mind, "spirited part" (will), and desires. Because creation necessarily reflects its Creator, images of the Trinity will necessarily appear everywhere.

Father

The Creed mentions three of the most important things we can know about God: that he is the Father, that he is almighty, and that he is the Creator. What does each of these three things mean?

We may think that Father is a metaphor, but it is not. God's fatherhood is not the metaphor; ours is. That is what Saint Paul tells us: "I fall on my knees before the Father, from whom every family in heaven and on earth receives its name" (Eph 3:14). He is not made in our image; we are made in his. He is not like us; we are like him. Father means first of all what the first Person of the Trinity is to the second by nature and to us by grace. Earthly, biological fatherhood is the metaphor, the translation of the primal fatherhood into the lesser language of dust and clay. (That language is a beautiful one, for God invented it; but it is not the primal one.)

The world invariably interprets God the Father as an anthropomorphic projection of human qualities into God, as wishful thinking, as finitizing the infinite. Some think it is a good projection, others a bad one. Feminists tend to resent the fact that the Bible calls God Father and not Mother (though many of them resent motherhood too) and the fact that he has a Son, not a Daughter. Shouldn't we put an end to this male chauvinism?

First of all, it isn't male chauvinism. The Bible is clear that the image of God is "male and female" (Gen 1:27). The greatest merely human being who ever lived was a woman, and the greatest merely human act of choice ever committed was her Yes to God, which brought down God himself and our redemption into her body.

But, most simply, we can't stop the "sexist" language (which is not chauvinistic) because we didn't start it. We call God Father rather than Mother or neuter Parent because we believe that God himself has told us how to speak of him. The fundamental issue in the dispute with the feminists about Scripture's language is not male chauvinism, which no one defends, but the authority of Scripture, which the Church defends. Is Scripture God's words about us or our words about God? The world is full of human words about God, full of reasonable human preferences. They are all inadequate. God cut through them all and told us things we would never have come up with if left to ourselves. That is the fundamental issue: Have we been left to ourselves or has our divine Lover proposed to interfere with our aloneness?

What does God the Father mean? Obviously not biological fatherhood but something like it. What does a human father give to his children first of all? Something even more primordial than love, time, care, education, or anything else: life, human life. To have God as our Father is therefore to have been given a share in God's life, divine life.

This is the incredible mystery the word of God reveals to us, "by which have been given to us exceedingly great and precious promises, that through these you may be partakers of the divine nature" (2 Pet 1:4). This mystery is also taught in the prayer of consecration over the chalice in the Mass: as the water is mingled with the wine, God has raised our humanity to share his own divinity. Unthinkable glory—to become God's children, not by metaphor but in fact!

When we call God "Father", then, we really refer to three

things. First, in the Trinity, the first Person is Father to the Son, his eternal word. Second, God fathers us by creating us in his image. Third, God becomes our Father and we become his children if and only if we are born again by faith and baptism.

People often confuse these last two meanings and ask whether God is not everyone's Father. If so, why is it necessary to believe in Christ to be saved? The answer is that by the creating fatherhood of God we have his image but not his life, somewhat as a picture or a statue has the image of a person but not the life of a person. When God gives us his very life, we become, like Christ the Son of God, sons and daughters of God, sharers in God's own divine life. The life of heaven, the kingdom of heaven, begins in seed form right now on earth. If it is not planted here, it will not be harvested there.

The image of Father includes the idea of origin but also of authority based on origin (*authority* means author's rights) and, most important of all, the idea of self-giving love. The combination of these three things, not just the idea of origin, not just the idea of authority, and not just the idea of love, is the image of God. It is originating, loving authority; originating, authoritative love. One reason we live in such a godless world today is that we see so few images of this godlike combination around us. We see instead authority without love and love without authority. That is why we need to see Jesus, who reveals the Father to us. No one was ever more loving than Jesus, but no one was ever more authoritative either. We need to see that love is authoritative, love is not limp.

How privileged and exalted a thing it is to be a father—it images God himself. If children do not have a good image of their earthly father to start from, it will be much harder for them to come to know God as a loving heavenly Father. Saint Augustine had a very bad relationship with his father, and he could not bring himself to address God as Father for a long time. Every father is a priest, like it or not, a good one or a bad one, mediating an image of God to his children.

Freud objects to the notion of God as Father on the grounds that it seems to him to be an obvious case of wishful thinking. This sort of God is exactly what we need and want. As Voltaire said, "If

God did not exist, it would be necessary to invent him." Isn't it a suspiciously perfect fit between our need for a Father's love, protection, and power, and the idea of God as just such a Father?

It is indeed—just as suspicious as the fit between a glove and a hand, or a key and a lock. There is obviously design here. But it is just as reasonable to say God fulfills our needs because he designed us to need him as it is to say that we designed him. More reasonable, in fact, for fathers "design" children before children can invent or design any imaginary fathers.

But, the objector may go on to say, isn't the notion of God as Father imperfect? How can such an imperfect human image fit the all-perfect God? The answer is a question: What is more perfect than a person? A force? If so, it is better to call God a force than a Person. Let's see. Would you rather be a person, with consciousness and free choice, or a great unconscious, blind force, like gravity? If you had to kill either a person or a force, which would you kill and which would you spare? Which would you in practice treat as the more valuable?

But, the objector may continue, aren't persons necessarily finite? Thus aren't we making God finite to call him Father and Person? No. Oriental religions usually think of God as a force rather than a Person for this reason: because they think of personhood as necessarily finite. The reason they think this is quite profound: it is that an I, a self, a person, is an I only relative to a Thou, an other self, while God is not relative to anything else. Only the doctrine of the Trinity answers this objection. Because God is a Trinity of persons, each I in God is relative to a Thou and yet infinite because it is relative to an infinite Thou.

Omnipotence

The creed goes on to call God "almighty". Not just "mighty", like the pagan gods, but all-mighty, omnipotent. "With God all things are possible." This is not just omnipotence, but the omnipotence of God the Father; not just power but the power of loving fatherhood exercised for the benefit of his children. That is why "all things work together for good to those who love God."

The creed puts "Father" before "almighty" because we are to worship God first for his goodness, not for his power. If it were possible to separate the two attributes, which it is not, and have two gods, one all-good but not all-powerful and the other all-powerful but not all-good, we should worship the one who is all-good even if he is not all-powerful. The motive for our worship should be love, inspired by God's goodness, not fear, inspired by his power. But in fact these two attributes are not only united in one God, but united in each other in him. God's power is the power of goodness.

And it's strictly a no-sweat power. The most powerful deed in history, the creation of everything from nothing, the creation of this staggeringly vast universe, was accomplished simply by his word, his thought and will. He simply said, "Let it be!", and it was. Is there any power greater than that? Kierkegaard says there is. "Do you think it was a great thing for God to create the world out of nothing? I will tell you a greater thing: he makes saints out of sinners." Kierkegaard is right. Nothingness had no will to resist God when God made the universe out of it. We resist. Only love wins us over.

Creation

The creed concludes its statement of faith in God the Father with the words "creator of heaven and earth". Creation is the distinctive act of God and the distinctively biblical, Jewish idea. All other gods form or shape an already-existing world. Only the God of the Jews, only the God of the Bible creates the very existence of the world, creates matter itself. Creation out of nothing is, quite simply, an idea that has never occurred to the mind of man without divine revelation.

Creation forms the essential dividing line between God and everything else. God exists eternally, without beginning or end.

The material world has both a beginning and an end. Human souls (and resurrection bodies) have a beginning but no end.

Because God is Creator, the world is real and precious. No one can love the world as much as a Jew or a Christian (or a Moslem), who knows who made it. Paradoxically, it is the Bible's demoting of the world to a second-rate status as creature that makes it precious, for then it is God's creature.

All those who "worship the creature rather than the Creator", who place the world or anything in it in the highest place, spoil the world. They who idolize the world do not have a higher view of the world but a lower, lesser one. To idolize anything—world, drink, money, sex, ambition, hobby—is to miss out on its proper pleasure and beauty and goodness as well as that of God, whom the idol replaces.

What difference does the doctrine of creation make? First, it makes a difference to our knowledge of God. We know God is generous with the gift of existence, omnipotent in being able to create being out of nothing, and creative, like an artist.

Second, it makes a difference to our knowledge of the world. We know the world is real, not an illusion, as the great Eastern religions teach. And we know the world is ordered, designed, rational. That is why science arose in the West, not the East. And that is why Judaism and Christianity are historical religions, where God deals with us in history rather than calling us out of matter and time into flights of spiritual escapism.

Third, it makes a difference to our knowledge of ourselves. We know we are precious because we are God's. He is the author of our very existence; therefore we are totally dependent on, and indebted to, God. We have no rights over against God.

How refreshing to have nothing to stand on over against God! It gives us the opening for God's grace to enter. The name of that grace is Jesus.

20

The Apostles' Creed: God the Son

The section on Christ is the longest in the creed because it is the most important to us. It concerns our salvation, the point of our lives.

Pascal, one of the greatest Christian philosophers of all time, said: "Not only do we only know God through Jesus Christ, but we only know ourselves through Jesus Chirst. We only know life and death through Jesus Christ. Apart from Jesus Christ we cannot know the meaning of our life or our death, of God, or of ourselves."

Christianity is Christocentric as Buddhism is not Buddha-centered, Islam is not Mohammed-centered, and Confucianism is not Confucius-centered.

Where Christ said, "Come unto Me," Buddha said, "Look not to me, look to my teaching." Where Christ claimed to be far more than a prophet, Mohammed claimed only to be the "seal" of the prophets. Where Christ claimed to be the Truth, Confucius claimed only to teach the truth.

The creed summarizes the four essential things that God's word tells us about Christ: his name, his origin, his history, and his destiny—i.e., his identity, his preincarnate life, his incarnate life, and his postincarnate life.

1. His name is Jesus (Savior), "for he shall save his people from their sins." Anyone who does not know that does not know *Jesus*. Anyone who calls Jesus a great man, a prophet, a teacher, a leader, an example, a philosopher, a moralist, or even a god but does not know him as Savior knows him in vain.

Christ (Greek, *Christos*) means messiah or anointed one. This name connects him with his Hebrew past, God's people specially chosen to be the earthly womb of the Incarnation. In Jesus, the Hebrew "chosen people" speak their supreme word to the whole world. His Greek title (*Christos*) is in the universal language of the ancient world because he is the universal Savior. His earthly origin is Jewish, but his purpose is universal.

2. Through telling us of Jesus' double origin, from God and from Mary, the creed tells us of Jesus' double *nature*. This truth was later to be more explicitly defined by Nicaea and Chalcedon when heretics challenged it, but the doctrine of Christ's two natures was not invented or discovered by Nicaea. No creed ever says anything new but only newly clarifies the original "deposit of faith".

Because Jesus is God's only begotten Son, conceived not by Joseph but by the Holy Spirit, and also born of the Virgin Mary, he is therefore truly God (not just God*like*) and truly man (not just in human *appearance*).

As G. K. Chesterton says, he is not like an elf or a centaur, half human and half something else, but "wholly God and wholly man". As God, he is the word that spoke the entire universe into being: "And God said . . . and it was." "In the beginning was the Word." As man he shared all our weaknesses, even death—sin's consequence and penalty—but not sin itself.

3. His life follows his name and purpose: He "suffered under Pontius Pilate, was crucified, died and was buried" *because* he was the Savior. Anyone who does not know him as Savior does not understand the great events of his life and death. To the humanist, his sufferings are simply another tragedy like that of Socrates or Mahatma Gandhi or Martin Luther King, Jr. To the Christian, his agony and death are celebrated as *Good* Friday!

History's greatest tragedy or its greatest triumph? On Calvary, Christian and non-Christian cease to have common ground. If Jesus were only a great man, then he was not even a great man, but a wicked or foolish man because he claimed to be God. If Jesus did not rise from the dead, thereby proving his divine power, then there has never been a greater failure than Jesus Christ: misunderstood by his disciples, crucified as a common criminal, betrayed by his friend, denied by the one he made leader, even abandoned by God ("My God, my God, why have You forsaken me?"). But. . . .

The Resurrection is the great "but". After descending to earth, to death, and to the grave ("he descended into hell" in the original creed meant not the place of eternal torment but the place of the dead [see 1 Pet 3:18–20]), "he rose again from the dead." Here is the good news, the capstone on the great story of salvation, the winning stroke in the battle. Christ's Resurrection, of course, proves his claim to be God; but it also wins our salvation, our eternal life. That is the central point of every sermon in Acts.

The good news that set the world afire was not "love your neighbor" or "God is one" or even "God is good"—these great truths wise men already knew—but the incredible news that God had become a man, died to save us from sin, and rose to save us from death. "If Christ is not risen, your faith is vain."

If only the present doubters in his own Church who obfuscate or nuance the greatest and most eternally important event in all of time would become honest little children again, accept 1 Corinthians 15:12–20, and blow the trumpet! The world will never hearken to "an uncertain [or nuanced] trumpet". What we need is not an unspecific Easter faith, but "Christ is risen." And not only "Christ is risen in the apostles' hearts" but Christ is risen in the real world. It really happened, right here in our world.

The most important task of our lives from now on is to announce this news, "make disciples of all nations", and live in union with the risen Savior, incorporated into his body by faith and baptism, fed by his eucharistic body and blood. Everything in Christianity—salvation, missions, faith, Church, sacrament—has as its point the resurrected Christ.

Ascension completes Resurrection. By ascending, Christ takes humanity to heaven as his trophy (Ps 68:18).

Our place at his table is waiting for us. Heaven will not seem strange, but home. We will feel exactly as Malcolm Muggeridge said he felt becoming a Catholic: it was like responding to a banquet bell and coming to a banquet place long set.

4. The story is not over. Seated in glory, triumph, and power (how unfashionable!) with the Father, he will come again. One would think that with events as great as these in their past,

Christians would be backward-looking people. But no. Expectation and hope have been their hallmarks from the beginning. And when this hope again inflames our world, a new Christian era will dawn.

When we stop merely trying to conserve and instead march forth to conquer; when we work as John the Baptist to prepare for his Second Coming by gathering his harvest; when every Christian becomes the missionary Christ expects him to be, *then* we will win the world and (even more importantly) do his will.

For he *is* coming. The Bible's last word, *maranatha* ("Come, Lord Jesus"), mirrors reality. He, the Truth, will shine once more, this time not veiled. No one will be able to doubt him then—not Pharisee or Sadducee, not Jew or Gentile. The light will judge all hearts, and the only important question that life presents to every individual will then be answered with unarguable openness and unchangeable eternity: "What think you of Christ?"

He comes to judge the living and the dead. There are only two kinds of people, the living and the dead. Many of the so-called dead are part of the living, and many of the so-called living are spiritually dead. Christ poses—and Christ is—life's one ultimate issue: "He who has the Son has life. He who has not the Son has not life."

There is no third possibility, only evasion. But death—the death of the world at his Second Coming and the death of each individual before that, which is like Christ's Second Coming in each individual life—removes forever the possibility of evasion.

Let us now explore some of the theology behind the creed's claims about Christ. The doctrine of the Trinity developed as a response to a problem that arose for Christian theology in the first six centuries A.D. It had arisen first for Christ's contemporaries. The problem is: What are we to make of Christ? Christ himself put the question to the Pharisees in Matthew 22:42: "What do you think of the Christ? Whose son is he?" When the Pharisees replied, "David's son," he asked, "How is it then that David, inspired by the Spirit, calls him Lord?"

Christ claimed divinity in many ways: by changing Peter's name (in Judaism, only God can change your name because your name is your identity); by forgiving sins, all sins ("Who can forgive sins but God alone?"); by uttering the forbidden word, the divine name Yahweh, I AM (Jn 8:58), the name only God can utter; by calling himself the Son of God (thus claiming to have the same nature as his Father); by promising to come at the end of time to judge the whole world; by performing miracles, especially his own Resurrection.

However, he is clearly human. He gets tired, hungry, even angry. He weeps over Jerusalem. He can die, and does. He calls himself the Son of Man.

The doctrine of the two natures in one person, the doctrine that Christ was fully divine and fully human, was stated with such force and clarity in the great creeds (the Nicaean, the Chalcedonian, and the Athanasian) that one would think no Catholic would be able to fudge the issue again. Yet we have seen a very strong resurgence in our own time of the old Arian heresy: the denial (or, in more modern fashion, the nuancing) of Christ's full divinity. It is the essence of Modernist theology, and it continues to draw official condemnations from Rome, whether its teacher is Arius, Hans Kung, or Schillebeecx.

The Arians had a case, however, not just from reason but also from Scripture. They pointed to the subordinationist passages in the Gospels, those passages where Christ clearly subordinates himself to the Father: "I come not to do my own will but the will of my Father." "My teaching is not mine but it comes from him who sent me." "I can do nothing on my own authority." "The Father is greater than I."

The Church has never sacrificed one point of its rich deposit of faith to another, but reconciled them, as she reconciles persons with God and each other. So rather than selecting the subordinationist passages or the equality passages, where Christ claims equality with the Father, as the more basic, the Church insisted on the whole Gospel. To do this, a distinction was needed: what was subordinated to the Father in Christ was not his nature but his will;

what was equal with the Father was not his will but his nature. His task on earth was to obey. But the person who obeyed was equal in nature to the Father.

What practical importance can such theological niceties have? How do abstractions like this cut into our ordinary lives? In the most crucial and practical way possible. The principle of theology that the early Church formulated to reconcile the subordinationist and equality passages is the key to the salvation of the modern world, the survival of Western civilization, in the following way.

The three fundamental human relationships in all times and places are the husband/wife relationship, the parent/child relationship, and the ruler/citizen relationship. Every time Saint Paul gives general advice about human relationships, he mentions these three. These three relationships have broken down or are in the process of breaking down in the modern world; that is the chief reason why the modern world is breaking down. Marriages and families especially, the foundations of society, are cracking in pieces at a horrendous rate and taking a tremendous toll in human suffering.

Christ came to make all things new, especially relationships. Outside of Christ, there are only two possible relationships: the order of power and superiority or the order of justice and equality. What about love? Outside Christ, love is a mere feeling or sentiment, incapable of providing the tough, solid foundation of order for all of life. But in Christ, love is as strong as God. In Christ love and order meet; a new order appears, the order of love. Order is no longer loveless and love is no longer orderless.

Take the most controverted of all relationships, the husband/wife relationship. Certainly, the most unpopular verse in the whole Bible today is "Wives, obey your husbands." It is unpopular because the next three words are forgotten or not understood: "in the Lord". Feminists of every kind are outraged at this idea because they think it is male chauvinism, the attitude that women are somehow inferior. They demand equality instead—a perfectly just and reasonable demand. But they don't see that to obey does not mean inferiority or inequality in value because they think of "obeying" in the worldly sense rather than in the revolutionary new sense Christ brought into the world.

Christ obeyed the Father. He subordinated his will to the Father. But Christ was equal to the Father. Therefore subordination of will, of role, is not a mark of inferiority or of weakness. Was Christ inferior? Was he weak? He was very God of very God, yet he obeyed.

Rather than enslaving the one who obeys, obedience liberates. The wife, the child, or the citizen who obeys the husband, the parent, or the ruler is not inferior. Christ liberated women, children, and citizens so that they are fully equal in value to men, parents, and rulers. But he did so without sacrificing order, authority, and obedience, as modern radicals think they have to do. They see only two possibilities: chauvinism or egalitarianism, order and authority based on superiority or lack of order and authority, based on equality. Christ's relationship with his Father is the third possibility, the principle of all stable, loving human relationships. The modern family can be saved by the dogma of the Trinity!

The Godhead of the Son tells us two things we did not know before: first, that God is more than just one person, that God is more than Father, he is also Son; second, that Christ is more than man, he is God too.

The consequences are radical. The consequences for our notion of God are that plurality, society, relationship, otherness, and love go all the way up into ultimate reality. And the consequences for our attitude toward Christ are equally radical. This man is God! Christ is not just a Jewish carpenter. He created the world (Col 1:16). He is the center and meaning of all reality. He is the cosmic Christ.

Three very practical consequences of this doctrine are the salvation of "anonymous" Christians, the spirituality of daily work, and a philosophy of values.

1. If Jesus is only human, then only some human beings know him: those who met him and those who learned about him. But he

claimed to be the only Savior (Jn 14:6). If he is not the universal divine Truth or preincarnate Logos, those who have not heard about the incarnate Christ have no chance for salvation. Only if Christ is also "the light that enlightens everyone who comes into the world" (Jn 1:9) can Socrates or Buddha or any Truth-seeking pagan be saved by him. They did not know the incranate Christ, but they may have known and loved the preincarnate Christ, the divine Truth and Goodness dimly perceived as their God.

2. If Jesus is not the universal light, then the little lights we pursue in our little daily works have little or nothing to do with Jesus. But if Jesus is cosmic, then when we wash the dishes, we do it for him and in him.

3. If Jesus is not the universal source of all good, then there can be goods, values, apart from him. But if he is the sole Creator and designer of all good, then every value anyone ever seeks, every truth, every goodness, and every beauty, is a sunbeam from the Son; it is Christ we all seek in everything we seek. He is, literally, our all.

How can we understand something of what this divine Logos is? The word itself is so rich that it is nearly untranslatable. At least thirty-two different English words have to be used to translate the single Greek word *logos* in different contexts: word, mind, speech, language, reason, concept, thought, understanding, principle, meaning, intelligibility, intelligence, argument, discourse, science, dialogue, conversation, relationship, responsibility, account, unity, point, purpose, explanation, cause, essence, form, species, manifestation, expression, revelation. The unity among all these meanings is intuited more than defined.

The closest single word, perhaps, is *thought*. And here we find a parallel in our daily experience to trinitarian theology. Just as our thoughts, or inner words, are *one* with us, yet one *with* us: just as they are ourselves and yet things we produce out of ourselves and dialogue with; so God's word is both "*with* God" and *is* God (Jn 1:1–2).

Another parallel is our conceiving characters in a story. We do that because we are made in God's image and God does that. We are his characters and history is his-story. The difference is that we are not quite so creative as to give our characters life outside our minds. He is. But we do create, or rather procreate, real people: our children. That is also because God, in whose image we are made, is the model for all generation. We biologically generate many children in time who reflect only parts of ourselves; he spiritually generates one Son in eternity who reflects all of the Father (Col 1:19).

Great writers, like Shakespeare, know that the characters they invent seem more as if they were discovered then invented—they take on a life of their own, they seem almost real. Even a mediocre author often has the surprising experience when telling a story of having some of his characters tell him who they are rather than vice versa. Some characters in fiction, even in classic television series like "M.A.S.H." or "Star Trek", are so real that we genuinely care about them. We are creative because we are God's image, and God is creative: he not only created the universe but also generated his Son. His Son is the paradigm for all persons, the thing our characters approach.

One last piece of "relevance", or connection with our lives: the Father's love for the Son is infinitely real, certainly no less real than a human father's love for his son. Most human fathers would suffer more if their sons suffered than if they could suffer in their place—like David mourning the death of his son Absalom: "O my son Absalom, my son, my son Absalom: Would I had died instead of you, O Absalom, my son, my son!" (2 Sam 18:33). That makes Calvary infinitely poignant: see how much the Father loves us. We must never contrast the gentle, loving Son with the stern, unbending Father—an ancient and still-popular heresy. No, "he who has seen me has seen the Father" (Jn 14:9).

The Patripassian heresy held that the Father literally suffered on the Cross with the Son. It is not true, for the Father did not become incarnate in time and passivity. But it is near the truth, for the

Father showed his infinite care and love and mercy to us in Jesus. One of the most beautiful verses in Scripture is the shortest: at his dead friend Lazarus' grave, "Jesus wept" (Jn 11:35). Jesus is the tears of God. Tears flow from two eyes. In God, love flows from two *I*'s and eternally becomes a third *I*, the Holy Spirit.

21

The Apostles' Creed: God the Holy Spirit

Eternally, the Holy Spirit is the love between the Father and the Son. Historically, the Holy Spirit is the love between God and the world. From the moment of creation, the Spirit has been brooding over the face of the waters, inspiring, in-breathing, in-spirit-ing his love into history. We must explore these two aspects of the Spirit who is love: his eternal nature and his historical work.

First of all, the Spirit is God. Scripture clearly ascribes divine names and prerogatives, both in the Old Testament and in the New, to the Spirit. Because the Father is God and the Son is God and the Spirit is God, God must exist in and consist of all three Persons.

Second, the Spirit is not it but he. He is a Person. He can be grieved (Eph 4:30). Jesus promises to send a "he", not an "it" (see Jn 16).

Third, the Spirit eternally (since God is eternal) issues, or proceeds, from the Father; he is the Spirit *of* God the Father (Mt 10:20). But he is also the Spirit of Christ (Phil 1:19). Thus he proceeds from the Father and the Son. The first major split in the Church, between East and West in 1054, was formally over the *filioque* ("and the Son") clause in the creed, the Western Church maintaining that the Spirit proceeded from the Father and Son, and the Eastern Church maintaining that he proceeded only from the Father.

Our thoughts and our loves, the two distinctively human acts that no animal can perform, issue forth from us but do not become distinct persons unless aided by the flesh. In God, they are so real that they are the two additional Persons in God: God's word, or self-expression, is so real that he is the second Person in God, and the love between Father and Son is so real that he is the third Person. Human creativity, both mental and biological, is the image of the Trinity. That is one reason why the family is holy; it bears the intimate stamp of the very inner nature of God, the life of trinitarian love, the two becoming three in becoming one.

The history of the Holy Spirit's work with this earth is the real, but hidden, story of history. To tell history as it really is is to tell the story of the Spirit. Take a few hours some time to sit down with a concordance and read every passage in Scripture, from Genesis to Revelation, where the Spirit of God is mentioned. You will be following the golden thread through the maze of events, the skeletal structure behind the mass of flesh that is what history looks like from the outside.

All three divine Persons are present from the beginning. The God who "in the beginning . . . created the heavens and the earth" (Gen. 1:1) was also the word who spoke "let there be" (the word through whom the Father created) and the Spirit who "moved over the face of the waters" (Gen. 1:2).

All life is the Spirit's special province and provenance, for the very word in Hebrew (*ruah'*) means both breath (of life) and spirit. The same is true in New Testament Greek with the word *pneuma*.

All divine in-spiration is the Spirit's work. The Spirit is constantly active throughout the Old Testament, gently but powerfully moving men and women to breathe God's spiritual air, swim downstream in God's living waters, open their eyes to the heavenly light. All true prophets, or mouthpieces of God, are spirit-moved; they speak God's word (the Logos) only when breathed on by God's Spirit.

Christ comes only because the Spirit prepares the way, filling Mary, substituting for Joseph (we confess that Christ was "conceived of the Holy Spirit, born of the Virgin Mary"). His public ministry begins when the Spirit descends on him at John's baptism. All four Gospels introduce him by comparison with John the Baptist by using the same formula: John baptized with water, but Jesus will baptize with the Holy Spirit.

Before the outpouring of the Spirit at Pentecost, the apostles are still huddled fearfully in the upper room. Jesus tells them not to leave Jerusalem and begin converting the world until after the

Spirit descends (Acts 1:4) because until then they lack power (Acts 1:8). It is the missing ingredient. It is essential, "for our gospel came to you not only in word, but also in power and in the Holy Spirit" (1 Th 1:5).

All of human history is a three-act play: creation, fall, and redemption. The third act has three scenes: Old Testament times, the revelation primarily of the Father; Gospel times, the revelation primarily of the Son; and the age of the Church, beginning with Pentecost, the revelation of the Spirit. First God *outside* us, then God *beside* us, then God *inside* us—three stages of love's intimacy. It is never either/or, of course. The Father reveals himself only through his word and Spirit. The Son reveals the Father and sends the Spirit. The Spirit reveals the Son and through him the Father. Yet in a sense we can divide history into the age of the Father, the age of the Son, and the age of the Spirit. We live in history's last age.

The three ages, and the three essential human tasks corresponding to them, are summed up in Acts 2:38. Peter—the new, Spirit-filled Peter, no longer the spiritual klutz with foot-in-mouth disease whom we know from all four Gospels—just preached his great Pentecost sermon, in the power of the Spirit. Three thousand were converted. The listeners ask him the essential question: not what they should think but what they should do (Acts 1:37). When Cicero addressed the Roman senate, the senators applauded and said, "How beautifully he speaks!" When Demosthenes addressed the troops, they arose, clashed swords upon shields, and shouted, "Let us march!" Peter now has the power of Demosthenes. And in answer to their question—"What shall we do?"—Peter says three things: First, repent—the one-word summary of all the Old Testament prophets, culminating with John the Baptist. Then, believe in Jesus and be baptized for the forgiveness of sins—the Gospels in one sentence. Finally, "you shall receive the gift of the Holy Spirit" (Acts 1:38).

The Spirit is the third part of God's package deal for us, not only for the apostles or the first-generation church. Peter scans the centuries and sees the descendents of his audience, spiritual as well as physical, including ourselves, as implicated in this New Covenant when he adds, "For the promise [of the Spirit] is to you and to your children and to all that are afar off, as many as the Lord our God calls to him" (Acts 2:39). We were there at Calvary ("Were you there when they crucified my Lord?"), and we were there at Pentecost.

When Paul visits the church in Ephesus (Acts 19), he notices something missing—I think he would notice exactly the same thing in most of our churches and preach the same sermon—and he asks them, "Did you receive the Holy Spirit when you believed?" (Acts 19:2). Why would he ask that unless he saw a power shortage? Why did twelve fishermen convert the world, and why are half a billion Christians unable to repeat the feat? The Spirit makes the difference.

The difference is perhaps best explained by a parable. A family of poor European immigrants saved for years to buy tickets to America. On the ship, they had nothing but the clothes on their backs and a few loaves of bread and wedges of cheese that they had bought before sailing. It was all they could afford. After three days of nothing but cheese sandwiches, the little boy approached his father with an ultimatum: "Dad, I *hate* cheese sandwiches. If I don't eat anything else before we reach America, I'm going to die." His father took pity on him and gave him his last nickel to go to the ship's galley and buy an ice-cream cone. (This was 1910!) He didn't return for hours, and his father was getting worried.

Finally, he showed up with a fat stomach and a fat smile. "Where were you?" "The ship's galley, getting something to eat." "What did you eat?" "Three ice-cream cones, and then a steak dinner because I was still hungry." "You bought all that with a nickel?" "Oh, no. Here's your nickel back. The food is free. It comes with the ticket."

The steak of the Holy Spirit comes with the ticket of our faith. But most of us are making do on cheese sandwiches. It will get us there, as the cheese sandwiches would get the immigrants to America. But why not eat the steak? It's free.

"The Spirit and the Bride [the Church] say, 'Come.' And let

him who hears say, 'Come.' And let him who is thirsty come, let him who desires take the water of life without price" (Rev 22:17). "The water of life" is the Holy Spirit. (See Jn 7:37-38.) Our qualification for receiving this water is simply our desire, our thirst. (Cheese sandwiches make you thirsty.) All we need do is ask. Read Luke 11:9-13. Do you believe this or not?

We received the Spirit by faith and baptism. "Anyone who does not have the Spirit of Christ does not belong to him" (Rom 8:9). But we need the release, the empowering, the anointing of the Spirit. Such empowerment is probably what the New Testament means by baptism in (or of or with) the Holy Spirit. It is supposed to happen at confirmation. Apparently, it usually does not. Millions of confirmed Catholics receive it afterward, usually in charismatic prayer meetings or seminars. The charismatic movement is obviously God's answer to Pope John XXIII's prayer for a new Pentecost. Popes Paul VI and John Paul II both blessed it but said that it will fulfill its purpose only when, like the early liturgical movement, it ceases to have a separate identity of its own and is absorbed into the whole Church. In other words, every Catholic should be a charismatic, baptized in the Spirit, empowered like the apostles.

The difference this baptism in the Spirit makes is not primarily in any particular charismatic gift, such as tongues. Paul clearly says not to get hung up on tongues (1 Cor 12-14). The difference is far greater: like the difference between a picture and a live person, between dead orthodoxy and living truth, between words and power. If we are not certain that Jesus Christ is present in us, working, acting, making a difference, rather than just being a teacher, an example, a lovely but remote historical figure, then we need Pentecost. And when that happens, the world will be won again.

22

The Apostles' Creed:
The Holy Catholic Church,
The Communion of Saints

Church in the original Greek is *ekklesia,* which means called out. The Church is those people who are called by God out of the world.

God created the world so he could create the Church. This universe is not a great machine that just happens to have humans in it. On the contrary, *we are its point.* The universe "peoples" as a flower flowers.

The Church is an object of faith: "I *believe* in the holy catholic Church." But we are not to place our faith in things human ("put not your trust in princes"). So it follows that the Church is, in a sense, divine.

Of course, it is human too, as Christ is. And it is therefore possible for the world to deny the divine nature of the Church as it denies the divine nature of Christ. But like Christ, the Church is divine in origin, nature, and destiny. Divine in origin because it is a divine work, not a human one. Divine in nature because it is really "the mystical [invisible] body of Christ", not only the visible mess it appears to be. (Whoever laid eyes on *organized* religion?) Divine in destiny because the last event in history, we are told by Scripture, will be the marriage of the lamb to his bride, the Church. Thus will be fulfilled the unimaginable and almost unendurable joy pronounced by the prophet: "Your Creator shall become your husband."

The Church is also our mother: Holy Mother Church. Thus the Blessed Virgin Mary is a symbol for the Church, and vice versa. In her, Christ comes to us.

The Church, God's bride and our mother, has marks to identify her. Two are mentioned in the Apostles' Creed ("holy" and "catholic") and two more are added in the Nicene Creed ("one" and "apostolic").

How is the Church *one?* Invisibly, as Protestants claim, or visibly, as Catholics claim?

Both. The Church is the *mystical* body of Christ. Like a human being, the Church's soul is invisible. External eyes see only external bodies; it takes inner eyes to see the soul, whether in the Church or in any human being. You see my soul with your soul; your body sees only my body.

But the Church is a visible reality too, just as we are. It is there, in history, objective and identifiable. And it is "one" on this level too. When Christ comes again at the end of the world, he will marry the Church, not churches. He is no bigamist. He does not have a harem, but a bride. And that bride is not an angel, a pure spirit. She has a body—*one* body.

As one soul goes with one body (the Holy Spirit is the soul of the Church) and as one husband goes with one wife (Christ is the husband of the Church); as there is "one Lord, one faith, one baptism" (Eph 4:5), there is one church. Many of its best brethren are tragically and temporarily separated brethren, but believing and baptized Protestants too are members of the one Church. They are Catholics without realizing it.

The Church's second mark is *holiness.* The creed calls her "the communion of saints". *Saints* does not mean the opposite of sinners; *saints* means *saved sinners.* The Church is the communion (common union) of sinners who have repented and received God the Father, Son, and Holy Spirit. All men are sinners. Some know it, repent, and are saved. They are the Church.

There are only two kinds of people, after all: saints, who know they are sinners, and sinners, who think they are saints. And there are only two "cities", as Augustine says in *The City of God.* A *city* is a community united by what its inhabitants love. Members of the city of God (the Church) love God above themselves. Members of the city of the world (everyone else) love themselves above God. The greatest truths in the world are that simple.

The Church is *holy.* The word means set apart. The most

unpopular mark of the Church today, especially in America and other nations where egalitarianism is worshiped, is its distinctiveness. We hate being different more than anything else, even sin. But to be a Christian is necessarily to be different. "If any man is in Christ he is a new creation." "Be not conformed to the world, but be transformed."

It is God who has set us apart as holy, not ourselves—that would be self-righteousness, not righteousness. God is love, and true love is monogamous and jealous. "The Lord God is a jealous God", he himself assures us. (How comforting! Would we want him to be uncaring or polygamous?) He has set us apart for himself: "You shall love the Lord your God with all your heart and soul and mind and strength. This is the first and greatest commandment."

The ultimate reason why we are holy is because, by faith and baptism, we have been really, ontologically united with Christ the holy one. We are his body: that is no metaphor. These bodies of ours are the metaphors. We are not only *his,* we are *him:* cells in his body. That is why Saint Paul sees a sin like sexual infidelity as blasphemous: "Do you know that your bodies are members of Christ? Shall I therefore take the members of Christ and make them members of a prostitute?"

But to be *holy* is not to be *perfect* yet. The Church's obvious human imperfections have been an occasion for scandal and apostasy for millions down through the centuries. But paradoxically this very fact is also a powerful argument for her divine nature. This is cleverly brought out in Boccaccio's story of Abraham, the medieval Jewish merchant in *The Decameron.* Abraham is contemplating becoming a Catholic. He tells his friend, the bishop of Paris, who has been trying unsuccessfully to convert him, that he has to go to Rome on business. The bishop is horrified: "Don't go! When you see the stupidity and corruption there, you'll never join the Church." (This was the time of the Medici popes, who were notoriously worldly and corrupt.) But Abraham is a practical man. Business calls. Upon his return to France, he tells the bishop he is now ready to be baptized. The bishop is astounded, but Abraham explains: "I'm a practical businessman. No earthly business that stupid and corrupt could last fourteen weeks. Your Church has lasted fourteen centuries. It must have God behind it."

The third mark of the Church, *catholic,* means universal. It is one Church worldwide, not a local sect. G. K. Chesterton says there is something just a bit provincial about a missionary asking an Outer Mongolian to become a Southern Baptist.

The Church is for all, equally. The only entrance requirement is repentance and faith. "In Christ there is neither Jew nor Greek, male or female, slave or free."

But how can we claim to be *universal* when we are only one *particular* religion, one of many in the world? The universal God chose to reveal himself to particular men and women as a particular man. That is a fact. If our attitude cannot digest it, we must alter our attitude; we cannot alter the fact. Christ is the particular person for all people. And his Church is the one particular people for all people. It is particular in origin but universal in its end.

The fourth mark of the Church is *apostolic.* This means both that it is founded on Christ's apostles, by apostolic succession, *and* that it is essentially a missionary Church, for *apostle* means one sent [on a mission]. The Church is thus apostolic in both its origin and its end.

Its apostolic origin is its real, literal, historical continuity with Christ's first apostles, who were the first missionaries, the first witnesses to Christ and his Resurrection. Thus the Church's apostolic origin and apostolic end (mission) are one.

The Church is essentially the witness to the Resurrection. The apostles saw and believed; blessed are we who have not seen and have yet believed. But we are blessed not because our faith is groundless and unreasonable. We believe for a reason: because we have been told by those who saw.

In addition to being witnesses, the apostles and their successors in the Church have the God-given authority to bind and loose (Mt 16:19), and to forgive sins (Jn 20:23). No Protestant church makes that claim. Asked why he became a Catholic, Chesterton replied, "To get my sins forgiven".

The claims the Catholic Church makes are a little like the claims Christ makes: so superhuman that it becomes impossible to take a comfortable, middle-of-the-road attitude toward them, unless we are either sleeping or dishonest. The man who claimed to be God is either God or a lunatic and blasphemer. And the Church that claims to be the body of the God-man, with divine authority to teach infallibly, to forgive sins, to make Christ sacramentally present at Mass—this Church is either God's own or it is the devil's own.

The old Protestant anti-Catholic propaganda, though often hateful in heart, was at least honest in head. It forms a good starting point for prospective converts, who should then read the writings and lives of the saints and see that this is *not* the devil's Church. The conclusion is inescapable.

23
The Apostles' Creed:
The Resurrection and Life Everlasting

"Life everlasting." How our hearts open wide with wonder when we hear this promise!

Everlasting life is life with God, and our hearts thirst for this because God designed our hearts to be "God-shaped vacuums". As Augustine says, "Thou hast made us for Thyself, and [therefore] our hearts are restless until they rest in Thee."

Life everlasting means more life *qualitatively*—livelier life. Mere unending life is not a blessing but a curse, as our legends of the Wandering Jew, the Flying Dutchman, and the curse of the undead suggest. Unending life without God is not heaven; it is hell. So for the Christian, life everlasting means sharing in God's own life.

The creed culminates with this idea because we ourselves do. It is the destiny we were created for: to share the life of the perfect one. Never in the history of the world has any destiny as exalted as this entered the mind of man.

This everlasting life is not in our natural reason because it is not in our nature. Plato was wrong: We are not by nature immortal but mortal. We are not by nature souls imprisoned in bodies, but creatures of body and soul, which fall apart at death.

Only by grace are we given everlasting life, which is natural for God but supernatural for us. Thus, all hopes for life after death hinge on the divine deed of Resurrection and on God's gratuity. This gratuity in turn comes only through the man who said, "I am the Way, the Truth, and the [everlasting] Life: no one can come to the Father but by me." Christ's Resurrection is the only door to our immortality: "I am the door."

How does this work? The God-man rose from the dead more than 1,900 years ago. I am here today, doomed inevitably to die. What's the connection?

Scripture tells us that only through Christ are we given eternal life; but it does not tell us by what "spiritual technology" God accomplishes this. Theories about how salvation works are not the thing itself and not the object of our faith. Yet the question is legitimate: How does salvation work?

Scripture's clue is that tiny word in. God puts us in Christ. Someone once observed that if we only knew all of what God meant when he inspired his Scripture writers to use the word in, there would be no mysteries left.

We are literally (though not physically) incorporated *into* Christ, into his mystical, invisible body, the Church. That is how salvation works. That's why the Church is essential and why "outside the Church, [there is] no salvation." This does not mean that all Protestants, Jews, Hindus, and atheists will go to hell—but if they are saved, they are saved by being incorporated into Christ's Church, either through implicit, unconscious faith or through explicit, conscious faith.

No one but God reads hearts. Therefore no one but God knows how many are saved. Christ refused to reveal heavenly population statistics when his apostles asked him, "Are many saved?" Instead, he pointed them back to their essential task: ensuring their own eternal destiny rather than speculating about their neighbor's. He replied, "Strive to enter in."

But what's certain is that we are given life everlasting only by being put into Christ. Perhaps the best natural analogy for this supernatural reality is the family. We are not born into the world independently, but from a family and into a family. Heredity counts for more than environment: it gives us our human nature and essence. Thus Jesus used biological birth as an analogy for salvation. "You must be born again." We are born by faith into the family of God. We become brothers and sisters of Christ, adopted children of God.

The connection, then, between Christ and life everlasting is that there is only one perfect man, one saved man, one everlasting man—Jesus Christ. We share his destiny by sharing his nature.

We do not merely imitate him; we share in him. This is far more organic than *imitation;* it is *incorporation,* or engrafting (Rom 11:17–24). "I am the vine, you are the branches." The same life—everlasting life—runs through vine and branches, head and body, Christ and Christian.

The Resurrection of Christ is central to every sermon in Acts. Paul says, "If Christ has not been raised, then our preaching is void of content and your faith is empty too. . . . If Christ was not raised, your faith is worthless. You are still in your sins. . . . If our hopes in Christ are limited to this life only, we are the most pitiable of all men" (1 Cor 15:14, 17, 19).

Note that we're talking about the resurrection of the body. Life everlasting is a *bodily* life. This is another surprise. Human reason came up with five guesses about what happens at death: (1) annihilation (death ends all); (2) angelism (the immortality of the separated soul); (3) pantheism (we are parts of the divine whole); (4) ghosts (survival of a pale half-self); and (5) reincarnation (back to other bodies on earth). Christianity fulfilled none of these popular expectations but only the divinely revealed Jewish prophecies about God raising the dead bodily (e.g., Dan 12:2).

God invented bodies. Bodies are glorious. Christ wept at Lazarus' grave not only, I think, because he had lost a friend but also because he had designed that body for an eternal destiny and now he saw what the fall had done to his masterpiece: maggots and stench. This decaying thing is not meat but man, a child of God, designed for shining glory.

But even Lazarus' resurrection was only a pale foreshadowing of ours for it was only a resuscitation, not a true resurrection. The body he rose with was mortal and had to die again. But the body we will rise with will be like Christ's glorified body: immortal and perfect yet truly body, as Thomas found when he touched the Lord's wounds. To prove he was no ghost, the resurrected Christ *ate*—once in the upper room and once on the shores of the Sea of Galilee.

The resurrected body of Christ was the same as, yet different from, his mortal body. It was the same: the mortal body did not lie behind in the tomb. No one ever produced it. (How easy it would have been for any of his many enemies to kill once and for all the Christian "superstition" of the Resurrection by simply producing Christ's dead body!) However, it was so different that Mary Magdalene, the Emmaus disciples, and Peter in the boat on the Sea of Galilee did not recognize him at first. Of course, they soon *did* recognize him: "It is the Lord!" Yet he is now the Lord glorified, able to ascend into heaven like iron filings to a magnet: the same, yet different.

Everything in heaven will be the same, yet different. For "world" is correlative to "body". The resurrected body includes "a new heaven and a new earth" (Rev 21:1). We will not change our species to angels or ghosts. As C. S. Lewis describes it, "The old field of body, matter, space, and senses is to be tilled for a new crop. We may be tired of that old field; but God is not." (Incidentally, I know of nothing more helpful on the Resurrection than the chapter in Lewis' *Miracles* entitled "Miracles of the New Creation.")

Whatever God has in store for us in life everlasting, one thing is sure: It will be better, not worse, than our best guesses. "Eye has not seen, ear has not heard, nor has it entered into the heart of man, the things God has prepared for those who love him." When we are on our deathbed, we have barely begun.

24
The Four Last Things: Death

I never realized what death is until the doctors told me my daughter was dying. They were wrong, thanks to God and to the prayers of hundreds of friends. But their mistake taught me a deep truth: "All men are mortal" does not tell you what death is. "The ones I love are mortal" does. Love brings the truth of our own mortality home to us, where it belongs.

How could we forget it? It is life's one certainty. Augustine says in one of his sermons: Listen to the relatives and friends at a baptism speculating about the future of this baby: "Will he be famous? Perhaps so, perhaps not. Will he be happy? Perhaps so, perhaps not. Will his life be long and healthy? Perhaps so, perhaps not." But no one ever says, "Will he die? Perhaps so, perhaps not!"

Death is our one certainty in an age of scepticism, our one absolute in an age of relativism, our one inescapable brush with otherworldliness in an age of *this*-worldliness, our last link with the sacred in an age of secularism. To secularize death, as our culture is doing, is the last blasphemy.

Saint Francis called her, with astonishing affection, "Sister Death". She is an enemy—our last enemy—yet she becomes our sister, our friend, and our teacher if we are honest enough to seek the Truth. In the face of death, Truth's voice acquires sudden volume. We're usually making too much noise to hear her still, small voice; but when the great silence of death comes near, we are able to hear some of the deep truths that are so close to us that we forget them, like the nose on our face.

But there are at least three sets of earmuffs we often wear, and if you're wearing any of them, I am asking you now, gently and in fear and trembling, to take them off.

The first earmuff is specifically un-Christian; it is secular society's only way to cope with death in the absence of any assurance of immortality. Our society reduces death, as it reduces sex, from a high and sacred mystery to a mere fact, a natural event, which we are supposed to "come to terms with", "cope with", and "accept" as "natural", contrary to all the myths, all the religions of the world, and all our instincts. There is nothing so dreary and horrifying as the plethora of books now crowding our shelves that try to level the last vertical spire that remains in a horizontal age, that try to pull the teeth of the great monster, our last connection with the transcendent. Death is *not* natural and *not* acceptable; it is a horror and an obscenity. Not to admit this is to lose one's intellectual virginity and honesty.

A second earmuff is the common confusion between Christianity and comfort, peace of mind, happiness, or success. To look death in the face does not, apparently, lead to these goals. Many people therefore simply look the other way and even condemn as "morbid" the interest in death. It is, of course, just the opposite: it makes you come alive and appreciate life's preciousness. As Dr. Johnson said: "Being hanged wonderfully concentrates the mind."

The third earmuff is the Christian faith in immortality itself, coming too soon; the solution without the problem, the assurance without the doubt, the "fear not" without the fear. Christ is God's solution to the twin problems of sin and death; but to look away to the solution before looking squarely and honestly at the problem is to miss the whole tang and bite and glory of the solution.

Honesty, though not the greatest virtue, is the necessary soil for the growth of every other virtue. Truth *must* be faced, sooner or later. Even hell is truth, faced too late. So why not face the immense fact of your mortality now, this moment? Look at your hand. Look also at the truth that this hand will, in less than a hundred years, be a skeleton's hand. Look at people passing by. Notice their faces, their irreplaceable individualities. Look also at the fact that every one of these faces will one day be a skull, including your own. *Memento mori.*

Why? *Why* remember death? Why look? Because it is true. For the same reason men climbed Mt. Everest. Because it is there.

Christ looked, and conquered: *veni, vidi, vici.* Caesar has infinitely less right to those great words than Christ: "I came, I saw, I conquered." Christianity is the religion of the conquest of death. Christ came to change death from an enemy to a friend, from a hole to a door, from a juggernaut to the golden chariot sent by the King to fetch his beloved Cinderella-bride to his castle to live with him in joy forever. The Christian can stick his tongue out at death and give it a Bronx cheer, like Saint Paul: "Oh death, where is they sting? Oh grave, where is thy victory?" "The sting of death is sin", and death is now a stingless bee, for its stinger has lodged in the body of Christ on the Cross.

Death is separation—from body, from friends, from world. But Christ has made it the opposite: meeting. For this meeting he has arranged every detail in our lives; death becomes the consummation of his betrothal to us.

But it must first be enemy before it can be friend. The no-problem approach is infinitely farther from Christianity than the no-answer despair. The existential anxiety of the honest atheist confronting eternal nothingness is infinitely more noble than the vapid, bland platitudes of pop psychology about acceptance, coping, and getting your life in order. Just as modern psychology substitutes "no sin" for the forgiveness of sin, substitutes "there's nothing to forgive" for "you are forgiven", so it substitutes an aspirin for an operation when dealing with death.

The unique message of Christianity about death is like the sudden happy ending of a fairy tale: a grace, a joy, a "good catastrophe". A Christian does not have the high-minded resignation of the stoic or the low-minded peace-of-mind mongering of the secular psychologists because he has faced the honest despair of the pagan and answered it with the fact of the Resurrection.

Death changed its meaning two thousand years ago, when the emptiness that had reigned since Adam was shattered by the Big Bang of a new kingdom on the first Easter morning.

25
The Four Last Things: Judgment

Sign on campus: "Prepare for your finals. Read your Bible." As with death, judgment requires that we face facts. Nothing can be done without light.

The fact here is justice—God's justice. Yes, God is merciful. But he is also just. "Justice and peace shall meet together, righteousness and truth shall kiss each other." He reconciles both justice and mercy at Calvary. That's why Christ had to die. If God were only merciful and not just, he could have breezily said "forget it" instead of "forgive it". Forgiveness is costly. If you owe me $1,000 and I forgive your debt, I have to pay my creditors $1,000 out of my own pocket. The debt must be paid. Justice *is*.

Judgment, therefore, is an eternal necessity, not an arbitrary whim. Judgment *must* fall—somewhere, sometime, on someone, somehow. Instead of here, at my death, on me, and as reason expects, it falls on Calvary, two thousand year ago, on Christ, in God's great mystery. But it falls. The "wages of sin is death," and Christ shoulders it all. The death here includes spiritual death, alienation from God, and hell itself. No soul in hell suffers more than the one who cried, "My God, my God, why hast thou forsaken me?"

Modernity cannot understand why Christ had to die because it does not believe in justice and judgment. The typically modern mind sympathizes with the clergyman in hell in C. S. Lewis' *The Great Divorce*. Granted a day's vacation in heaven, he chooses to return to hell because "we have a little theological society down there" and the paper he is to present that night deals with the question of what Jesus' mature views would have been if it hadn't been for that tragic accident of the Crucifixion!

Our only escape from judgment is in the one who did not escape it. We are saved *in* Christ. Not by *imitating* Christ, or by being

externally "clothed" with Christ, so that God blinds his own eyes
by looking at us but seeing Christ instead (Luther's notion), but
rather by being incorporated into Christ.

Life is full of warnings to prepare for the Last Judgment.
Psychoanalysis furnishes a fine example: push a problem down into
the unconscious and you don't bury it dead, you bury it alive, and it
rises from the dead and haunts you. There is justice in every act in
our lives: the same stroke of the axe that weakens the tree
strengthens the lumberjack. And the same blow of the club that
softens the victim's body hardens the mugger's soul. For every
action there's an equal and opposite reaction—in the spiritual
world as well as the physical. There's no free lunch.

We hear little about this today—about justice and judgment in
this life, much less in the next. One reason is our loss of
metaphysics; our disbelief that the human mind can know
objective reality. Justice is reduced to vengeance, a subjective
motive. Religion itself is reduced from objective truths to
subjective comfort.

Another reason is the prevalence of some very odd theologians
among writers and opinion makers. Partly as a reaction against
those who emphasized judgment to control people by making them
feel guilty, modern theologians shy away from the idea of
judgment. But *abusus non tollit usum:* abuse does not take away use.
The misuse of a fact does not make the fact any less true.

A third reason we hear so little about judgment is an implicit
monism in our thinking. How could life present us with ultimate
choices with diverging paths? Shouldn't it be a mountain where all
paths meet at the top? The mind naturally wants to think so. Yet
God has told us not. He has told us that life is like a tree, not like a
pool. It's full of forks. And though there are countless forks and
choices and roads, there is none that does not eventually bring us to
one or the other of the only two final destinations. Psalm 1 sets the
tone for all Scripture: there are two ways, not one. Two
destinations, not one. That's the reason for judgment: to separate
the sheep from the goats.

We will not be able to argue with God's judgment, for it will be simply truth, simply light. Hell is light hated, and truth is torture to souls who hate it. Heaven is the same light loved. It's like two people at a symphony. For one it is hell; for other it is heaven. Thus, judgment is not changeable. It is not arbitrary will or whim. It is simply the truth about who we are.

Yet it's personal too; it is a relationship. God is not light in an impersonal sense. God *wills* light. Faith—acceptance of God's revealed light—is like the choice to accept a marriage proposal. Unfaith is the willful refusal of that offer. Apostasy is spiritual divorce. Judgment is no more impersonal than it is arbitrary, for God the judge is both personal and perfect.

Because God is just and justice is eternal, it is not set aside by Christ, but fulfilled. The law, God's unchangeable demand for perfection ("Be ye holy as I the Lord your God am holy"), is fulfilled only by Christ, and our eternal destiny is totally dependent upon our relationship to him. The thing Saint Paul calls "the justice of God" or "the righteousness of God" is the gospel, the good news that the most unjust thing that ever happened—deicide—resulted in our salvation.

God is a very tricky fellow, you see. Because he's love. Love will do *anything* to get its way. *Amor vincit omnia:* love conquers all, love always finds a way. God's amazing way of satisfying the demands of justice is the very thing atheists hurl at him as an objection: the innocent suffer the desserts of the guilty. His reply: Yes, the innocent one suffered the desserts of the guilty, and that is your only hope of enduring my judgment.

26
The Four Last Things: Heaven

Quo vadis? Where are you going? That's the most important question for a traveler. And we the living are all travelers. Death calls us all and moves us on. Stability is illusion. So those who cannot abide illusion must raise the question: *Quo vadis?*

If heaven is not the answer to the question, our whole faith is false, and Jesus was a fool. If it is, then there's nothing that is more important in the whole world. Indeed, the whole world is only heaven's womb.

Why do we hear so little about this today, even from the pulpit? Why are we told by our "leading theologians" that we must take our eyes off the clouds and keep them on the ground? Why is it so outrageously irresponsible to think more about heaven than politics? Because these leading theologians are really *following* theologians, with their noses to the tail of the modern world. They are in fact upside down: not only are their eyes stuck in the mud, but their feet are kicking up in rebellion at the sky. They want to turn Christianity—which in the clear teaching of its founder was an otherworldly religion of faith, hope, and charity—into a this-worldly religion of prosperity and success (the Right with its electronic Church) or of political revolution (the left with its liberation theology).

But these shams don't satisfy for long. Prosperity is boring. The suicide rate in Sweden is something like a thousand times that of Haiti. And even revolution is finally boring. No revolution can survive its own success. Every revolution turns into a new tyranny, and Ecclesiastes' cycles return like the clouds after a rain.

The big, blazing, terrible truth about man is that he has a heaven-sized hole in his heart, and nothing else can fill it. We pass our lives trying to fill the Grand Canyon with marbles. As Augustine said: "Thou hast made us for thyself, and our hearts are

restless until they rest in thee." That's the greatest sentence ever
written outside Scripture because it tells us the secret of our
destiny, our happiness—and our unhappiness. It is, however, not
only unfashionable but terribly threatening. It tears the band-aid
off our wound. It shows up our false gods for the tiny things they
are compared with our own hearts. People do not take kindly to
idol smashing. Look what they did to the prophets.

But we should be encouraged. Even the sceptic who does not
believe in heaven has a heaven-shaped heart. The deck is stacked
and the dice are loaded, loaded with the love of heaven. *Amor meus,*
pondus meum, said Augustine: "My love is my weight." The gravity
of his own heart pulls the sceptic in heaven's direction, even while
the antigravity of sin pulls him away.

But the head must often be outwitted, for it is entangled in
verbal prejudices. Talk about heaven and you'll get sneers. But
talk about a mysterious dissatisfaction with life even when things
go well—*especially* when things go well—and you'll get a hearing
from man's heart, even if his lips will not agree.

No one longs for fluffy clouds and sexless cherubs, but *everyone*
longs for heaven. No one longs for any of the heavens that we have
ever imagined, but everyone longs for "something no eye has seen,
no ear has heard, something that has not entered into the
imagination of man, something God has prepared for those who
love him."

We are still children, however hard we try to cover that up.
There are no "grown-ups". When we get old, we only exchange
our toys: business for bats, sex for sleds, power for popguns. At
death our Father calls: "Come, little one. Time to put away your
toys and come home."

Home—that's what heaven is. It won't appear strange and
faraway and "supernatural", but utterly natural. Heaven is what
we were designed for. All our epics seek it: It is the "home" of
Odysseus, of Aeneas, of Frodo, of E.T. Heaven is not escapist.
Worldliness is escapist. Heaven is home.

People think heaven is escapist because they fear that thinking
about heaven will distract us from living well here and now. It is

exactly the opposite, and the lives of the saints and our Lord himself prove it. Those who truly love heaven will do the most for earth. It's easy to see why. Those who love the homeland best work the hardest in the colonies to make them resemble the homeland. "Thy kingdom come . . . on earth as it is in heaven."

The pregnant woman who plans a live birth cares for her unborn baby; the woman who plans for an abortion does not. Highways that lead somewhere are well maintained; dead ends are not. So if we see life as a road to heaven, some of heaven's own glory will reflect back onto that road, if only by anticipation: the world is charged with the grandeur of God and every event smells of eternity. But if it all goes down the drain in death, then this life is just swirls of dirty water, and however comfortable we make our wallowing in it, it remains a vanity of vanities.

The existence of heaven, the desire for heaven, the nature of heaven, and the relevance of heaven are all important questions. But there is only one question that's absolutely essential, one question compared with which how we might save the world from a nuclear holocaust is trivial: "What must I do to be saved?" When I'm honest enough to look through the door of death, infinite joy or infinite joylessness loom up as my only two possible destinies. What decides for joy? What is heaven's entrance ticket? What is the Way, the Truth and the Life?

I am horrified to report that I've asked this question of hundreds of Catholic college students, and far fewer than half have known the answer. This means that the Church's religious education has been not a failure but an inexcusable disaster. Most reply either "God is good to everybody" or "I'm basically a good person."

If anyone out there is unsure of the correct answer, then for the love of God get out your Bible and study for your finals! To save you time—since you may die while reaching for your Bible—I will quote God's scandalously simple answer to the most important question in the world, how to get to heaven: "Believe in the Lord Jesus Christ and you will be saved" (Acts 16:31).

27
The Four Last Things: Hell

The hell with hell! says the modern mind. Of all Christianity's teachings, hell is certainly the least popular. Non-Christians ignore it, weak Christians excuse it, and anti-Christians attack it.

Some, like Bertrand Russell in his famous essay "Why I Am Not a Christian", argue that because Jesus clearly taught it, he was not a good moral teacher. (Russell's essay, by the way, makes fine devotional reading for a Christian. My college roommate was about to lose his faith until he read it; he said to me, "If those are the arguments against Christianity, I'd better be a Christian.")

Why do we believe there's a hell? Not because we're vindictive. "Vengeance is mine, I will repay, says the Lord." Why, then? Simply because we've been told, by Christ himself. There's a popular fallacy that Jesus spoke only comforting words and that the fear of hell began with Saint Paul. The textual truth is the opposite: Jesus uttered many "hell fire and damnation" sermons, while nearly all the passages that offer any hope to the universalist (who believe all men will be saved in the end) are from Paul.

Fear of hell is not a base motive. As George MacDonald says, "As long as there are wild beasts about, it is better to be afraid than secure." God's graciousness accepts even the "low" motive of fear of hell for salvation if that's the best we can muster. His arms are open to all prodigals. He is not high-minded, like some of his detractors. All's fair in love and war. And life is both.

Hell follows from two other doctrines: heaven and free will. If there *is* a heaven, there can be a not-heaven. And if there *is* free will, we can act on it and abuse it. Those who deny hell must also deny either heaven (as does Western secularism) or free will (as does Eastern pantheism).

Hell and heaven make life serious. Heaven without hell removes the bite from life's drama. C. S. Lewis once said that he never met a single person who had a lively faith in heaven without a similar belief in hell. The height of the mountain is measured by the depth of the valley, the greatness of salvation by the awfulness of the thing we're saved from.

What is hell? The popular image of demons gleefully poking pitchforks into unrepentant posteriors misses the point of the biblical image of fire. Fire *destroys*. *Gehenna*, the word Jesus used for hell, was the valley outside Jerusalem that the Jews used for the perpetual burning of garbage because it had been desecrated by heathen tribes who used it for human sacrifice. In hell you make an eternal ash of yourself. Hell is not eternal life with torture but something far worse: eternal dying. What goes to hell, said C. S. Lewis, is "not a man, but remains".

The images for hell in Scripture are horrible, but they're only symbols. The thing symbolized is not less horrible than the symbols, but *more*. Spiritual fire is worse than material fire; spiritual death is worse than physical death. The pain of loss—the loss of God, who is the source of all joy—is infinitely more horrible than any torture could ever be. All who know God and his joy understand that. Saints do not need to be threatened with fire, only with loss. "All your life an unattainable ecstasy has hovered just beyond the grasp of your consciousness. The day is coming when you will wake to find, beyond all hope, that you have attained it— or else that it was within your grasp and you have lost it forever" (C. S. Lewis).

Jesus does not tell us much detail about hell. He tells us that it exists, that it's horrible, that any man can go there. Judas seems to be one, for Jesus says of him, "It would have been good for that man if he had not been born." If no one goes to hell, it would seem to be inexcusable for Jesus to give us so many fearful warnings about it. But he does not give us population statistics. To his disciples' question "Are many saved?" he does not answer with estimates but with a forceful appeal to the will: "Strive to enter in."

Jesus says the way to hell is broad and many find it and that the way to heaven is narrow and few find it. And he means it: you don't get to heaven simply by being born, by being nice, or by oozing into an eternal growth experience. But "few" here does not mean that less than half of mankind will be saved. For God speaks as our Father, not our statistician. Even one child lost is too many, and the rest saved are too few. The good shepherd who left his ninety-nine sheep safe at home to rescue his one lost sheep found even 99 percent salvation too "few".

The most important question about hell, as about heaven, is the practical one: What roads lead there? They are interior, of course. In fact, heaven and hell may be the very same objective place— namely God's love, experienced oppositely by opposite souls, just as the same opera or rock concert can be heavenly for you and hellish for the reluctant guest at your side. The fires of hell may be made of the very love of God, experienced as torture by those who hate him: the very light of God's truth, hated and fled from in vain by those who love darkness. Imagine a man in hell—no, a ghost— endlessly chasing his own shadow, as the light of God shines endlessly behind him. If he would only turn and face the light, he would be saved. But he refuses to—forever.

Just as we can attain heaven by implicit as well as explicit faith ("Saint Socrates, pray for us," says Erasmus), so hell too can be reached without explicit rebellion. This is the terrible—and terribly needed—truth taught by C. S. Lewis in *The Great Divorce* and Charles Williams in *Descent into Hell*. We can drift, slide, even snooze comfortably into hell. All God's messengers, the prophets, say so.

We desperately need to hear this truth about hell again, simply out of honesty, because it is there. And also out of compassion. For when an abyss looms ahead, the *least* compassionate thing to tell the traveler is "peace, peace, when there is no peace". Out of love for god and man, let us tell the truth about hell!

Sure, we'll be mocked as vindictive, manipulative, or funda- mentalist. Let it be so. Sometimes it seems that we're more afraid of sharing our Lord's holy unrespectability than of hell itself. It's a small price to pay for the salvation of a single infinitely precious soul. And that is the business we're supposed to be in.

PART TWO

CODE: FUNDAMENTALS OF CHRISTIAN LIVING

A. CHRISTIAN VIRTUES:
THE THREE THEOLOGICAL VIRTUES

28
Faith

Faith, hope, and charity are, quite simply, the three greatest things in the world. We cannot possibly overemphasize their importance. Together they make up the "one thing necessary". We must speak of them in the same imperious and imperative terms Jesus used when he said, "If your right eye causes you to sin, pluck it out and throw it away; it is better that you lose one of your members than that your whole body be thrown into hell." Nothing is more important than faith, hope, and charity because they make the difference between heaven and hell, eternal life and eternal death, and there is no difference as great as that.

They are called the three theological virtues because they have God (*theos*) as their object. They are the glue that attaches us to God. They are the three-doored entrance to heaven. It is not that God refuses entrance at heaven's gate to anyone; these *are* heaven's gate. Anyone who has no faith in God, no hope in God, and no love of God cannot go to heaven because heaven would be hell to him. He could not endure or enjoy the presence of God after death anymore than he did before death.

Faith, hope, and charity are the three legs of a single tripod that supports the whole Christian life. Each leg depends on the others. Faith without the works of love is dead, according to Scripture, and false—not real faith at all. Love not motivated by faith is not *agape* but mere feeling and sentimentality (often masked by the code word *compassion*), dependent on the whims and winds of human change. Hope without faith is mere wishful thinking, "the power of positive thinking", optimism. Hope is not the same as optimism; some of the great hopers are pessimists by temperament, like Evelyn Waugh. Hope's opposite is despair, which is a deadly sin, not pessimism, which is a psychological trait. Love without hope is desperation, Stephen Crane's "open boat" of doomed castaways able only to huddle close for warmth before death, the end of everything. Hope without love is isolating and selfish; it is the Phariseeism and self-righteousness of every tyrant and architect of a "brave new world". Faith without hope is simply impossible, for the God we believe has given us an astonishing bag of promises.

This tripod is the foundation of all other virtues. The other virtues all depend on these three because these are the key to the very life of God within our souls, and all other virtues are characteristics of that life, not self-improvement programs that we whip up within ourselves. Honesty, justice, patience, chastity, self-control, even love of neighbor, all come from the prior presence of God in us, which in turn comes only through faith, hope, and charity. We do not practice the virtues in order to get to heaven; we practice the virtues because heaven has already gotten to us. Love of God, for instance, will always send us to love of neighbor, while love of neighbor will not always send us to love of God, for God always sends you to your neighbor, but your neighbor does not always send you to God. Both commandments are absolutely necessary, but there is an order—not of importance, for love of God without love of neighbor is just as worthless and false as love of neighbor without love of God—but an order of priority, of precedence. First things first. Foundations first. Back to basics.

It is appropriate for us to turn back to these basics of the Christian life now because the society we live in does not understand them. We live in a post-Christian world, and many of us are not sufficiently aware of that fact. Our modern world is in fact a clear countersign to these three virtues. Doubt, despair, and selfishness are the pillars of modern life, not faith, hope, and charity. Our world sees faith as naiveté, hope as Pollyanna-style wishful thinking, and charity as weakness. We see around us a growing materialism, which is unbelief in practice; a rising suicide rate and depression, which is despair in practice; and a rising respectability for the me-first philosophy for which charity is a totally unintelligible alternative, a radical foolishness. It is therefore high time for us to go back to our spiritual basics, lest we sink into the dark waters that surround us and disappear into me-tooism, lest our salt lose its saltiness and deserve only to be trodden under foot, like rock salt thrown on snow or ice.

Kant said that there are only three absolutely necessary questions that everyone must answer, implicitly or explicitly: What can I know? What should I do? What may I hope? The three theological virtues are God's answer to these three most important human questions. We can know God and all that is necessary for our salvation by faith in what God has revealed to us; we can know our essential moral obligation as charity to God and neighbor; and we can know what to hope in by what God has promised us.

These three virtues are also called the supernatural virtues to distinguish them from the natural virtues, the virtues that do not require the saving presence of God's own life in the soul for their existence (though they do require that for their perfection). The four cardinal, or "hinge", virtues in the natural order are prudence (practical wisdom), fortitude (courage), temperance (moderation), and justice (fairness and harmony within and without).

Without the supernatural virtues, the natural virtues cannot flourish. Augustine went so far (too far, I think) as to call the natural moral virtues of pagans like Socrates "splendid vices". But it is true that, for instance, without charity, which goes beyond justice, it is very hard even to be just, for we cannot fulfill the just requirements of the natural law of fairness to our neighbors except by the power of love. "Love is the fulfillment of the law", as Saint Paul says, not because love substitutes for the law, as if we did not need to do works of justice once we had charity, but because love fulfills the law, for when we love someone we want them to receive perfect justice.

Another example of the same principle: it is very difficult to be courageous without hope of heaven. Why risk your life if there is no hope that your story ends in anything other than worms, decay, and forgetting? Also, no one can be truly wise without faith, for faith sees higher and farther and deeper than reason or experience can. It sees "through a glass, darkly", but it sees truly. And no one can practice temperance or self-control without God's grace, for we are all addicted to sin and self-indulgence, and it is very difficult to break an addiction by just trying a little harder without help from without.

The point is simply that without God's grace, which comes only through faith, hope, and charity, no one can be very good. Without love, justice turns to cruelty. Without hope, courage turns to blind despair and rage. Without faith, this-worldly wisdom becomes foolishness in God's eyes.

Faith first, because it is first. It is the root, hope is the stem, and charity is the flower. The flower is the fairest, the stem does the growing, but the root must come first. What is faith?

We can speak of faith (1) in a very wide, general sense, as the world speaks of it; or (2) in a biblical sense, as saving faith, or the condition for salvation; or, finally, (3) in its most technical theological sense as one of the three theological virtues.

1. Faith in the most general sense is simply a feeling of trust in or reliance on someone (or even sometimes on no one, as in the poster where a tiny knight with a tiny sword tremblingly confronts an enormous dragon, and the caption says, in Gothic letters, "Have faith"). This is indeed naiveté. "Have faith in me", says the used-car salesman or the presidential candidate or the incompetent doctor with the divinity complex.

2. Faith in the biblical sense of saving faith is the act by which we receive God's own eternal life (or "sanctifying grace", in technical theological terms). It is our fundamental option of saying Yes instead of No to God with our heart, our will, our personal center. To believe in this sense is to receive (Jn 1:12 parallels the two terms), to receive God himself.

Saint Paul argues in Romans that faith (in this sense) was even in Old Testament times the condition for salvation, for our justification with God. Abraham was justified by his faith. Go back even farther: the fall was first of all a fall of faith. Only because Eve first believed the serpent when he told her she would not die if she ate the forbidden fruit, rather than believing God when he told her that she would—only because of Eve's faithlessness within— did she practice the faithlessness without that was the actual act of disobedience, the eating of the forbidden fruit. Faith is the root of obedience; the lack of faith is the root of disobedience. If we totally believed that obedience always worked to our blessedness, we would not disobey. Only because we must pray "Lord, I believe, but help my unbelief" do we sin.

Saint Paul contrasts faith with sin when he says, "Whatever is not of faith is sin." We usually think of sin as the opposite of virtue, and faith as the opposite of doubt. But virtue is a moral term, and doubt is an intellectual term. The opposite of moral virtue is moral vice, and the opposite of intellectual doubt is intellectual belief. Faith is deeper than either moral virtue or intellectual belief. Sin is deeper than either moral vice or intellectual doubt. Faith is a fundamental Yes to God with the center of our being, and sin—the state of sin as distinct from particular acts of sin—is the fundamental No to God with the center of our being. Faith is the opposite of sin. Faith is to sin what light is to darkness.

Belief is an intellectual matter. I believe the sun will shine tomorrow: I believe I am in good health, I believe my textbooks. This is mere opinion. Faith is not mere opinion. Opinions do not save us. Trust is an emotional matter. I trust my surgeon or my psychiatrist or my children. This is a precious feeling, but it is a feeling. Faith is not feeling. Feelings do not save us. Faith, however, results in or expresses itself in both belief and trust, for the prefunctional root that is the very essence of the self expresses itself in the two branches or functions of the intellectual (belief) and the emotional (trust). But faith is deeper. That is why even some people who seem on an intellectual level to be unbelievers may on this deeper level be believers, and we may be surprised to see some famous so-called atheists in heaven. And it is why some people who seem to have very little emotional faith—little trust, serenity, consolation—may nevertheless be people of great, even heroic, faith. Only God sees hearts.

3. The third and most specific, most technical sense of faith is the sense we learned from the Baltimore Catechism. Faith is the act of the intellect, prompted by the will, by which we believe the truth of all that God has revealed on the basis of the authority of the one who has revealed it. This is essentially the definition used by Saint Thomas Aquinas and medieval scholastic theology.

At the time of the Protestant Reformation, each side used a different language system, and the most important and tragic split in the Church's history resulted. Protestant reformers, using faith in the biblical sense, as saving faith, insisted that the Bible clearly taught that faith alone was sufficient for salvation. They formulated their slogan *sola fides* (faith alone), on the basis of Romans and Galatians. They thought that the Catholic Church's insistence that good works were also necessary for salvation was a pagan doctrine, a compromise of the very essence of the gospel. Most evangelical and fundamentalist Protestants to this day justify their disagreement with the Catholic Church more fundamentally on this basis than on any other. They sincerely believe that Catholicism is another gospel, as Paul called Galatian legalism, and many wonder whether Catholics are even Christians.

But James clearly says in his epistle that faith without works is dead and that we are justified by works (good works, the works of love) as well as faith, working together with faith. James and the Catholic scholastic theologians were using faith in its third, narrowest sense: as just one of the three theological virtues. In this sense, hope and charity must be added to faith for salvation. Paul and the Protestants were using faith in its second, broader sense: as the root or center of all three theological virtues, not as an act of the intellect (as in the Baltimore Catechism definition) but as an act of the heart (in the biblical sense) or spirit or personal center. Both sides were (and are) right, as Pope John Paul II made quite clear to the Lutheran bishops of Germany on his visit there in 1983.

In other words, the essence of the Protestant Reformation was a misunderstanding. What hope for reunion lies in that fact!

To clarify the different meanings of faith in another way, remember that we exist on three levels. Saint Paul in two places in his letters refers to them as "spirit, soul, and body". Body is our relationship with the physical world, the level of reality that is less than ourselves. Soul is our relationship with ourselves (self-consciousness) and with others, our equals. Spirit is our relationship with God, the reality that is greater than ourselves. There is a form of faith on each of the three levels. Faith in the bodily sphere is the works of love and obedience without which, according to James, faith is dead and false. This is the aspect emphasized by the writer of the epistle to the Hebrews in the classic chapter on faith, chapter 11. The faith of each of the Old Testament heroes was defined or manifested in what they did. Faith in the sphere of the soul includes both intellectual belief and emotional trust. Finally, faith in the spirit, where faith begins, is the basic Yes to God that is the condition for salvation. This is an act of the will, but it is not always consciously rational and intellectual.

Saint Thomas, like the New Testament, sometimes uses faith in the technical and intellectual sense, as an act of the intellect. But sometimes he uses faith in the broader and deeper sense, the Pauline sense, just as the Protestant reformers did—for instance, when he says that "the object of faith is not a proposition but a person." In other words, God himself is the object of faith; the propositions in the creed express its content. We believe not just ideas about God but God. It is essential to know things about God, but it is more essential to know God. "This is eternal life", says Jesus in his high priestly prayer in John 17:3, "to know Thee, the only true God." The creeds are like accounting books, God is like the actual money.

Though the root of faith is not intellectual, one of its fruits is. "Faith seeking understanding" (*fides quaerens intellectum*) was the operative slogan for a thousand years of Christian theology.

"Unless you believe, you will not understand"—faith first. Then, "In thy light we see light"—understanding follows. How accurately the saints know God; how foolishly mistaken are the unbelieving geniuses! Reason may run ahead of faith, as John ran ahead of Peter to the empty tomb, but faith first enters the secret of understanding, as Peter first entered the tomb. Faith is more active than reason. Reason passively reports data, like a camera. Faith takes a stand, like an army. Faith leaps into God's arms, answering his proposal of spiritual marriage.

There is a kind of faith that Saint Paul lists as one of the charismatic gifts. This is special, miracle-working faith. It is available to all but found in few. When we have this kind of faith, we do not pray from the human platform of uncertainty and pleading but from the divine platform of operative certainty. The word of this kind of faith is not "please" but "be it done." Many radio and television preachers have confused listeners by confusing this special kind of faith with ordinary saving faith, making listeners think they are guaranteed miracles and if miracles do not happen they just do not have real faith at all. This may be an honest mistake, but it is a cruel one. Jesus' own disciples had faith smaller than a grain of mustard seed, Jesus said. Yet they were accepted. "Lord, I believe; help my unbelief" is a good, honest prayer, like the prayer of the publican, "God be merciful to me a sinner." Let us be content to run before trying to fly.

The most pervasive mistake the modern world makes about faith is to subjectivize and psychologize it, as if believers constructed their religion out of their own psyches: "I'm feeling rather religious today; do you have anything for me to believe in?" This mistake occurs because the modern mind has things inside out. It starts with the human rather than the divine. Thus its values are "my values" (don't impose them on anyone else, please!), and even truth is "truth for me". Both the Bible and common sense say differently. We must conform to reality, not vice versa. We must be honest. There is only one honest reason why anyone should ever believe anything: because it is true. God is, and God has acted, and

God has spoken. Now I must respond. That is the true situation. Do I respond Yes (faith) or No? That is the simple question.

Faith is very simple. Saying all this is perhaps too much. Much of what is written about faith is like snowflakes on a bell: it muffles the sound. Just say Yes to God. It's the simplest thing in the world.

29
Hope

No one can live without hope. Only angels do not need hope, for they do not live in time and have no future. They possess the whole of their reality at once. But we creatures of time are constantly moving into the future, and our eyes are usually facing forward. Hope is like headlights. It is not easy to drive without headlights in the dark.

To be human is to be growing. We are all spiritually babies, and the most spiritually mature of us are the first to admit that fact. There are no grownups. Life is a continual pregnancy, and death is like birth. To live without hope is like being pregnant with a dead baby.

Hope is the life of the soul. A soul without hope is a dead soul. The Russian novelist Gogol wrote a story with the haunting title *Dead Souls*. I find the phrase unforgettable, especially when I look carefully into the eyes of some street people and also some very famous people. There really are such things as dead souls. Just as the body is dead when its source of life, the soul, is gone, so a soul is dead when its source of life is gone. That source is the spirit. The spirit's life-giving work in the soul is to give it a reason to live and a reason to die, in other words, hope. Hope is the soul's food. Without it the soul simply cannot live.

Freud says, sagely, that the two things everyone needs are love and work, and work means hope: a reason to get out of bed in the morning, a reason for doing anything. Our modern society finds it harder to find reasons for getting out of bed than any other society that has ever been. It also finds it easier to find reasons for getting into bed than any other society that has ever been. We know no reason to get out of bed and every reason to get in.

Hope is the forgotten virtue of our time because hope—real hope, the theological virtue of hope, as distinct from the vague sentiment of hopefulness, or optimism—means something scandalously transcendental, something offensively supernatural, to the modern mind. That mind dare not raise its eyes to the sky; its nose-to-the-grindstone worldliness cannot understand or respect the otherwordly goal. It can do nothing but invent sneering names for the goal like "escapism" and "pie in the sky bye and bye". The New Testament appeals to heavenly hope on nearly every page. It is continually reminding us that our citizenship is in heaven. Modernity sees this not only as escapism and wishful thinking, but as traitorous: If our citizenship is not in this world, how can we be loyal to it? That is like thinking that if an unborn baby hopes to be born out of the womb, it is a traitor to the womb.

Hopelessness means living in a squashed, low, flat, one-dimensional world, a ranch-style universe, where the sky is only a flat, painted ceiling a few feet above your head. Hope, on the other hand, means living in a universe in which it is possible to climb mountains and stand outdoors, where the terrifying and wonderful winds of heaven whip through your hair. The silliest of all the many superstitions of unbelievers is that Christianity is a dull, wimpy, boring batch of platitudes; that a Christian is something like a worm: flat and squashed and "humble" as Uriah Heep was "humble". Rather, "we are never so tall as when we bow." Hope gives us height, and room. It puts us outdoors, outside this stuffy little idol called society, in a cosmos that sprouts turrets and spires.

In an age of hope men looked up at the night sky and saw "the heavens". In an age of hopelessness they call it simply "space". Emptiness has replaced fullness. Where our ancestors heard "the music of the spheres" our contemporaries hear only "the eternal silence of those infinite spaces that fills me with terror", as Pascal pointedly puts it.

The concept of hope has been hopelessly trivialized by the modern mind, just as the concept of faith has. Just as "I believe" usually means merely "I feel", so "I hope" usually means only "I wish" or "wouldn't it be nice if. . . ." But Christian hope, the theological virtue of hope, is not a wish or a feeling; it is a rock-solid certainty, a guarantee, an anchor. We bury our dead " in the sure and certain hope of the resurrection". Feelings are subject to every wind of chance and change, from politics to digestion. But Christian hope has a foundation. It is a house built upon a rock, and that rock is Christ. "The hopes and fears of all the years are met in thee tonight", we sing to the "little town of Bethlehem", the "house of bread" from which our souls are fed.

For Christian hope does not come from us. It is our response to God's promises. It is not a feeling welling up from within, something we can whip up at will. It is saying Yes to God's guarantees. It is the alternative to calling God a liar. It is the simple and commonsensical acceptance of all God's promises on the ground that, as Saint Thomas Aquinas put it in the great hymn "Pange Lingua", "than Truth's own word there is no truer token."

The object of hope is God himself, just as God is the object of faith. The creeds formulate faith, and God's promises formulate hope. But hope's object is not the abstract promises but the concrete God, the person who made them. God is always first, always the initiator. Even our seeking him is the result of his first seeking us. Therefore hope too must be our response to his initiative. God is not the response to human hope; our hope is the response to him and his promises.

Hope is thus definite and specific, not vague, because God has promised definite and specific things. That does not mean that these things are always clear rather than mysterious, or that they do not require a leap of faith or a lot of waiting or testing. But it means that God, who is not fuzzy and woolly but sharp and specific, makes promises that are not fuzzy and woolly but sharp and specific. The promises are written in Scripture, not just in our psyches. Hope is specified by a book, by words, rather than by feelings. If you had the time, it would be an amazing exercise to go through the whole of Scripture just noting and counting the promises. There are well over three hundred of them, three hundred distinct promises, many of them repeated many times in different forms.

Our God is thus a God of promises. And he keeps every one to the letter. Promises come true. The scriptural notion of truth is not, like the Greek notion, a timeless formula, something abstract and static. Rather, it is something that happens in history, it comes true. The Messiah is not an ideal but a person. Creation, fall, Incarnation, death, Resurrection, ascension, Second Coming— these are not myths or images or meanings merely, but actual events. Truth is dramatic; it happens; we see it. John begins his first epistle with words that still invoke awe at this incarnation of truth in time: "That which was from the beginning, which we have heard, which we have seen with our eyes, which we have looked upon and touched with our hands . . . we proclaim to you."

Yet, though hope is not vague, it is universal. Though specific, it is also generic. There is a cosmic dimension to Christian hope that overarches and transcends and environs particular events. Gabriel Marcel, the French Catholic personalist philosopher, defines this hope as "the affirmation that there exists, beyond all data, all inventories, and all calculations, a mysterious principle [*principium*, source, origin, not abstract statement or formula] that is in connivance with me, that cannot but will that which I will if what I will deserves to be willed and is in fact willed with the whole of my being". This rather obscure but profound definition means that our deepest needs, values, longings, and ideals, which flow from our God-given nature, from the image of God in us, are not just facts about us but also facts about objective reality; not just subjective blips on our mental screen but realities detected by our inner radar; not just flotsam and jetsam on the sea of the human psyche but rocket ships that really touch other worlds.

Hope means that the reason I must choose life is that at the heart of reality life is chosen. Hope means that when I say "it is better to be than not to be", I am not expressing a prejudice or even a feeling but a fact; that all things that exist join me in a cosmic chorus of approval. Hope means that my implicit desire for God, however obscure or unconscious, is God's own trace in my being. Hope means that the agony and ecstasy of longing for a joy this world can never give is a sure sign that I was made by and for one who is joy itself, and him alone.

Thus when I hope against hope that my friend will recover from a disease the doctors assure me is fatal, I am not playing the game of predictions and statistical averages against the doctors but prophetically asserting something about the nature of ultimate reality: that it is on my side in willing life over death, that death is the rind or epidermis or outer appearance of life, not vice versa; that ultimate reality is not this indifferent cosmos but an infinitely caring and loving will.

One cannot overemphasize hope because the only alternative is despair, which is worse than death. Better to die in hope than to live in despair, as Charles discovered at the end of Dickens' classic *A Tale of Two Cities,* when he said of his chosen martyrdom, "It is a far, far better thing I do than ever I have done." Despair is the silhouette of hope: it defines the shape of hope by its absence. You never appreciate a thing as sharply as when it is taken from you. For this reason we cannot be too grateful to the great despairers in literature, from Ecclesiastes ("vanity of vanities, all is vanity") to Jean-Paul Sartre. One could almost construct a theology from the writings of the great atheists. The God who is not there is sometimes clearer than the God who is.

A revitalization of the forgotten theological virtue of hope would go far toward healing the tensions in the Church between liberals and conservatives. For liberals emphasize love, often at the expense of faith, and conservatives emphasize faith, often at the expense of love. Hope builds bridges between the two other theological virtues, thus between liberals and conservatives. If you start with love, hope prods you into faith, for if you love someone, you want the dogmatic, glorious, supernatural truths of the faith about human destiny to be true. And if you start with faith, hope prods you into love, for if you believe what the Church teaches about human destiny, your love for God must become also love for his image in your neighbor, who is destined to share divine life. Hope builds bridges—between faith and love, between conservatives and liberals, between present and future, between earth and heaven.

30
Love

Without qualification, without ifs, ands, or buts, God's word tells us, straight as a left jab, that love is the greatest thing there is (1 Cor 13:13). Scripture never says God is justice or beauty or righteousness, though he is just and beautiful and righteous. But "God is love" (1 Jn 4:8). Love is God's essence, his whole being. Everything in him is love. Even his justice is love. Paul identifies "the justice of God" in Romans 1:17 with the most unjust event in all history, deicide, the crucifixion, for that was God's great act of love.

But no word is more misunderstood in our society than the word *love*. One of the most useful books we can read is C. S. Lewis' unpretentious little masterpiece *The Four Loves*. There, he clearly distinguishes *agape,* the kind of love Christ taught and showed, from *storge* (natural affection or liking), *eros* (sexual desire), and *philia* (friendship). It is *agape* that is the greatest thing in the world.

The old word for *agape* in English was charity. Unfortunately, that word now means to most people simply handouts to beggars or to the United Fund. But the word *love* won't do either. It means to most people either sexual love (*eros*) or a feeling of affection (*storge*), or a vague love-in-general. Perhaps it is necessary to insist on the Greek word *agape* (pronounced ah-gah-pay) even at the risk of sounding snobbish or scholarly, so that we do not confuse this most important thing in the world with something else and miss it, for there is enormous misunderstanding about it in our society.

The first and most usual misunderstanding of *agape* is to confuse it with a feeling. Our feelings are precious, but *agape* is more precious. Feelings come *to* us, passively; *agape* comes *from* us, actively, by our free choice. We are not responsible for our feelings—we can't help how we feel—but we are responsible for our *agape* or lack of it, eternally responsible, for *agape* comes from us; feelings come from wind, weather, and digestion. "Luv" comes from spring breezes; real love comes from the center of the soul, which Scripture calls the heart (another word we have sentimentalized and reduced to feeling). Liking is a feeling. But love (*agape*) is more than strong liking. Only a fool would command someone to feel a certain way. God commands us to love, and God is no fool.

Jesus had different feelings toward different people. But he loved them all equally and absolutely. But how can we love someone if we don't like him? Easy—we do it to ourselves all the time. We don't always have tender, comfortable feelings about ourselves; sometimes we feel foolish, stupid, asinine, or wicked. But we always love ourselves: we always seek our own good. Indeed, we feel dislike toward ourselves, we berate ourselves, precisely because we love ourselves; because we care about our good, we are impatient with our bad.

We fall in love but we do not fall in *agape*. We rise in *agape*.

God is *agape,* and *agape* is not feeling. So God is not feeling. That does not make him or *agape* cold and abstract. Just the opposite: God is love itself; feeling is the dribs and drabs of love received into the medium of passivity. God cannot fall in love for the same reason water cannot get wet: it is wet. Love itself cannot receive love as a passivity, only spread it as an activity. God is love in action, not love in dreams. Feelings are like dreams: easy, passive, spontaneous. *Agape* is hard and precious like a diamond.

This brings us to a second and related misunderstanding. *Agape's* object is always the concrete individual, not some abstraction called humanity. Love of humanity is easy because humanity does not surprise you with inconvenient demands. You never find humanity on your doorstep, stinking and begging.

Jesus commands us to love not humanity but our neighbor, all our neighbors, the real individuals we meet, just as he did. He died for me and for you, not for humanity. The Cross has our names on it, not the name "humanity". When Jesus called himself the Good Shepherd, he said he "calls his own sheep by name" (Jn 10:3). The gospel comes to you not in a newspaper with a Xeroxed label, "Dear Occupant", but in a handwritten envelope personally addressed to you, as a love letter from God to you alone. One of the saints says that Jesus would have done everything he did and suffered everything he suffered even if you were the only person who had sinned, just for you. More than that, he did! This is no "if"; this is fact. His loving eyes saw you from the Cross. Each of his five wounds were lips speaking your name.

A third, related, misunderstanding about love is to confuse it with kindness, which is only one of its usual attributes. Kindness is the desire to relieve another's suffering. Love is the willing of another's good. A father can spank his child out of love. And God is a father.

It is painfully obvious that God is not mere kindness, for he does not remove all suffering, though he has the power to do so. Indeed, this very fact—that the God who is omnipotent and can at any instant miraculously erase all suffering from this world deliberately chooses not to do so—is the commonest argument unbelievers use against him. The number one argument for atheism stems from the confusion between love and kindness.

The more we love someone, the more our love goes beyond kindness. We are merely kind to pets, and therefore we consent that our pets be put to death "to put them out of their misery" when they are suffering. There is increasing pressure in America to legalize euthenasia (so far only Nazi Germany and now Holland have ever legalized euthenasia), and this evil too stems from the confusion between love and kindness. We are kind to strangers but demanding of those we love. If a stranger informed you that he was a drug addict, you would probably try to reason with him in a kind and gentle way; but if your son or daughter said that to you, you would probably do a lot of shouting and screaming.

Grandfathers are kind; fathers are loving. Grandfathers say, "Run along and have a good time"; fathers say, "But don't do this or that." Grandfathers are compassionate, fathers are passionate. God is never once called our grandfather, much as we would prefer that to the inconveniently close, demanding, intimate father who loves us. The most frequently heard saying in our lives is precisely the philosophy of a grandfather: "Have a nice day."

Many priests even sanctify this philosophy by ending the Mass with it, though the Mass is supposed to be the worship of the Father, not the Grandfather.

A fourth misunderstanding about love is the confusion between "God is love" and "love is God." The worship of love instead of the worship of God involves two deadly mistakes. First it uses the word *God* only as another word for love. God is thought of as a force or energy rather than as a person. Second, it divinizes the love we already know instead of showing us a love we don't know. To understand this point, consider that "A is B" does not mean the same as "A equals B." If A = B, then B = A, but if A is B, that does not mean that B is A. "That house is wood" does not mean "wood is that house." "An angel is spirit" does not mean the same as "spirit is an angel." When we say "A is B", we begin with a subject, A, that we assume our hearer already knows, and then we add a new predicate to it. "Mother is sick" means "You know mother well, let me tell you something you don't know about her: she's sick." So "God is love" means "Let me tell you something new about the God you know: he is essential love, made of love, through and through." But "Love is God" means "Let me tell you something about the love you already know, your own human love: that is God. That is the ultimate reality. That is as far as anything can ever go. Seek no further for God." In other words, "God is love" is the profoundest thing we have ever heard. But "love is God" is deadly nonsense.

A fifth misunderstanding about love is the idea that you can be in love with love. No, you cannot, any more than you can have faith in faith, or hope in hope, or see sight. Love is an act, a force, or an energy, but persons are more than that. What we love with *agape* can only be a person, the realest thing there is, because a person is the image of God, who is ultimate reality, and God's name is I AM, the name for a person. If anyone says they are in love with love, that love is not *agape* but a feeling.

A sixth misunderstanding about love is the idea that "God is love" is unrelated to dogmatic theology, especially to the doctrine of the Trinity. Everyone can agree that "God is love", it seems, but the Trinity is a tangled dogma for an esoteric elite, isn't it? No. If God is not a Trinity, God is not love. For love requires three things: a lover, a beloved, and a relationship between them. If God were only one person, he could be a lover, but not love itself. The Father loves the Son and the Son loves the Father, and the Spirit is the love proceeding from both, from all eternity. If that were not so, then God would need us, would be incomplete without us, without someone to love. Then his creating us would not be wholly unselfish, but selfish, from his own need.

Love is a flower, and hope is its stem. Salvation is the whole plant. God's grace, God's own life, comes into us by faith, like water through a tree's roots. It rises in us by hope, like sap through the trunk. And it flowers from our branches, fruit for our neighbor's use.

Faith is like an anchor. That's why it must be conservative, even a stick-in-the-mud, like an anchor. Faith must be faithful. Hope is like a compass or a navigator. It gives us direction, and it takes its bearings from the stars. That's why it must be progressive and forward-looking. Love is like the sail, spread to the wind. It is the actual energy of our journey. That's why it must be liberal, open to the Spirit's wind, generous.

Agape is totally defenseless against an objection like Freud's: "But not all men are worthy of love." No, they are not. Love goes beyond worth, beyond justice, beyond reason. Reasons are always given from above downward, and there is nothing above love, for God is love. When he was about six, my son asked me, "Daddy, why do you love me?" I began to give the wrong answers, the answers I thought he was looking for: "You're a great kid. You're good and smart and strong." Then, seeing his disappointment, I decided to be honest: "Aw, I just love you because you're mine." I got a smile of relief and a hug: "Thanks, Daddy." A student once asked me in class, "Why does God love us so much?" I replied that that was the greatest of all mysteries, and she should come back to me in a year to see whether I had solved it. One year later to the day, there she was. She was serious. She really wanted an answer. I had to explain that this one thing, at least, just could not be explained.

Finally, there is the equally mind-boggling mystery of the intrinsic paradox of *agape:* somehow in *agape* you give yourself away, not just your time or work or possessions or even your body. You put yourself in your own hands and hand it over to another. And when you do this unthinkable thing, another unthinkable thing happens: you find yourself in losing yourself. You begin to be when you give yourself away. You find that a new and more real self has somehow been given to you. When you are a donor you mysteriously find yourself a recipient—of the very gift you gave away.

There is more: nothing else is really yours. Your health, your works, your intelligence, your possessions—these are not what they seem. They are all hostage to fortune, on loan, insubstantial. You discover that when you learn who God is. Face to face with God in prayer, not just a proper concept of God, you find that you are nothing. All the saints say this: you are nothing. The closer you get to God the more you see this, the more you shrink in size. If you scorn God, you think you're a big shot, a cannonball; if you know God, you know you're not even buckshot. Those who scorn God think they're number one. Those who have the popular idea of God think they're "good people". Those who have a merely mental orthodoxy know they're real but finite creatures, made in God's image but flawed by sin. Those who really begin to pray find that compared with God they are motes of dust in the sun. Finally, the saints say they are nothing. Or else (Saint Paul's words) "the chief of sinners". Sinners think they're saints and saints think they're sinners.

Who's right? How shall we evaluate this insight? Unless God is the Father of lies (the ultimate blasphemy), the saints are right. Unless the closer you get to God the wronger you are about yourself, the five groups in the preceding paragraph (from scorners to saints) form a hierarchy of insight. Nothing is ours by nature. Our very existence is sheer gift. Think for a moment about the fact that you were created, made out of nothing. If a sculptor gives a block of marble the gift of a fine shape, the shape is a gift, but the marble's existence is not. That is the marble's own. But nothing is our own because we were made out of nothing. Our very existence is a gift from God to no one, for we were not there before he created us. There is no receiver of the gift distinct from the gift itself. We are God's gifts.

So the saints are right. If I am nothing, nothing that is mine is anything. Nothing is mine by nature. But one thing is mine by my free choice: the self I give away in love. That is the thing even God cannot do for me. It is my choice. Everything I say is mine is not. But everything I say is yours is mine. C. S. Lewis, asked which of his many library books he thought he would have in heaven, replied, "Only the ones I gave away on earth and never got back". The same is true of our very self. It is like a ball in a game of catch: throw it and it will come back to you; hold onto it and that ends the game.

31
Our Father

Saint Thomas Aquinas says that everything a Christian needs to know is contained in three things: the Apostles' Creed, the Ten Commandments, and the Lord's Prayer—what to believe, what to do, and what to pray. The Lord's Prayer is the perfect prayer because it comes from the Perfect Pray-er; it is our Lord's prayer. He invented it, gave it to us, and told us to use it. That must be our fundamental reason for praying it: not to get God to do our will but to do God's will. We can give God something he wants, a Christmas present: our heart, wrapped in prayer.

Do you know what Jesus is doing right now? Don't read the next sentence yet; see whether you know the answer. The answer is that he is at his Father's side praying for us, for you and me, by name. Romans 8:34, Hebrews 7:25, and Revelation 3:5 tell us that wonderful but forgotten fact. We can answer his prayer for us by fulfilling his desire for us. His desire for us is that we learn to pray. And we learn to pray by going to Jesus' school of prayer, where the textbook is the Lord's Prayer. Therefore to pray the Lord's Prayer is to answer the Lord's prayer. The Lord is pure love. His desire, his prayer, for us is that of a lover: the happiness of his beloved. We fulfill his desire and attain our happiness simultaneously when we pray the prayer he desires us to pray.

We should pray this prayer for the same reason we do everything: "Whether you eat or drink or whatever you do, do all to the glory of God" (1 Cor 10:31). We should pray it to obey "the first and greatest commandment", to imitate the simple secret of

189

all sanctity, Mary's one word: *fiat,* "be it done unto me according to thy word."

The ideal prayer is in words. This ideal surprises some people. Don't all the saints and mystics agree that wordless prayer is higher? Ah, but these words are from *the* Word, and lead us back to him. He is the one thing necessary: the Word, not the words. The words are no magic formula; they must express and foster our relationship with him.

Eastern religions rank meditation higher than prayer. Now meditation is a fine thing, and all of us could use a lot more of it in our hectic lives, but it is no substitute for prayer. For meditation is only within yourself; it is psychological. Prayer is between you and God; it is theological.

The superiority of prayer over meditation is also shown by the fact that there are techniques for meditation but not for prayer. Jesus did not give us a technique; he gave us a prayer, for prayer is from the heart, and the heart is foreign to techniques. (The heart in Scripture does not mean the feelings but the will, the self, the I, the image of God.) Only the functions have techniques, not the prefunctional root, the heart. Thinking, feeling, and acting have techniques. In Hinduism there are four yoga techniques, one for the body, one for thinking, one for feeling, and one for acting. Techniques are useful, like church buildings or fund-raising programs. But Jesus gave this perfect prayer not into our hands or our heads but into our hearts because that is the only setting worthy of this gem.

Therefore we must pray this prayer not just with our lips or even just with our minds but with our hearts. In fact, if we do not pray it with our hearts, then we will not understand it with our minds. Only when our will lines up with God's will can our mind line up with God's mind. Jesus tells us: "If your will were to do the will of my Father, you would understand my teaching." It is the pure of heart who see God.

The ideal prayer has only fifty-six words in it. Jesus obviously means for us to use them over and over. He cautions us against meaningless repetitions in prayer (Mt 6:7) but not against meaningful repetitions, like the whispers of lovers. If mere recitation of the words were prayer, then we could make prayer wheels, as the Buddhists do, and twirl them around to repeat the words, like portable Xerox machines. But the words of this prayer are not like a tape to listen to passively, but like a piece of sheet music to interpret actively and play on our own instrument. They are not like a science textbook but like a laboratory manual: directions for doing. We should use them like Christmas trees. We are invited to festoon them, to put our own personal decorations on them.

The words are a map; we must make the journey our own. They are the guidelines, and the Holy Spirit is our guide, but we are the travelers. When you make your journey down the river of this prayer, your diary of exploration will be different from anyone else's, even though we all travel the same river through the same jungle and empty out into the same divine sea. This essay—any essay—on the Lord's Prayer is not that journey or a substitute for it. The most important thing about prayer, like the most important thing about faith and love, is simply to do it. I love the story about the theologian who died and was given a choice between going to heaven or going to a lecture about heaven. He chose the lecture. I love that story because I need it: it laughs at me.

In the first two words of the Lord's Prayer, more treasures are contained than in all the other words in this world. Saint Teresa found it almost impossible to get beyond these first two words when she prayed because they were like a beautiful country that she never wanted to leave. Until we feel that way, we have not understood these words. We must walk round and round them, toss them up and down, heft them, swim in them, sink into them, taste them, chew them, digest them, smell them, caress them, let them caress us, until we begin to understand Saint Teresa's wonderful difficulty.

One of the greatest of all mysteries is contained in that first little word, *our*. It is the mystery of solidarity, the mystery of the Mystical Body. Each individual who prays this prayer is to call

God not only "my Father" but "our Father". Each individual is to pray in the name of the whole Church. When you pray the Our Father, all the presence and power of the Mystical Body of Christ is praying with you, helping you. God sees you praying alongside the Pope and Mother Teresa and Jake Grubb (never heard of him? God did!) and Saint Francis and Saint Augustine and Saint Peter and the Blessed Virgin Mary herself. For none are dead or past to God, the eternal contemporary. (See Lk 20:37–38.) Solidarity is a fact, not an ideal. Each believer is an organ in his body. Saint Paul says, "If one member [organ] suffers, all suffer together; if one member is honored, all rejoice together. Now you are the body of Christ and individually members of it."

Therefore we are each responsible for all, when we work and when we pray. This is not just a pious feeling but an awesome fact. When I pray, I have effects on my grandchildren, on some stranger I have never met, on the most abandoned soul in the world. When I bake an act of charity in the oven of the Church, that is bread to some starving soul across the world. My prayer or work, ascending like mist today, in this place and time, will come down like rain at some other place and time, whither God directs it, where thirsty soil needs it most. Just as my money can really save lives in Ethiopia, my prayer can really save souls in China or Purgatory. Spiritual transportation systems are just as real and just as effective as physical ones, for the spiritual universe is just as real and just as much one, just as much a *uni*-verse, as the physical universe; and its connecting thread, its spiritual gravity, is just as strong, as subtle, and as pervasive as physical gravity.

Thus, I share in the responsibility for all the good and all the evil of the human family. I am rightly ashamed of Adolf Hitler because Hitler was my brother. I dare not say "Am I my brother's keeper?" because God our Father has made me just that. Dostoevsky says, "If I had been a little better, even the birds at my side would be a little happier." So I must ask forgiveness even of the birds. (Perhaps that was what Saint Francis was doing when he preached to them.)

Every time Scripture describes our ultimate destiny, heavenly worship, it is communal. What we will do eternally is the fulfillment not of the mystic's quest for private ecstasy but of the Father's quest for family love.

And then comes that blessed word *Father*. Before Jesus came, God was not our Father. He was the same, of course, but we were not, and therefore our relationship with him was not. Jesus changed that relationship: he made us children of God, and thus made God our Father. God is not regularly called our Father in the Old Testament. Ever since the fall, we have been orphans. Now we can come back home to Daddy. Not just Father but Daddy. In fact, Da-da. That is the meaning of the Hebrew word *Abba*. A Jewish friend half-seriously told me that Aramaic Hebrew must have been the language we spoke in Eden because babies still remember it: their first word is usually "Ab-ba". Jesus begins the restoration of Eden's intimacy, when God walked with us in the garden in the cool of the evening. He teaches us to call God "Da-da". ("Unless you become as little children, you cannot enter the kingdom of God.")

We appreciate how incredible this intimacy is only after we have learned the opposite lesson, God's awesomeness and infinite otherness, the distinctively Jewish revelation of God as transcendent Creator. Only after we are Jews can we be Christians; only after we know God in awe can we know God in intimacy. "The fear [awe] of the Lord is the beginning of wisdom" and filial intimacy is the end.

Because of Jesus, this utterly, unimaginably, incomprehensibly, and infinitely awesome abyss of eternal perfection, this dazzling light of Truth that designed the entire universe down to each grain of sand and still guides the paths of each falling hair and sparrow— *this* God is now our Daddy! Christians are the kids of the King.

Even more, Father means giver of life. Oyster fathers give oyster life, cat fathers give cat life, human fathers give human life—and God the Father gives divine life, his own life. We are called to share in the divine nature without losing our human nature, to become like Jesus our brother: human and divine. This is not heresy or pantheism; it is the teaching of Scripture (2 Pet 1:14) and the Church (the prayer over the gifts in the Mass).

Father is the word Jesus consistently used for God, and he did not choose his words carelessly. What else does Father mean to us? Let's look at connotations as well as denotations, feelings as well as definitions. Father connotes both security and challenge. A good father, says George Macdonald, is "easy to please but hard to satisfy". That's God all over: pleased even with the first faltering steps of his toddler, not yet satisfied even with the heroics of his saints, ever sculpting their souls into more and more love. Jesus is the perfect mirror of the Father, and he has both attributes in greater strength and in greater union than any man who has ever lived. He is terribly tender and terribly demanding, terribly loving and terribly stern, terribly soft and terribly hard. He is the two things every girl dreams of in her ideal man: strong and gentle, like a chivalrous knight. How hard it is for us to combine those two attributes, to be gentle without being weak and strong without being harsh.

Jesus is both infinitely gentle and infinitely demanding because that is what the Father is, and like Father, like Son. Our Father is more soft-hearted than any liberal and more hard-headed than any conservative. His compassion is absolute and unconditional, but so are his demands: "Be ye holy as I the Lord your God am holy." That's why Jesus weeps over his native Jerusalem and its temple but whips the moneychangers out of it. That's why Jesus calls the Pharisees whitewashed tombs but weeps at Lazarus' tomb. "He who has seen me, has seen the Father", who weeps when a sparrow falls but sends his saints like steel through Job's tortures.

There are many voices today even in the Church who quarrel with the word *Father* because they see it as being sexist. They forget that the masculine imagery comes not from the Church, not even from the apostles, but from Jesus himself. Was Jesus a sexist pig? Was God incarnate unable to transcend the sins of his culture? Christians call God Father because they believe that God himself has told us what to call him.

This is no slight on women. The Mother of God was a woman;

the Father of God was not a man. Furthermore, God is masculine because we are all feminine to him, as the mystics say. He impregnates our souls with his life, as he impregnated Mary's body. Mary is us; Mary is the Church; Mary is the bride in the Song of Songs; Mary is the soul. God's deepest desire is to marry us. "Your Creator shall become your husband." How could our imagery about that relationship be sexless? God is our Father and our husband, rather than our mother or our wife.

God is also our Father rather than our grandfather. Never once does Scripture call God our grandfather. "God has no grandsons"; we inherit his life not through our parents but directly from him. And his love is that of a father, not a grandfather: demanding and intense and intimate. A student said to me the other day, "I cannot buy the God of the Bible. I prefer a God I can feel more comfortable with." There are some bits of foolishness that are so appalling they make me speechless. I should have remembered what C. S. Lewis said:

> What would really satisfy us would be a God who said of anything we happened to like doing, "What does it matter so long as they are contented?" We want, in fact, not so much a Father in heaven as a grandfather in heaven—a senile benevolence who, as they say, "liked to see the young people enjoying themselves" and whose plan for the universe was simply that it might be truly said at the end of each day "a good time was had by all."

The most often-heard wisdom in our day is: "Have a nice day." The least often-heard wisdom in our day is: "Be ye perfect, even as your Father in heaven is perfect." We can freely choose between these two destinies.

32
Hallowing God's Name

As far as I can tell, the average catechism class makes little or no impression on kids. But one day my daughter came home from catechism (she was about seven or eight) with a real insight. With a twinkle, she greeted me with "Hello, my father on earth." She had learned the wonderful fact that we adults usually forget or forget the wonder of: that we each have two fathers, one for each of our homes, one temporary, one permanent.

"In"

What does it mean to call God "Our Father in Heaven"? Is God in some place? Where is heaven? It doesn't appear on any map. God is not contained in any place because he is infinite. He is not even contained in all places, like air or light or space. He is not contained in anything, least of all space. He contains everything, but not spatially. He contains everything spiritually by knowing it and loving it. So you can't get to heaven by rocket ship.

Is heaven then only a state of mind? No, for then heaven would be contained not in space but in your mind. Heaven is not a mere idea, concept, thought, belief, or feeling. It is as real as earth, more real than earth, in fact. It is objectively real, independent of our minds. What's out there is not just atoms and molecules, you know. If you think that, you're a materialist. God, angels, and other human minds are objectively real, not just in your mind. But they're not made of matter.

So where is heaven? Not somewhere (in space) and not nowhere (only subjective), but (like God) everywhere. Heaven is where God is, and God is everywhere, so heaven must be everywhere.

Why don't we see it then? My answer is a guess and subject to correction by wiser theologians, but I suspect it is for the same reason an unborn baby doesn't see the world yet. To the baby, the world seems to be outside the womb and after birth, but actually the baby is already in the world by being in the womb, which is part of the world. I suspect that after we die and look back at our earthly lives from the vantage point of heaven, we will feel a bit like a baby who has just been born: "I was always here, in this larger world; I just didn't see it when I was in that little dark womb." Perhaps that's one reason why heaven will feel like home, not like a strange, far country.

So heaven is not in this world, but this world is in heaven, for all who end up there. Emily in Thornton Wilder's *Our Town* realized something like this when she signed her schoolbooks with this address:

Grovers Corners
New Hampshire
United States
Western Hemisphere
Planet Earth
Solar System
Milky Way Galaxy
Universe
Mind of God

"Heaven"

Heaven is like God in that we can be much clearer about what it is not than about what it is. But what is it? It is God's mode of existence, God's metaphysical place. God's revelation does not tell us much that the philosopher would want to know about heaven because revelation is addressed not to our intellectual curiosity but to our hearts and lives. It tells us how to get there. There's time enough once we are there to understand. One thing we are told is that heaven is our home. To be with God in heaven is our destiny. Jesus is even now preparing for us our apartment, our "mansion", or "room" in heaven, a different one for each of us (Jn 14:1–6; Rev 2:17).

Heaven is the answer to the most practical question of all, *Quo vadis?* Where are you going? The answer to that question makes a total difference here and now because my destination changes the meaning of every step I take. Pascal says, "All our actions and thoughts must follow such different paths according to whether there is hope of eternal blessings or not that the only possible way of acting with sense and judgment is to decide our course in the light of this, our ultimate objective." It's not escapism but realism to think about heaven. Life is one long slide down the slippery slope of time into the abyss of nothingness—or is it into the soft, strong, everlasting arms? What fool dares to say it makes no difference?

God is in heaven. What difference does that make?

1. We are not pagans; our God is transcendent, the Creator, not part of the cosmos. We adore him, we worship him. We cannot worship an equal, a chum, a big brother, a team leader, a chairman of the board. The fundamental impetus of Modernism and Humanism is to deny transcendence, to flatten out God, to democratize reality, to expect a cocktail party or a committee meeting with God rather than ever to say, with the prophet, "I fell at his feet as one dead."

2. God's transcendence allows humility as well as awe. Heaven is the exorcism of arrogance. The sign over heaven's gate reads, "Only one know-it-all lives here."

3. Ecclesiastes says: "God is in heaven and you are on earth, therefore let your words be few." Awe is not chatty. Worship's words are words of power and depth because they emerge from the silence, not just from other words. Jesus was a man of few words. His prayers were short, his parables were short, his sermons were short, his answers were short, his commands were short. Mother Teresa said about some theologians: "They talk too much. Pick up a broom and help someone sweep the room; that says enough."

"Hallowed"

What do we pray when we pray that God's name be hallowed? This is an old English word, and we have forgotten much of its meaning, both in our minds and in our lives. The word has disappeared from our language because the reality has disappeared from our lives. Let us try to help rehabilitate the reality by rehabilitating the word.

It means "made holy"; and *holy* means set apart, sacred, special, superior, worthy of bowing down to. We modern egalitarians find it hard to bow. We have no earthly training for the necessary entrance to heaven. Only little children enter; heaven's gate is low, and those who refuse to come in on their knees will not come in at all. I hope we will not be shocked or disappointed to find that heaven is an absolute monarchy, not a democracy.

Our response to the holiness of God is adoration. Adoration is a psychological necessity. Modern man is bored, depressed, neurotic, and suicidal because he does not worship. Worship and adoration are the purest self-forgetfulness. Self-forgetfulness is the purest ecstasy, in the double sense of standing outside yourself (the literal meaning of the Greek *ek-stasis*) and joy, of a quality different in kind, not just degree, from pleasure, contentment, or even happiness.

Here is a piece of divine psychiatry that we never hear from our secular psychiatric establishment: "Turn your back on your problems! Turn your face to me. Let my light shine into your darkness rather than standing in your own light and making shadows." Even a small moon can eclipse the great sun because it is so close to the earth. Even a little problem can distract us from God because it is so close, so *ours,* so subjective. We need to "get away from it all"—not from earth or others or circumstances, but from ourselves. "Hallowed be thy name"—worship, adoration—does that. Our problems come from ourselves, not from others or circumstances. Attempted suicides who have a near-death experience often say they learned this dazzling lesson: whichever way you turn, you always have your own rump behind you.

Our faces need not always have ingrown eyeballs. The solution to every great problem, even horrible ones like Job's, is to stand face to face with God. Once Job saw God, all his agonizing questions died away, and he got something far better than answers: the Answerer.

In adoring God we all become mystics. There is a difference only in degree, not in kind, between the simplest act of self-forgetful worship and the greatest mystic's greatest flight from self to God. The tiny spark of joy that every act of adoration ignites in our soul is a spark from the very same fire that consumed the greatest saints and will consume us in heaven, when we "enter into the joy of thy Lord" as into the infinite and eternal fire of absolute reality.

"Be"

We must *will* adoration. We must long for God's name to be hallowed. We must have a passion for praise. This passion is one of God's most precious graces and one we should pray for much more than we do. (When was the last time you asked God for this one?) For it is a grace. As Augustine says right at the beginning of his incomparable *Confessions:* "*Thou* dost so excite him that to praise thee is his joy, for thou hast made us for thyself, and our hearts are restless till they rest in thee."

If we have a passion to praise our earthly beloved or even our favorite baseball or football team or even our favorite movie star or rock star, why do we think it square or hokey to get excited about God? If we give three cheers to toast a friend, why won't we give even one cheer for God? Talk about repression!

Joseph Grigg wrote about this repression:

> Jesus, and shall it ever be,
> A mortal man ashamed of thee?
> Ashamed of thee, whom angels praise,
> Whose glories shine through endless days?

> Ashamed of Jesus! that dear friend
> On whom my hopes of heaven depend!
> No, when I blush, be this my shame,
> That I no more revere his name.
>
> Ashamed of Jesus! Empty pride!
> I'll boast a Savior crucified,
> And, oh, may this my portion be,
> My Savior not ashamed of me.

Jesus had even stronger words: "Whoever is ashamed of me and of my words in this adulterous and sinful generation, of him will the Son of Man also be ashamed when he comes in the glory of his Father with the holy angels" (Mk 8:38).

I think most of us are not ashamed of Jesus but of ourselves, of the shoddiness of our praise, at the utter inadequacy of our words and our lives, rather as we are ashamed of shoddy religious art. But isn't even shoddy praise better than none? If we are silenced from praising him, Jesus says, the very rocks will do it for us (Lk 19:40). The only place there is no praise is in hell.

The motive for our praise and adoration must be objective, not subjective: because God deserves it, not because we feel like it. We worship not to play a good little psychological trick on ourselves but to make an honest response to reality, to God's real praiseworthiness. Paradoxically, when we forget ourselves and do this, only then do we find joy. We find ourselves only by losing ourselves. That is why God commands us to worship him: for our sakes, not for his, as if he needed our worship. But our motive must be his sake, not ours. Thus the two of us exchange places, so to speak: he for us, not for himself; we for him, not for ourselves. Thus we share in the deep secret of the very life of the Trinity and its joy. "He who loses himself shall find it; he who finds himself shall lose it."

"Thy"

As we have just seen, true worship must be God-centered, not self-centered. "Not my name but Thine be praised." "Not my will but thine be done." We find fulfillment only when we forget about finding fulfillment. We stand tall only when we bow.

We must begin with God, not self or even others because that is the way reality is ordered. God is first, and to treat him as second, to treat the Absolute End as a means to any other end at all—self-fulfillment or the needs of the world or any other high and valid end—is to have a false God, an idol. And all idols break. You can't even fool Mother Nature much less Father God.

The first and greatest commandment is to love God with your whole heart. The second is to love your neighbor as your self. The third is taken for granted: love yourself. This is the secret of joy: J-O-Y, Jesus first, Others second, Yourself third.

Because we must begin with God, we must begin with praise. Praise is the light that makes the rest of any prayer true. Any thanksgiving, confession, intercession, or petition that is not in that context is false, for it is not God-centered. If we are God-centered, we will inevitably praise because no one can stand in the presence of God—the real God, as distinct from a comfortable concept or feeling of our own—and not praise. If wonder and awe are not our inescapable reactions, then what we are reacting to is not God.

The greatest prayer book, the Psalms, is primarily a book of praises. The greatest Christian classics, like Augustine's *Confessions* and Pascal's *Pensées,* however deeply they dip into human darkness, begin and end with praise. Literally—look at the first and last sentences. The Bible itself, most realistic of books because it follows the order of reality itself, begins with creation praising God and ends with the new creation doing the same, with an invitation to us to join the music. All of history is a pause between those two notes of praise.

It is not only realistic but practical to be God-centered and praise-centered, for praising God, saying "hallowed be thy name", is what we will be doing for eternity. It's practical to get practice in now.

Praise is an acquired taste, a habit, a second nature. Our fallen nature does not want to put God first. That's why it's very difficult for us to pray this petition: it's contrary to our nature. The clearest proof of original sin, of our fallenness and abnormality, is the difficulty we experience in self-forgetful adoration of God. Adoration is like a glass mountain to us: when we try to climb it, we slide back down to habitual self-consciousness. God could not have made us this way, with such an anti-God gravity.

It takes repeated effort to adore God, even though this is our supreme joy. It is a measure of the insanity of our sinfulness that even when we know with certainty, by both faith and experience, that self-regard does not bring joy and that self-forgetful adoration of God does—in fact, that it brings a joy incomparably greater than any other we can ever experience—we still run away from it, from prayer, as if it were a deadly plague, sniffing out the tiniest excuses as if they were truffles. We have a formidable enemy within to overcome. Life is a school. God has to educate us a long, long way between here and heaven. We must be ready for some shattering changes.

"Name"

Hallowed means made holy; but we do not make God holy. God *is* holy. We only recognize and conform to the objective fact of his holiness. But we do make his name, his reputation, his being known on earth holy. Or unholy. Saints make God's name holy. The unanswerable argument for Christianity is saints.

Unfortunately, as G. K. Chesterton says, it is also true that "there is only one unanswerable argument against Christianity: Christians." Asked to write a letter to the London *Times* on "What's Wrong with the World", Chesterton wrote the world's shortest letter:

> Dear Sirs:
> I am.
> > Yours truly,
> > G. K. Chesterton

We make God's name holy or unholy. We are God's advertisements. God is not dependent on us, but other people are dependent on us for their knowledge of God. They cannot see God, but they can see us. They cannot see our faith except through our works, our lives, our love, and our joy. The world's most effective advertisement against God is joyless Christians.

Praying this petition and meaning it is turning our mirrors to the light. We can do nothing to darken the light that is God, but we can turn away and put ourselves and others in the dark. When we turn our faces to God, when we think more about God than about ourselves, we become mirrors to his light, as Jesus is. When we turn our backs to God, we run into our own shadow.

When we pray this petition, we stand at one corner of a triangle, related to God and others. We ask God's name be hallowed for God's sake because he deserves it; but God commands it for our sake because we need to worship; and for others' sakes because they need to see God through us for their sakes, so that they can praise too. This is the priesthood of all believers. This is our "weight of glory", about which C. S. Lewis says:

> It is a serious thing to live in a society of possible gods and goddesses, to remember that the dullest and most uninteresting person you can talk to may one day be a creature which, if you saw it now, you would be strongly tempted to worship, or else a horror and a corruption such as you now meet, if at all, only in a nightmare. All day long we are, in some degree, helping each other to one or the other of these destinations. . . . There are no *ordinary* people. You have never talked to a mere mortal. Nations, cultures, arts, civilisations—these are mortal, and their life is to ours as the life of a gnat. But it is immortals whom we joke with, work with, marry, snub, and exploit—immortal horrors or everlasting splendours.

33
God's Kingdom Coming

"Thy"

There are only two kinds of people in this world, says C. S. Lewis: those who say to God, "Thy will be done", and those to whom God says, in the end, "*Thy* will be done." Every person who has ever lived has had one and only one absolute choice, one fundamental option: "thy kingdom come" or "my kingdom come." We are here to do someone's work, to establish someone's kingdom, someone's lordship; the only question is: ours or his?

God is terrifyingly fair: He gives all of us what we want. If we want ourselves and our kingdom, not him and his, then that is exactly what we will get. And that is the definition of hell. But if we want him and his kingdom, then that is what we will get. And his kingdom is heaven. "All who seek find"—that's his solemn promise or threat and our infinitely serious choice.

"Kingdom"

God is King. That fact is not changed by proud individuals playing king of the mountain with God or by egalitarians resenting the fact that the structure of spiritual reality is not democratic. But populists can take heart: his kingdom is people. We are his kingdom. And this king is no remote and egotistical tyrant, but a Father who created and re-created us, a Son who loved us to death, and a Spirit who lovingly longs to live within us in utter intimacy.

His kingdom is first of all in our hearts, our souls, our spirits. Secondly it is in our lives and works; they are its colonies. But first things first: the colonies depend on the homeland. "What must we do to do the works of God?" Jesus was asked, and he replied, "This

is the work of God: that you believe in the one whom he has sent."
We make "thy kingdom come" first by faith, then by works.

The reason for this priority is simple: God is love, and a lover
wants above all not just a certain kind of work but a certain kind of
person. A machine could do the work. Our works are important
above all in God's eyes for their rebound effect on the worker: the
works of love construct God's kingdom in the heart of the lover
first of all and only then in the world outside.

I remember vividly the liberating sense of exultation I felt upon
first encountering that simple insight. (It was in C. S. Lewis' *Mere
Christianity*.) It frees us from the slavery of legalism but not into the
worse slavery of relativism. It is more demanding, not less, to think
of God's kingdom as persons than as deeds. The Pharisees were
really the lax, the minimalists, the less demanding ones. They
demanded only exact deeds. Jesus demanded personal perfection:
"You must be perfect, even as your Father in heaven is perfect."
Lovers are perfectionists because lovers believe in crazy things.
Lovers are also blissfully happy with far less than perfection. A
father's love is "easy to please but hard to satisfy" (George
Macdonald).

"Come"

We must pray for God's kingdom to come because we are in time,
in history, in "his story". We are his kingdom, which comes to be
in time; God does not grow. Process theology is simply silly: it
confuses the Creator's eternity with the creature's growth. God is
the home port; we are the ship on the stormy sea. Our lives enact
the fundamental plot of all stories: homecoming. (That's why *E.T.*
is the world's most successful movie: that heartbreaking, magic
word *home*.) The coming of God's kingdom to us is our homecoming to him. We must long for this coming as the lost ship longs for
its home port, as the deer longs for springs of water. The early
Christians had this longing for the Parousia, the completion of the
story, the Second Coming. But today, small fringe groups of

fundamentalists seem to be almost the only contemporary
Christians who have this passion. We forget Christ's imperative to
pray the imperative verb *come*.

We must revive this lost virtue of hope. Our lives and our faith
are dreary and dull when it is lacking. Where the early Christians
saw gold and glory when they peered into the future, we see only a
gray mist. Freud was right: every life has two absolute needs—
love and work. Loving and working for the greatest thing that can
ever happen on this earth, God's kingdom, fulfills both needs more
perfectly than anything else in this life ever can.

"Thy"

But there is an obstacle to "thy kingdom come", and it is "my
kingdom come". For instance, it is absurdly hard to begin to pray,
to put aside our many things and turn to the one thing necessary.
That turning must be done again and again. It is the easiest thing in
the world to understand and the hardest thing in the world to do,
this simple turning of our attention and our will to God, saying
"thy will be done" and meaning it with all our heart. But it
absolutely must be done. It is what we were made for, and Love
will not settle for anything less. There are no side roads or
shortcuts up this mountain.

I remember the first time I ever realized this simplicity. I was
about seven or eight, I think, and very confused by the many
mysterious and threatening things I had associated with my
religion. By a gift of grace, I suddenly realized that it all came
down to one simple thing, and I asked my father, "Dad, all those
things we have to remember, all those things God wants us to do,
they're only one thing, aren't they?" "What do you mean?" "I
mean we only have to think about one thing, don't we?" "What's
that?" "To think What does God want me to do now? and then do
it." "Why, yes, that's it all right." Life is so simple that only a child
can understand it.

"Will"

My simplicity, my oneness, my center, my I is in my will. It is not in my mind, as Greek philosophy thought, nor my feelings, as modern psychology supposes, nor my will power, but my will. But sin means that my will is divided from itself as well as from God. How can my divided will be made one? How can I become truly myself? By this petition: "Thy will be done." I can become one by being united to God, who alone is perfectly one and the source of my oneness. "Thy will be done" unites me to myself by uniting me to him. It gathers the scattered pieces of my being, like the pieces of a broken mirror, and allows it once again to reflect the divine light that it was created to reflect, the glory of God. Kierkegaard said, "Purity of heart is to will one thing"; and Jesus said, "Blessed are the pure of heart, for they shall see God." Their mirror, their will, now one, reflects the light of *the* One.

The God of popular religion is a mind but not a will; an "it" rather than a "he". This is "nature's God" or "the force" of *Star Wars*. The Bible knows nothing of such a God. Its God wills the world into being, wills the law, wills his own death for our life, and wills our heart's response, longs for our free love. Such a passionately demanding God is not nearly as comfortable as the "force" we can turn on or off like an electric light bulb.

To will God's will is not a matter of will power but of will, not trying to do it but doing it. Scripture hardly ever uses the word *try* but very often uses the word *trust*. Willing is choosing, committing, saying Yes. The thing is so simple and fundamental that there is no perfect word in the language for it except *yes*. It is like the answer to a marriage proposal. It is the answer to a marriage proposal.

"Be"

We are to pray that God's will be done. But isn't God's will always done? Yes, but in two different ways, just as there are two different ways to obey the law of gravity. You obey it in one way by walking or even by flying; in another way by falling off a cliff. Earth is like walking, heaven like flying, hell like falling. And we can walk either to the airport to fly or to the cliff to fall. God's will is not frustrated, but ours can be. Goodness, the object of God's will, is always done in the long run, but it matters whether it is done in the best way or the worst way, by our salvation or our damnation, by fulfilling the greater good of love or by fulfilling the lesser good of justice.

"God is not willing that any should perish, but that all should come to repentance" (2 Pet 3:9). But he has left this thing he wills most of all, our eternal salvation, to our free choice. The "be" in "thy will be done" is to be not only prayed and willed but also achieved (precisely in the act of willing it) by us. The fulfillment of God's own will is put into our hands! God has given us the incredible responsibility of being co-causes with him of our own true selves in this world and of our eternal destiny in the next.

Kierkegaard says that this fact, the fact of our free will, "is the cross that philosophy could not carry but was left hanging from". What a paradox it is—that it is up to us whether Omnipotence's will will be done! But that is what freedom means. There is one thing that even Omnipotence cannot give to himself: our own free choice to love him. Our *amen* is a sacramental word, a word of power, a word that operates. Our prayer is not a mere thought or wish but an act, like a sacrament.

In fact, the whole Lord's Prayer is sacramental. Each petition, if honestly meant, effects what it signifies. When we say and mean "our Father", that ratifies our sonship. (Saint Paul says that no one can call God Father except by the power of the Holy Spirit.) When we pray "hallowed be thy name", we are by that act actually hallowing it. When we pray "thy kingdom come", that makes it come, for the kingdom is first of all in the praying heart. When we pray "thy will be done", the very desire is its own fulfillment, for that is his will: that we pray and mean "thy will be done". When we pray "give us this day our daily bread", we are already receiving our daily bread, our primary need, which is prayer, and truth—the truth that all good comes from God. When we pray "forgive us our trespasses as we forgive those who trespass against us", we are forgiving others, for if we are not, then we are asking God for our own damnation.

The Lord's Prayer is not a sacrament in the strict sense, for its grace does not work *ex opere operato,* from the outside in, so to speak. Nevertheless it is a real sacramental, perhaps the most powerful of all sacramentals. Great graces are given through it, though from the inside out, dependent on our own hearts. The more we put into it, the more we get out of it. It is a spiritual investment. It pays higher rates of interest the more we invest in it. It is like the offering of the Mass: the more we identify ourselves with Christ the victim, the more we are identified with his victory. The more of ourselves we put on the altar with him, the more of ourselves we find resurrected and transubstantiated into him.

"Done"

But why do we petition God for his kingdom to come and his will to be done? Do we make it happen, or does he? Who does the deed we pray to be done? Does God come to us or do we come to him? The answer is that we must both meet, freely, like lovers. He has come an infinite distance, from heaven to earth, to meet us; and he has brought us an infinite distance to meet him, from nonbeing to being by creation and from spiritual death to spiritual life by salvation. Now we must ratify this salvation; we must take one more step into his arms. It is really up to us, that last step. Though we can't do it without him, he won't do it without us.

The petition "thy will be done" is the primary one, for it is the first and greatest commandment, to love the Lord God with our whole heart and soul and mind and strength. It is Saint Ignatius' prayer, "Take, O Lord, all my liberty. Take my memory, my understanding, and my entire will." When we give our will to God, he gives it back to us; when we yield our freedom to him, we become truly free; when we die to ourselves. we become for the first time truly ourselves. That is the whole reason we have the gift of freedom: to freely give it back to the Giver and thus receive it again, the more to give back, and the more to receive, forever, in the endless exchanges of love.

When we say "thy kingdom come" and "thy will be done", is this active or passive? Does his kingdom come by our working in the world or by our submission to him? It must be both, for activity in the world that is not submitted to God's will is our kingdom, not his; and submission to a God who does not send us out to the world, to our neighbor, is not submission to the God of Jesus Christ but to a figment of our own imagination. When we say Yes to God, he says Yes through our lives. He comes in one end of us and out the other: in by faith and out by the works of love, in by contemplation and out by action. Christianity perfectly integrates the two halves of our personality, the receptive and the active, *anima* and *animus,* yin and yang.

"On Earth as It Is in Heaven"

When we pray "on earth as in heaven", we realize the relevance of heaven. It is the model for this earth. Nothing could be more relevant, less escapist, than heaven. When God's will is done perfectly on earth as it is in heaven, then earth will become heaven, for heaven is essentially that: where God's will is perfectly done. All the Utopian dreamers in history are profoundly right: this earth can and should and must and will become heaven. And they are also profoundly wrong: there is no other way to that goal than through the willing of God's will. The only way to Utopia is death, the only way to yea-saying God's will is nay-saying self-will. God and his kingdom cannot be added to our lives and our earth like a second layer to a cake. He transforms and takes possession of it all. He is God, after all, not a means to our Utopian dreams or a convenient symbol of them.

What we pray for in these petitions is the most beautiful, noble, joyful, wonderful, glorious, and desirable thing in the world—in fact, more desirable than the whole world—heaven, heaven on earth. Revelation reveals what this kingdom is: a golden, bejeweled city coming down out of heaven like a breathtakingly beautiful bride adorned for her adoring husband.

Alas, you say, we do not see this glory yet. Oh, but we do. In fact, there is a thing we can see right here and now, though not with the eyes of the body, that is even more glorious than this symbol: the reality it symbolizes—a human soul willing God's will. The most beautiful thing in all creation is the soul of a saint.

This kingdom is indestructible. The power of death and the gates of hell cannot prevail against it. No earthly king can take his kingdom with him when he dies. Alexander the Great directed that he be buried with his empty hand hanging out of his coffin, as an object lesson to the world that the man who had conquered the world and wept because there were no more worlds to conquer left this world as he entered it, naked.

> Only one life, 'twill soon be past.
> Only what's done for Christ will last.

34
Our Daily Bread

The structure of the Lord's Prayer and the structure of the Ten Commandments are similar because both follow the same model; the structure of reality, the real human situation in relation to God. Both are concerned with love above all because love is above all. Both are divided into two parts because we need to know two basic parts of love: love of God and love of neighbor. God asks Saint Augustine, "What do you want to know?" and Augustine replies, "Only two things: you and myself". "Nothing more?" "Nothing more."

The first three commandments are about loving God, the next seven about loving neighbor. The Lord's Prayer is also about loving God and neighbor. The first three petitions are the love of God expressed as adoration, worship, and praise. The second three petitions are the love of neighbor expressed as petitions for our neighbor's needs.

Our neighbors include ourselves. We are our own first neighbor. That's why Jesus commands us to love our neighbors as ourselves. Implied in "love your neighbor as yourself" is "love yourself as your neighbor."

Furthermore, the pronouns in the Lord's Prayer are plural, not singular. For instance, we are to pray, "Give us this day our daily bread" not "Give me this day my daily bread." Intercessory prayer for our neighbors has no separate petition in the Lord's Prayer because all three petitions of the last half of the prayer are equally for neighbor and for self.

We are now ready to move into the second half of the Lord's Prayer, from praise to petition. These are the two main purposes of prayer, though praise is usually subdivided into adoration, thanksgiving, and confession, and petition into petition for self and intercession for others, thus giving five purposes of prayer.

The word *pray* in our language often means simply petition, asking, with an implied "please". In fact, in older English the word *pray* often meant exactly the same as *please,* as in "pray come dine with me." *Please* was one of the first words we learned as a child. We learned that it was a kind of magic word. Remember your parents saying, "What's the magic word?" when you asked for something without saying "please"? It was indeed a magic word; i.e., it made a real difference; it was a word not just of meaning but of power. There really are magic words, you know, like "I love you" and "I hate you" (black magic) and sometimes "I give up" (especially when spoken to God).

But "please" is not magic in a technological sense; it is not automatic and mechanical. It communicates a felt need to a free person, and machines have neither feelings nor freedom. In this word *please,* i.e., in petition, is implied the three great mysteries of human free will, human interdependence, and human charity. "Please pass the mustard" is deeper philosophy than 99 out of 100 books of the philosophers. Jesus surely had these three mysteries in mind when he told us to ask our heavenly Father for our daily bread, our daily needs, for (1) God is a free person, no less free, surely, than our earthly fathers; and (2) we depend on him no less than on our earthly fathers for our very being; and (3) he is no less charitable, in fact he is charity itself.

But we must ask. "Ask and you shall receive; seek and you shall find. for all who ask, receive, all who seek, find." It is implied that if we do not ask, we will not receive. God often withholds good things from us until we ask for them, even things we need badly. Why? Why would Infinite Love do this? For only one reason: because he sees that we need prayer even more than we need the thing prayed for.

Think: Why did God institute prayer in the first place? Why didn't he simply supply us with all our needs without waiting to be asked? For the same reason an earthly father doesn't: to give us the gift of freedom, of being co-causes of our own fulfillment. "God instituted prayer", says Pascal, "to communicate to his creatures the dignity of causality." "Give a man a fish and you feed him for a day; teach a man to fish and you feed him for a lifetime."

Why don't we always get what we ask for? We do! All seekers find. That is his promise, and he is no liar. But what our heart most deeply seeks is not always what our tongue speaks or even what our mind knows. God grants every petition that comes from the heart, i.e., from the real I. He does it in his time and in his way. Sometimes he does not grant it until heaven. Sometimes he grants it the hard way rather than the easy way. But "God's way is the best way, though we may not see." This sounds like easy piety. It is piety (anything wrong with piety?), but it is not easy. Faith is not a security blanket; it is a leap, a life, a stormy marriage. Ask Job.

Sometimes we feel that this is the only part of the Lord's Prayer that we want to pray: when we feel so full of needs that we seem like baby robins with our mouths wide open waiting for momma robin to fill us with longed-for, fat, juicy worms. We then don't feel like praising, only petitioning. God is our momma robin, and we are hungry, and he does have food, and we should open our mouths and wait on him. "Open your mouth and I will fill it", he says. But we also need to praise, even when we don't feel like it, as Job did when he responded to his tragedies: "The Lord has given, the Lord has taken way. Blessed be the name of the Lord." Such praise is worth infinitely more than the praise that comes easily, comes from our feelings. Feeling is a beautiful follower, but a bad leader.

At other times we feel so content just to be with God that we want nothing more. We want only to adore, not to petition—like Job at the end, still on his dung heap but satisfied even before his fortunes were restored simply because of God's presence: "I had heard of you with the hearing of the ear, but now my eye sees you." When we feel like that, we want nothing more. But we need to petition then too, just as we need to praise when we feel only like petitioning, for praise and petition are two of our unchanging needs. That is why Jesus commands us to pray both at all times. When we feel like gods, we are still animals, with animal needs.

When we feel like baby robins, we are still sons and daughters of God, children of praise.

Whether we feel empty or full, we are to pray "give us this day our daily bread" and mean it, for prayer is not dependent on our feelings. I do not say merely that prayer should not be dependent on our feelings but that it isn't. Prayer has a certain nature of its own, whether we feel it does or not. It is not primarily an expression of our feelings, an externalization of what is in us, "getting it out", as we are constantly told by most psychologists and even by spiritual writers who listen to the prophets of our age more than to the prophets of God. No, prayer is not a little thing coming out of a bigger thing, an act of feeling/expression coming out of the self; rather, it is a little thing (ourselves) entering into a bigger thing. Prayer does not issue forth from us; we issue forth into it. It is like love: it's bigger than both of us. That's why we are in love, not love in us. Prayer is like an elephant that we ride. It is bigger than we are. When we pray, we put on kingly and queenly robes and become bigger ourselves. "We are never so tall as when we kneel." Prayer is our royal robes, and the most kingly robe of all is the one given to us by Christ the king.

Context can change everything. A human eye in a human body is quite different from the same eye in a test tube. "Fire!" means something quite different on a rifle range, a burning building, and Moses' burning bush. The context of adoration changes the meaning of petition in the Lord's Prayer. Adoration has to come first. Only after we get to know God, by adoration, can we know what to ask for and how to ask, for God cannot be a means for us to use to the end of getting what we want. That's the child's concept of prayer. We must turn that inside out, and realize that what we should ask for and how we should ask must depend on God, whom we know by adoration.

Let's be more specific about the difference adoration makes to petition. There are three possible attitudes in asking; adoration eliminates the first two and comes down squarely in the third. The three attitudes are demanding, cajoling, and trusting. We meet the demanding attitude in some loud and pushy preachers who scream at us to "claim the promises" or to "claim our inheritance" of total deliverance in this life from poverty, pain, and sickness—as if God had promised us a rose garden without thorns, and as if all the saints and martyrs had failed to claim their inheritance since they all suffered; they all received from God frequent "no" answers to their petitions.

We meet the cajoling attitude in the worried, hand-wringing fusser and complainer. If Jesus spoke Scots, he'd say to them simply, "Dinna fash yourself." The unctuously humble Uriah Heep and the brashly arrogant Elmer Gantry types are alike beneath their differences, for they are both self-centered rather than God-centered. That's why both froth at the mouth a lot. They have not learned first to adore, to "be still and know that I am God." They both say, in effect, "No, God, you be still and know that I am me."

If we know God, we will trust him. Our petition must be surrounded by trust. What does this mean, specifically? It means (1) honestly confronting and acknowledging our needs, both material and spiritual, just as our psychologists tell us to do— hiding from unpleasant truth comes from a lack of trust—but then (2) placing all these needs in his hands and leaving them there, turning our attention away from our problems, back to him. This is not as hard to do as we think it is, if only we have begun by adoring him, because if we begin by adoring him, we will not want to turn away for very long from the sunbeam of his face to the dust motes of our problems. We will want to face him and let him shine his light on our darkness rather than facing our own shadow with our back to his light.

A farmer was carrying a donkey to market on his back. A neighbor with a horse and cart saw him and said, "Come up onto my cart. You'll break your back if you carry that donkey all the way to market." The farmer accepted the offer, but when they reached the market, his back was broken anyway: he had come aboard the cart but had not put down the donkey! If we have a donkey (or a monkey) on our back, the Lord offers to take it away, not just to give us the additional burden of advice we can't follow.

He gives us more than advice. He gives us power. "The kingdom of God is not in words but in power", says Saint Paul. Giving him our worries is like giving him our sins: he really takes them away. We may still have troubles; he promised us that: "In this world you shall have tribulation." But he also added, "Be of good cheer: I have overcome the world." He is the living water in which we wash our hands; the dirt is really washed away.

There is a solid basis for such total trust: God has become our Father. We have been born again into his family. Now, then, Christ tells us, quite reasonably, if we ask our Father for bread, will he give us a stone? Not even our earthly father would do that. Does God love us less? Or has he less power to give us what we need than our earthly fathers do? Or less wisdom to know what we really do need? Put these three nonnegotiable dogmas of divine love, divine power, and divine wisdom together with the fact that this God is now our Father, and you get the most simple, reasonable, nonsentimental basis for total trust that can be.

So our prayer "give us this day our daily bread" is to be uttered in the utter certainty that it will be answered. Otherwise, Christ is a liar. For he promised to answer every prayer we ask in his name, and his own prayer is certainly in his name! When we do not get what we ask for, our only choices are to believe (1) that we know better than God, and that God is withholding from us what we really need, or (2) that God knows better than we do, and we are mistaken about what we really need. Perhaps in the light of eternity we appear to be little more than overgrown infants pouting, "I want what I want when I want it." This sounds cruel: Is it only infantile pouting to weep and wonder, "God, why did you do this to me?" after suffering a bereavement or the wreck of a relationship? Not from a human point of view; it is natural. But from the viewpoint of eternity, I suspect that we will look back on such agonized questions and see them as the inarticulate cry of a newborn baby.

Is that all our wisdom amounts to? Yes indeed, according to our wisest men. The greatest theologian of all time declared his own masterpiece, the *Summa Theologica,* only straw. When we hear a philosopher or theologian saying that we are "man come of age", we can be sure we are hearing a modern Pharisee, an infant pretending to a grownup, praying, "Lord, I thank thee that I am not like other men, or even like this humble theologian Aquinas. I am mature. I am a well-adjusted member of this world." We know what the Lord said about such people. How dare we think we creatures of a day know what we really need better than the eternal wisdom that designed all worlds? How dare we self-centered sinners think we love ourselves more than infinite self-abandoning Love loves us? One of us is the fool, ourselves or God. Would we really rather it be God? What hope would we have then?

We are to pray only for today's bread, for, Jesus tells us, "today's worries are quite enough for today." Jesus lived in the present, and we are to do the same. Otherwise, if we are always *planning* to be happy, we never are. "Tomorrow is always a day away", to quote a small, red-headed philosopher. Jesus warns us with striking strength and frequency against worry and fear: against worry because it leads to the deadly sins of avarice or despair; against fear because it is the enemy of faith, hope, and love, the three greatest things in the world.

Jesus' living in the present was dramatically shown just before his death, when he turned to the repentant thief on the cross and said, "Today you shall be with me in paradise." That thief had probably lived fifty years of a wasted, horrible life. But Jesus did not live in that past, only in the present, where he saw the present paradise, not the past hell, in the thief's repentant heart. Those who heard his words probably shook their heads, tsked their tsks, and murmured, "How can he forget the awful things that man did? It isn't fair."

But Jesus does that because he lives in the present; and he lives in the present because he comes out of eternity, which has no past or future but is all present. It's the only time he knows. And we are to be like him: today, we are to pray for today's bread. We will pray for tomorrow's tomorrow—that is, when tomorrow becomes today.

It is the acres-of-diamonds principle: there are acres of diamonds right in our own backyards, and we are fools to ignore them and search abroad. The spatial backyard here symbolizes the temporal present; the diamond in our own backyard is the eternity in the present moment, the sacrament of the present moment. Eternity intersects time only now, "now, while it is called 'today', . . . now is the time of salvation" and the time of prayer and of the answer to prayer. Jesus even tells us, "When you ask, believe that you have already received it, and it shall be yours", for God is not only everywhere but also everywhen. He even meets us from up ahead, from our future. He is already there; he has already taken care of tomorrow's needs.

Christ does not specify what needs we are to pray for. We are to give God the blank check, "our daily bread". It is not wrong to add specific needs, for we are assured that "my God will supply all your needs out of his riches in Christ Jesus", but we must give God room, give God a blank check for him to fill in the amount. He knows what we need, and the very first thing we need is to keep that fact firmly in mind.

Our needs and our wants are not identical. We need some things we may not want (perhaps to fast or to relax or to pray more or perhaps to suffer, to be tested), and we want many things we do not need (the million toys this world offers us to distract us from our real need, which this world can never supply). We need only one thing. "Only one thing is necessary", Christ tells us. That is why God offers us only one thing: himself in Christ. Christ does not just give us joy or life or salvation or resurrection; he *is* our joy, our life, our salvation, our resurrection.

When Saint Thomas Aquinas had finished his great treatise on the Eucharist, he was praying alone in chapel, watched in secret by his friend Brother Reginald, who testified that Christ spoke to Thomas from the crucifix: "You have written well of me, Thomas. What will you have as a reward?" And Thomas gave the perfect answer: "Only thyself, Lord." That is why Job was satisfied. That's why we shall be satisfied. Nothing else will do.

"Our daily bread" suggests the Eucharist, which is Christ. We are to pray for the gift God has already given to us. There is one simple way to be sure we get what we pray for, our daily bread. The most it would cost is a little time. All we need is Christ, and Christ in the Eucharist is only a few blocks away each morning. For us to pray "give us this day our daily bread" and to make no effort to receive the very gift we pray for when God has left it under our Christmas trees, in daily Eucharist, is like praying for light and not opening our eyes. Saint Francis' disciple, Brother Giles, said, "Who do you think is readier: God to give grace or we to receive it?" As we pray "give", let us take heed to receive what is being given.

35
Forgiveness

There is an oft-repeated story about C. S. Lewis that is probably apocryphal—which makes it even more significant, more deliberate. Lewis is supposed to have come late to a convention of theologians who had been discussing for hours the issue: Where, if anywhere, is Christianity distinctive? What Christian doctrine has no parallel in the other religions of the world? The professionals had despaired of an answer. Lewis, told the question, immediately replied, "That's easy: the forgiveness of sins."

The reason Jesus came and died, the reason God did all the things he did throughout biblical history, was this: to get us forgiven. Forgiveness solved the greatest of all problems: the problem of evil. The problem of evil is both the greatest theoretical problem—the most powerful objection against faith in an all-loving and all-powerful God—and also the greatest practical problem. But it is first of all a practical problem. Good philosophy can answer the theoretical problem, but something more than good philosophy is needed to answer the practical problem.

That problem seems insoluble because there are only three possible practical attitudes toward anything: affirmation, negation, or indifference; saying yes, no, or nothing to it. But if we say yes to evil, we condone it; if we say no to it, we condemn it; and if we say nothing to it, we ignore it. To condone it is to become a quisling, an accomplice. To condemn it is to become an inquisitor, a witch hunter, a hater, to fight fire with fire. And to ignore it is to become an ostrich. There is the practical trilemma of evil.

God's solution cuts through this problem like a sword through the Gordian knot. It is forgiveness. Forgiveness does not play ostrich because it faces the fact of evil. It does not play quisling because it labels evil as the enemy; it does not say, "Forget it, there's nothing to forgive", because there *is* something to forgive.

And it does not play inquisitor because it "resists not evil" but drains it away.

This tired old world of ours sometimes looks like a great, gaping wound. Everybody is hurting. Everybody hurts everybody else. Our history and our lives are largely the history of hurting, the history of victimization. Ever since the fall we have had this terrible, inescapable, senseless addiction to hurting each other. No matter how hard we try, we cannot break the habit. Our history is largely the history of war; and our marriages and friendships, our vaunted I-Thou relationships, are history written small and close, where it hurts most. The only way to avoid hurting is to secrete a shell around yourself, and that is the worst hurt of all: loneliness.

There is no solution but forgiveness. The only solution for Christian and non-Christian alike is forgiveness. Even if the world does not accept the Church or Christ or God, the world can still accept forgiveness. It is the most relevant and universal solution to the world's problems, and the simplest.

There are a thousand objections to forgiveness, but there is one argument for it that is stronger than all the objections: if we do not forgive each other, we will die. The alternative to forgiveness is murder, in one form or another. And in the age of the nuclear global village, the age when the world has become one not in love but in fear of total annihilation, the thing that happens to marriages or friendships when there is no forgiveness will also happen to the whole world. We must forgive one another or die. It is as simple, as black and white, as that.

What is called the forgiveness of sins is really the forgiveness of sinners. God cannot forgive sins; every sin must meet its due destiny: eternal expulsion from the presence of Pure Goodness. No darkness can possibly survive the heavenly light. But forgiveness dissolves the glue that sticks the sinner to the sin. Sins are inevitably burned in the eternal garbage dump called hell, or Gehenna, the valley of burning. Sinners are too if they stick to their sins, if they hold on to their garbage.

God and the sinner must freely cooperate to dissolve the glue that sticks the sinner to the sin. It is like a reverse epoxy: both parts

must mix together for this anti-glue to work. God forgives, and
that dissolves the glue from the side of sin; and the sinner repents,
accepts God's forgiveness, and that dissolves the glue from the side
of the sinner. God takes all sins and nails them to the Cross, justly
forgives them by his Son's sacrifice. His part is done: we are
forgiven. The gift is given. Our part is to receive the gift, to
repent. Repentance and forgiveness work together like husband
and wife to conceive a new birth, salvation.

But why did it cost God so much? Why did Jesus have to die?
Why couldn't God just forget our sins? Because God can't forget.
God is Truth. And truth about morality is justice. God is just. He is
not under the law of justice, subject to it, as we are; but neither is
he the arbitrary inventor of a moral law that could have been
different. Morality is as eternal, as unchangeable, and as necessary
as mathematics (though not, of course, as simple) because it is
based on the very nature of God, which is eternal, unchangeable,
and necessary. God can no more change the nature of justice than
he can change from being God to not being God. Justice cannot be
silenced or ignored. That's why God can't just forget our sins.

But there is more; there is love. Justice is an attribute of God's
essence, but love *is* his essence. Thus justice is an attribute of love.
These two things, which to us are often an either/or, are to God a
both/and. Both must be satisfied because both are absolute and
eternal. "Mercy and truth shall meet together, righteousness and
peace shall kiss each other", says the prophecy. How can God
accomplish this reconciliation? Justice and mercy are one in him, in
eternity; but they are tragically separated for us fallen creatures.
How can God accomplish that reconciliation in our lives, in
history? By a second reconciliation, one between heaven and
earth, as the same prophecy goes on to say: "Truth shall spring up
out of the earth and justice shall look down from heaven." The
Incarnation was his way to forgive our sins justly. The marriage of
heaven and earth was the way to the marriage of justice and peace,
justice and mercy.

Forgiveness is a miracle. But a miracle presupposes natural law.
If nature did not work by fixed laws, a miracle would not be a

miracle, an exception. Just as physical miracles presuppose physical laws, moral miracles like forgiveness presuppose moral laws. If there were no justice, forgiveness would not be a moral miracle but the mere easy dismissal that it is for the modern mind, which no longer believes in objective, eternal, absolute justice, and which finds it hard to forgive because it finds it so easy to say "there's nothing to forgive."

Christians who have come under the sway of the modern mind have gotten into the habit of thinking we have a right to God's forgiveness. That's why they don't know what to make of the God of the Old Testament, where justice and judgment and punishment are so strong and clear. Perhaps the most shocking teaching in Christianity to this mentality is its very central one, the heart of the gospel, namely the doctrine of salvation by grace, by free gift. That doctrine sounds very nice and not at all shocking until you realize that it implies that it is not justice, i.e., that it goes beyond what we deserve, i.e., that we deserve not to be saved, i.e., that we all deserve hell! God did not have to send his Son. It would have been perfectly just for him to leave us alone. And that is precisely hell: ourselves, alone, without God.

Because there is justice, forgiveness costs something. It cost Jesus the pains of hell on the Cross, the hell we deserved because we freely chose it: to be alone, on our own, forsaken by God. We said to God, "Leave me alone", and he left his own Son alone instead, so that we would never be alone. If there is a real debt, it must really be paid. If you owe me one thousand dollars and I forgive you your debt, that costs me one thousand dollars. Christ, in forgiving us our debts, assumed them all. The metaphor of the debt is not the only way to understand salvation, of course, but it comes from Jesus himself, not just from medieval theologians, as we are often told. Jesus put this metaphor right smack into the perfect prayer he gave us. "Forgive us our debts" is as accurate a translation as "forgive us our trespasses" (which is another metaphor: crossing a forbidden boundary line).

Praying for this forgiveness of our sins is the first and most necessary application of the previous petition, "give us this day our daily bread", for our most crucial need, our very first bread, is to have a right relationship with God, to have our sins, which separate us from him, forgiven. If not, if we are on the outs with God, then nothing else can follow. "Without me you can do nothing." The relationship must be restored before it can flourish. The road must be opened before anything can travel on it.

God has done his part. He has opened the road to heaven, to himself. He did that on the Cross. Now our part is to accept this strangely shaped vehicle of grace that comes to us along that opened road. We must get inside, and it will take us to heaven. There is only one car in God's fleet, and it is Christ. "I am the way. . . . No one can come to the Father but by me." Entering Christ means two things. His car has two doors, and we must open both in order to get in. They are repentance and faith, the two-word summary of the kerygma, from Jesus right down to the present day. The message never changes its essential structure. And repentance must come first, because repentance is like getting out of our broken-down car, and faith is like getting in his. Faith is receiving the gift. A gift is not a gift unless it is both freely given and freely received. If I offer you a million dollars and you do not have faith in me and take it, you are not a penny richer. So with the gift of Christ, in whom is forgiveness. If we freely choose not to receive it, we do not have it. That is why, though salvation is the free gift of God, it depends on our faith.

Forgiveness implies sin, for what is forgiven is sin: both sins and sin, both actual sins and original sin, both deeds and doer, what we do and what we are. Without the consciousness of sin, Christianity is meaningless: a needlessly complex divine operation for a nonexistent disease, a supernaturalistic mythology inexplicably encumbering a simple earthly ethic—that is what the modern world thinks of Christianity. Asked why he became a Catholic, G. K. Chesterton replied, "To get my sins forgiven". Until they perceive the disease Chesterton perceived, people will not come to the hospital Chesterton came to. Or if they come they will come for the wrong reason, thinking the Church a museum for saints rather than a hospital for sinners.

Jesus says, simply and starkly, "Those who are well have no need of a physician, but those who are sick. I came not to call the righteous, but sinners." This is deliberately ironic. Jesus is implying that those who think they are well are the sickest of all, in fact incurable. The unforgiveable sin can only be one thing: the refusal of forgiveness, final impenitence, for God is infinitely forgiving. Man cannot commit a sin greater than God can forgive. "Where sin abounded, grace did much more abound." Even deicide not only was forgiven but was the very means to its own forgiveness. Christ prayed for his murderers, "Father, forgive them", and then died for them. For us—the whole world was there, each of our sins a nail in the sacred flesh.

The way to come to know the first necessary truth about ourselves, that we are sinners in need of forgiveness, is to get to know the all-holy, all-just, uncompromising, unbribeable character of God. This is why the Lord's Prayer begins with adoration. We know God by adoring him, and we know ourselves in light of him rather than him in light of ourselves. Knowing God, we will then know our need for forgiveness. By human standards most of us are "good people", and we wonder "why bad things happen to good people". But by God's standards, there are no "good people": "There is no one righteous, no, not one" and the mystery is rather why good things happen to bad people.

We are to pray for forgiveness in the double conviction that we need it and that God wants to give it. We need it as much as the lost sheep needed the shepherd, and God longs to give it to us as much as the shepherd longed to bring his lost sheep home. We need him as much as the prodigal son needed his father, and he wants us as much as the father of the prodigal wanted his son home. More, infinitely more.

But there's a catch—a necessary catch. If we do not forgive others, God will not forgive us, cannot forgive us. This is the only petition in the Lord's Prayer that Jesus reinforces with a postscript: "For if you forgive men their trespasses, your heavenly Father will also forgive you; but if you do not forgive men their trespasses, neither will your Father forgive your trespasses." The reason Jesus comments on this one petition is evidently that his disciples needed to know something they didn't know. This is the surprise, this is the catch.

It's not an arbitrary but a necessary catch. It's not that God decided to make this one thing the qualification. Rather, it's intrinsically impossible for us to receive God's forgiveness if we do not forgive our neighbors. All things may be possible for God, but not all things are possible for us. And here is one thing that is not possible for us. It is no more possible for a person who is in a state of unforgivingness toward his neighbor to receive the forgiveness of God than it is possible for someone who ties his hands behind his back to avoid giving gifts to receive any.

We cannot receive God's forgiveness when we do not forgive others because God *is* forgiveness. Forgiveness is the only way we can understand God. We understand God as we understand a person rather than a concept: not with the head but with the heart. Imagine the heart of someone who believed he received God's forgiveness while he refused to pass it on to others; that person would immediately crush the life out of that gift of forgiveness. Forgiveness is like light; you can't possess it or bottle it. You can only reflect it, pass it on. Forgiveness is like water: if you refuse to pass it on, it becomes stagnant. Look at a map of Israel. You will notice that the very same water, the Jordan River, flows into the Sea of Galilee and into the Dead Sea. The Sea of Galilee is fertile and full of life; the Dead Sea is as dead as its name. The difference is that the Sea of Galilee passes the water on. It has an outlet, while the Dead Sea does not. God's grace in our soul is like the water of the Jordan River: it lives only if it is passed on. The gift can be received only if it is also given.

This realization is wonderful and terrible. All other sins can be forgiven if sincerely repented, but this one cannot, for it is impenitence itself. Quite simply, if we refuse to forgive our neighbor, we will go to hell. Please do not call me a fundamentalist for saying that, unless you call Jesus one too. It is terrible, but it is reasonable, for no unforgiving soul could possibly endure the light of heaven, which is forgiving love. One who stood on his rights could not stand heaven's forgiveness of wrongs.

Now notice how lovingly clever Jesus is in framing the words of this petition for us. We are to ask God to forgive us exactly as (*hos*) we forgive others. Thus if we do not forgive others, we are asking God for our own damnation every time we pray the Lord's Prayer! We cannot pray for forgiveness without forgiving others if we realize what we are saying.

No duty has ever been so seriously commanded as this. We absolutely, unqualifiedly, immediately must forgive everyone, with no ifs, ands, buts, or delays. If you have not done so, please do not read another word; get down on your knees and ask God's forgiveness for your unforgivingness to your neighbor and then get up off your knees and give it to him. Free him in order to free yourself. Lose not a minute.

It is not wrong to speak so urgently. Our urgency pales compared with that of Jesus. His is the urgency of infinite love, of a father watching his child dancing on the brink of the abyss. There is an abyss, and many have already perished in it. It is not the work of love to refuse to shout "Danger!" where there is thin ice for fear of upsetting people. The most compassionate thing we can do, the greatest work of charity, says Saint Thomas, is to tell the truth.

Jesus' forgiveness of sins was one of his clearest claims to divinity. He forgave all sins, whether against him or against God. I have a right to forgive you for harming me but no right to forgive you for harming someone else. Yet that is what Jesus did: he acted as if he was the one who was hurt in every sin—because he was. You do not understand that? Have you never seen a crucifix? There, on the Cross, all the sins of the world came together to be forgiven. That was the worldwide convention of sins. The Holocaust was there and the Gulag and Sodom—every sin since we lost Eden. How could such a thing really happen? How could all times be present at once? Because Christ, as God, is eternal and thus can in a moment of time suffer all the sins of history, for his eternity intersects all time. Thus we were there too, all our sins were there, in awful concert.

Were you there when they crucified my Lord?
Were you there when they crucified my Lord?
Oh, sometimes it causes me to tremble, tremble, tremble!
Were you there when they crucified my Lord?

The price of forgiveness was infinitely high. But it was paid. "It is finished", and we are free. To ask God for his gift of forgiveness now is to receive it. There is no gap, no delay, not for a second. Like the thief on the cross, we are in paradise the very day we repent and receive his forgiveness. The plant of paradise, the tree of life, grows in the most unlikely place: Golgotha, the "place of the skull". We are invited to eat its fruit, forgiveness.

36
Temptation and Deliverance

I think the first religious doubt I ever had was one occasioned by the petition "lead us not into temptation." I realized one day that it sounded as if God led us into temptation. If that was so, how could we trust him? How could he expect us to trust him when he commanded us to pray for an escape from the very thing that he led us into? What a cruel game! I desperately hoped that I was making some mistake. I remember the deep feeling of relief that came from reading the clear answer in Scripture: "Let no one say when he is tempted, 'I am tempted by God'; for God cannot be tempted with evil and he himself tempts no one, but each person is tempted when he is lured and enticed by his own desire" (James 1:13–14).

Later, I came to see that the word *temptation* is ambiguous. It could mean either (1) an attempt to inveigle someone to sin—which, of course, is the devil's work, not God's—or (2) a trial, a test of faith, like Job's—which often is God's leading. It is this second meaning of temptation that Jesus had in mind when he told us to pray "lead us not into temptation." It means "lead us not into trials like Job's."

Even the first kind of temptation is not itself sin, and many people confuse the two, thinking that to be tempted is to lose your innocence. Adam and Eve were tempted while they were innocent, before they sinned. They didn't have to sin, even though they did; to deny that is to deny free will. Jesus was tempted (by the devil in the wilderness) and did not sin.

Temptation, then, is not sin. The first kind of temptation is temptation *to* sin. The tempter wants you to sin. But this is not so with trials. God tried Job, like gold in the fire, desiring not that he should break under his trials but that he should become purified. Trials strengthen faith as exercise strengthens muscles. Rabbi Abraham Heschel says, "Faith like Job's cannot be shaken because it is the result of having been shaken." But why, then, if trials strengthen faith and thus are good for us, are we to pray to God to lead us not into them? Because we do not know our limits. God does. The petition comes from humility, both intellectual and moral. Intellectual, because we do not know how much fire our gold needs or can endure; moral, because we should not assume we are stronger than we are or even that we are as strong as we think we are. Everyone has his limits. We are all fallen creatures.

To see the rightness of this petition, consider the alternative: "Lord, please lead us into great trials because we are confident that our faith is so strong that it will endure them, as Job's faith did." That would be foolish, proud, and unnatural. It would be foolish because we usually underestimate our weakness. It was a saint who said of the drunk in the street, "There but for the grace of God go I." His companion was shocked, as we are shocked when we read Saint Paul calling himself "the chief of sinners". But saints are not fools. If we had only had Adolf Hitler's heredity and environment, we may well have committed Hitler's crimes.

It would be proud as well as foolish to pray "lead us into temptation" because the object of that faith is not God but ourselves, and our own faith. Faith does not mean faith in faith; faith means faith in God. Finally, the desire to go through trials is unnatural, and Jesus does not tell us to desire contrary to our God-given nature. The flight-or-fight response to trials is part of our nature. We are to pray to avoid trials for the same reason we are to fight poverty, sickness, and death. Jesus never says that these things are blessed but that those who suffer them are blessed. They are the divine surgeon's instruments, the divine sculptor's chisel strokes. We are to endure them in faith but not to ask for them. The willingness to suffer is heroism; the desire to suffer is usually masochism. Jesus himself did not ask to suffer. He prayed, before his crucifixion, "Father, if it be possible, let this cup pass from me." Only then did he add, "If this cannot pass unless I drink it, thy will be done" (Mt 26:39, 42).

But what of the saints who seem to long for suffering, to seek it out as a pig snuffles out truffles, as delicacies, to be offered to God?

My purely personal opinion, offered without much assurance and subject to correction by those with more experience, sanctity, and authority, is that this phenomenon, though precious in the saints, is dangerous for most of us and is not to be recommended for imitation except under very careful spiritual direction. The desire to suffer, I think, more often indicates a psychological disorder than heroic sanctity. It is disturbingly easy for us to delude ourselves that we are saintly because we admire the saints and aspire to be like them, easy to confuse sharing their ideals with sharing their character.

Compare the following two prayers and see whether you recognize anything familiar. (1) "Lord, I thank thee that I am not like other men. I can and will endure heroic sufferings for you. Please send them my way." (2) "God, be merciful to me, a sinner. I am weak. I can hardly endure even a little pain for you. Therefore please do not send me great pain." Self-delusion prays, "I am strong." Self-knowledge says, "I am weak." Self-knowledge says, "I am riddled with evils, physical, psychological, and spiritual, as with bullet holes or cancer. Therefore I need deliverance. Deliver me from evil."

Our poor world is a mass of bleeding wounds. Everyone is hurting out there. Everyone is hurting in here. Our role is that of the patient. God's role is that of the doctor. God tenderly bends over our wounds and kisses them and binds them up. He embraces us in our bleeding, in our leprous ugliness. How could we doubt it? The main thing Jesus did for three years was to heal people. And Jesus is the window to the Father; "he who has seen me has seen the Father." Therefore the healing ministries, whether physical, psychosocial, or spiritual, are extensions of the Incarnation, of Christ's own work. Every physician, every psychologist or social worker, and every priest is doing the very job Jesus is doing: delivering us from evil. Evil comes in many forms. Pain, weakness, and death are evil for the body, our foothold in the material world. All sorts of neuroses, psychoses, and hang-ups are evil for the psyche, our relationship to ourselves and each other. And sin is evil for the spirit, our relationship to God. Evil permeates our whole being. We need deliverance everywhere.

Every religion in the world promises deliverance. It is the only thing that unites all religions. Not all religions believe in God or life after death or a divine law or even the soul. Buddhism, for example, believes in none of these things. But every religion offers deliverance because only a fool is blind to that need.

But Christ puts the petition for deliverance from evil last in his ideal prayer. We tend to put it first. The child's first prayer is usually "Help!" This is not wrong, but inadequate, like the fear of God, which is the beginning of wisdom but not the end, as G. K. Chesterton sagely says. We must wrap petition in adoration. The God we petition without adoring is a divine machine. The God we petition after adoring is a lover. When we don't get what we want from a machine, we curse and kick the machine. When we don't get what we want from a lover, we do not curse or kick (though we may weep and wonder) but we trust.

Even within the petitions, Christ puts "deliver us from evil" after "give us this day our daily bread." There are two reasons for this order. First, so that we give God first the blank check of "our daily bread", in other words "whatever you see we need", and only then, within this context of trust, cry for help. Second, so that we begin with the positive and only then go to the negative. Good is more important than evil, getting real goods more important than getting rid of real evils. If we had to choose between having neither good nor evil or both, both would be preferable. (That's what God thought when he decided to create us with free will, foreseeing all the evils that would come but also all the goods.) Our first need is the good that is God; then, as a means to this, deliverance from the evil that keeps us from God. We first need the home at the end of the road, to make our journey worthwhile; then, we need to overcome the obstacles along the way.

We are to pray for deliverance from evil—all evil, bodily, psychological, and spiritual. (If you don't understand the difference between the last two, read Heb 4:12.) God's desire is to free us completely. Why then are we still bound? Because we are in time, in process, in a story. Our deliverance is not instantaneous because our being is not instantaneous. Religion is not an instant deliverance tablet; it is a love affair.

But it's so slow! Why are we still starving, lonely sinners? Who is holding back? God or us? Wrong question: it's not either/or. Our role is not 50 percent and God's 50 percent. His role is 100 percent, and our role is 100 percent. Deliverance is a cooperative activity, like marriage. He won't deliver us without our cooperation, and we can't deliver ourselves without his grace. The liberal emphasizes our activity and specializes in social action; the conservative emphasizes God's grace and specializes in faith and resignation to God's will. The dispute is like the one between the head and the tail of a coin.

As for our part, one of the most important principles of deliverance from evil of all three kinds, of body, soul, and spirit, is the principle Lao-tzu, the ancient Chinese sage, and Machiavelli, the modern Western sceptic, both formulated: when a disease is hard to see, it is easy to cure; but when it becomes easy to see, it is hard to cure. Sin is like cancer. It begins small, and if we attack it in its beginning, where it is hard to see, it is relatively easy to defeat. But if we wait until the cancer has spread and taken root, so that it is easy to see, it is very hard to cure.

Sin begins in our thoughts. Another ancient sage, Gautama the Buddha, said, "All that we are is made up of our thoughts. It begins where our thoughts begin, it proceeds as our thoughts proceed, and it ends where our thoughts end." Saint Paul recognized that sin begins in our thoughts too; that's why his prescription for deliverance from evil at its roots is to "bring every thought into captivity to Christ". If Eve had done that in Eden, all the problems in our world would never have started. If she had turned her thoughts to God instead of to the tempter, we would be doing the same today. Thoughts are like wild animals. They need tamers.

The false god of freedom of thought has beguiled millions into the false freedom of calling their thoughts their own and thus giving them up to the power of evil. If Christ is to be Lord of all, his lordship must begin in the most interior place of all, our will, and then the second most interior place, our thoughts, and spread out from there into our relationships and our world. As Jesus said, it is not what goes into us that defiles us but what comes out of us. Once our will is given to him (and if it is not, we are not his), the next gift must be our thought life. We must yield to him the very first thoughts and imaginations of sin. Hard as that seems, it is infinitely easier than anything else. Thoughts are like clouds: easy to lift to him in oblation. Once they harden into actions, they get a weight that makes them much harder to lift, and they fall like a deadly rain on our lives.

> Sow a thought, reap an act.
> Sow an act, reap a habit.
> Sow a habit, reap a character.
> Sow a character, reap a destiny.

As the cancer of sin grows, increasingly radical measures are needed. Eventually we are confronted with an incredible operation: the divine surgeon takes the cancer out of the patient by taking it into himself. God delivered us from evil by coming right smack into the heart of it, on the Cross.

He descended into all our hells because love wants to share everything, even suffering. That is why he came: to fulfill love's desire. Love's deepest desire is not happiness but withness, intimacy, union. "Better unhappy with her than happy without her"—that is the word of a lover. Love wants to be inside the beloved; love wants exchange. Thus God exchanged his deliverance for our evil, his garbage truck for our garbage. What happened on the Cross is no freak accident, no exception, but the universal principle of what love does. Love delivers the beloved from evil by taking it upon itself and soaking it up, like a blotter.

It is a bloody business, deliverance. Where do we find deliverance? There, in Christ's wounds. Remember the line of the great old (forgotten?) prayer "Anima Christi": "In thy wounds hide me." The devil dare not come there. He cringes from the blood. That is the safest place to be. Israel was taught that, symbolically, at the first passover, in Egypt, when the Israelites were protected from the angel of death only by the blood of the sacrificial lamb sprinkled on the doorposts of their houses. Our lives are the houses that we build to live in. The door is our openness to God. The blood of Christ must be there because that is the only way the all-holy God can come in to us and be the guest of our soul. Our deliverance is to be "washed in the blood of the Lamb". The Lord's Prayer ends with the gospel.

A very old form of the Lord's Prayer, not in Scripture but in the Church's liturgy from earliest times, adds the doxology "for thine is the kingdom and the power and the glory, both now and forever". Ironically, it was the Protestants who used this old Catholic liturgical formula and the Catholics who dropped it, here practicing the Protestant principle of *sola scriptura*. It has been reinserted into the Catholic liturgy, where it belongs—not just because it is a tradition but because it is a good tradition. It is good because it is right to end the prayer with praise and adoration, as we began, since our lives and the life of the universe itself begin and end with praise, with the heavens and the heart telling the glory of God the Creator and Redeemer, the Alpha and Omega.

God's kingdom, power, and glory are not as visible as ours. We can easily see our kingdoms: our finances, for instance, or our lands. We can see our power in our bodies and in the works of our minds. And our glory is seen by other people: the beauty of our works, our words, and our bodies. These are good, for they are God's gifts. But they are ours only on loan. Our very existence is not our own but is borrowed from Existence Itself, who created us. But we have a kingdom that is infinitely more glorious than all the kingdoms of history, and our Father has promised that we will rule it one day. We shall have powers that dwarf nuclear bombs because they are extensions of the power of God himself. We have far to go in our training before we can be trusted with such power, though even now we "taste the powers of the age to come" (Heb 6:5) in tiny, intermittent samples. And at the end of our training lies a "weight of glory"; if we saw it in anyone now, we would be strongly tempted to worship him. (That from C. S. Lewis' great, great sermon, "The Weight of Glory".)

The unthinkable power and glory will be ours; but only when we let it be his. Jesus himself refused to "grasp" his divinity but "emptied" himself (Phil 2:5–11). When we give up our own glory for God's, we attain our own, for we are mirrors, not lights. When we turn to the one Light of the World, the mirror of our soul reflects the dazzling light of the face of God. Those who have tasted the most intimate appetizers of that heavenly meal—the great saints and mystics—consistently report that in that union the light of God is so perfectly reflected in the mirror of the purified soul that it seems as if there is but one light, as if we are nothing but the place where his beams come to focus.

> Blow, blow, blow till I be
> But the breath of the Spirit blowing in me.

Finally, the word *Amen.* It means not just "I'm finished now" but "So be it!" It is not a mere wish but a word of command, of power. It is a sacramental word; it is efficacious. When a great king says "so be it", it is done. The greatest king of all has made us princes (Ps 45:16), and prayer is our staff of power. When we say "Amen", we wield our staff; we say, "Let it be done."

There are two things we must know about this power: that it is and is not like magic. Most of us already know how it is not like magic: it is not impersonal and mechanical but dependent on faith, on our personal relationship with the Source of that power. But many of us do not know that it *is* magic: it is real power, not just a psychological placebo. Scripture calls it *dynamis,* the origin of our word *dynamite.* Prayer is like dynamite. It should be used with great care, for when its power is released, it changes the world.

37
The Goal of Christian Living: What Is a Saint?

Why does the Apostles' Creed include "the communion of saints" as one of the twelve articles of faith, one of the twelve essentials of our religion? Because our fundamental vocation in life is to be saints. Because, as Charles Peguy put it, "life holds only one tragedy, ultimately: not to have been a saint." Because this whole world is a saint-making machine. Because the whole purpose of creation, revelation, Incarnation, Atonement, and Church is to make us saints. Because everything the Church does, from setting up bishops to setting up chairs, from raising money to raising martyrs, has no other purpose than this. Because life itself has no other purpose than this.

Saints are not far-out freaks, weirdos, or exceptions. They are the rule, the plumb line, the standard operating model for human beings. If we are *not* saints, we are the exceptions to the rule, whether we make up 1 percent or 99 percent of the human race.

In the biblical sense of the word, all believers are saints. Saints are not the opposites of sinners. There are no opposites of sinners in this world. There are only saved sinners and unsaved sinners. *Holy* does not mean sinless but special, set apart, called out of the world to the unthinkable destiny of eternal ecstasy in spiritual marriage to God Almighty.

In the popular sense of the word, sainthood is a matter of degree: a saint is someone who does something better than most of us. What thing? One thing with three sides: faith, hope, and love.

The Church's language is half biblical and half popular when she canonizes certain "saints", i.e., solemnly declares that certain known and named persons are both in heaven and worthy models for our earthly imitation. The modern world is a world without heroes. Saints are the answer. Saints are the true heroes.

What is a saint? A saint is first of all one who knows he is a sinner. A saint knows all the news, both the bad news of sin and the good news of salvation. A saint is a true scientist, a true philosopher: a saint knows the Truth. A saint is a seer, one who sees what is there. A saint is a realist.

A saint is also an idealist. A saint embraces heroic suffering out of heroic love. A saint also embraces heroic joy. (This is one of the criteria for canonization: saints must have joy.)

A saint is a slave of Christ, a doormat for Christ, a palm branch for Christ's donkey to march on. A saint is also a conqueror greater than Alexander, who conquered only the world. A saint conquers himself. What does it profit a man if he conquers the whole world but does not conquer himself?

A saint is so open that he can say, with Paul, "I have learned, in whatever state I am, to be content. I know how to be abased and I know how to abound" (Phil 4:11–12). A saint marries God "for better or for worse, for richer or for poorer, in sickness or in health, till death". A saint is also so closed-minded, so determined, so stubborn, that he will die before compromising the Truth, and will write *credo* in the sand with his own blood as he dies. (One saint actually did this.)

A saint is a sworn enemy of the world, the flesh, and the devil. He is locked in mortal combat with principalities and powers. A saint is also a friend and lover of the world. He kisses this sin-cancered world with the tender lips of the God of John 3:16. A saint declares God's war on this world, sinking the Cross into the enemy-occupied earth like a sword, hilt held by heaven. At the same time he stretches his arms out on that very Cross as if to say, "See? This is how wide my love is for you!"

A saint is Christ's bride, totally attached, faithful, dependent on him. A saint is also totally independent and detached from idols, from other husbands. A saint works among money, power, pleasure as a married woman works with other men, but will not marry them or even flirt with them.

A saint is higher than anyone else in the world. A saint is the real mountain climber. A saint is also lower than anyone else in the world. Like water, he flows to the lowest places, like Calcutta.

A saint's heart is broken by every little sorrow and every little sin. A saint's heart is also so strong that not even death can break it. It is indestructible just because it is so breakable.

A saint takes his hands off the steering wheel of his life and lets God steer. That's scary, for God is invisible. As saint also has the strongest hands, hands that move the world. He has feet that know just where to go and that move through the world with a sure step.

A saint does not let others play God to him, as the rest of us all do (especially in a democracy). A saint takes his orders from the General, not from the army. A saint also does not play God to others, as the rest of us all do in all societies since Eden, often in subtle ways. But saints are not subtle. Saints are simple.

A saint is a little Christ. Not only do we see Christ through his saints, as we see a light through a stained glass window, but we also understand the saints only through Christ, as we understand eggs only through chickens.

The saints are our family. We are one body. They are our legs and we are theirs. As Pascal says, "examples of noble deaths of Spartans and others hardly affect us, . . . but the example of the deaths of martyrs affects us, for they are our members. . . . We do not become rich through seeing a rich stranger, but through seeing a father or husband rich."

Finally, the saints are our destiny, our eschatology:

> And when the strife is fierce, the warfare long,
> Steals on the ear the distant triumph song,
> And hearts are brave again, and arms are strong.
> Alleluia!

I get goose bumps whenever I hear that hymn. The echoes of the song that is the saints come from Eden and from heaven, and all human happiness is an echo of that echo. When we suffer, when we despair, when we cry in rage or helplessness, when we are bewildered, bewitched, bedeviled, betrayed, besmirched, and besotted with the weight of the world, we need to listen to that echo from heaven.

The saints are present, not just past. "We are surrounded by so great a cloud of witnesses" (Heb 12:1) that we are never alone. We are watched and helped. Death is not so wide a river that heavenly hands cannot reach across it.

Sainthood is God's job description for us. It is the only job in town. It is not an option, something just for "religious people" (whoever they are). The most important thing in the world to know, therefore, is how to qualify for this job. First, anyone can qualify. Saints are made out of sinners. Only sinners need apply. Second, no one can qualify. No one can make himself a saint. Only God can do it. Our part is to want it, to choose it, to believe it, and to receive it, and to lie there and not wiggle while Doctor God operates on us.

But though we can't do it without God, God won't do it without us. We become saints by willing to. As William Law says, if you stop to consult your own heart in total honesty, you will see that there is one and only one reason why you are not even now a saint: you do not wholly will it. We become saints not by thinking about it, and not (certainly) by writing about it, but simply by doing it. There comes a time when the "how" question stops and we just do it. If the one we love were at our door knocking to come in, would we wonder how the door lock works, and how we could move our muscles to open it?

Saint Francis of Assisi told his monks that if they were in the beatific vision and a tramp knocked at their door asking for a cup of cold water, then turning away from the heavenly vision to help the tramp would be the real heaven, and turning away from the tramp to keep the blissful vision would be turning from God's face. A saint is one who sees who the tramp is: Jesus.

PART THREE

CULT: FUNDAMENTALS OF CHRISTIAN COMMUNITY

38
The Four Marks of the Church:
Oneness

Vatican II's two most important documents both concern the Church. They are *Lumen Gentium,* the "Dogmatic Constitution on the Church", and *Gaudium et Spes,* the "Pastoral Constitution on the Church". To understand these key documents we must first be familiar with what the Church has previously said about herself from her earliest creeds and councils, for that is the foundation on which all subsequent teaching rests. And that foundation is essentially the "four marks" of the Church.

The four marks of the Church are the Church's answer to the question: How are we to recognize the true Church, the fullness of the Church? Many groups of Christians, many churches and denominations, may possess much goodness, wisdom, piety, or Christian service, but only the Catholic Church is fully (1) one, (2) holy, (3) Catholic, and (4) apostolic. These are the signs by which the Church from its earliest centuries, creeds, and councils has identified herself.

What is meant by the oneness of the Church? I want to consider (1) six ways in which the Church is not one, though many people think she is; (2) six ways in which the Church is one, but not the essential way; and (3) six aspects of the essential way in which the Church is one. Thus we will move from the periphery to the center, from surface to depth.

First, the Church is not uniform. She is not an anthill. She does not discourage pluralism and individuality. Totalitarian political regimes may fear individuality, but the Church is the mother of saints, who are the most distinctive individuals the world has ever seen. Augustine's great motto is hers: "In essentials, unity; in nonessentials, diversity; in all things charity."

Second, the Church is not a unity brought about by force. Her unity is at root spiritual, therefore free. When churchmen forced Jews or pagans to be baptized against their will or forced heretics to recant by the threat of torture, they were acting contrary to the nature of the Church.

Third, the Church is not untroubled by schisms and heresies. Her history is "by schisms rent asunder, by heresies distressed". Only partially has she obeyed Saint Paul's command to "be of one mind". Yet the gates of heresy and even hell cannot prevail against her existence or her unity; for (as Saint Thomas Aquinas says) "everything guards its unity as it guards its existence."

Fourth, the Church is not one by being superior, detached, and indifferent to visible conflicts; not one by being purely spiritual. She is not one as the sky is one, but she is one as the earth is one.

Fifth, the Church is not the one and only visible church, the only candidate. "The scandal of particularity" is that she is (or appears to be) only one among many, just as Christ was one man among many.

Sixth, the Church is not one in some abstract, lowest-common-denominator sense, arrived at by dropping disagreements and skimming off the cream of common beliefs, or "fundamentals". Its unity is more concrete.

But wait. Doesn't the Apostles' Creed summarize the common essential beliefs of the Church? Yes, it does; but it is not a lowest common denominator or even a highest common factor. It is not even a number of common ideas. The creed is not ideas, not concepts; it is realities.

But creeds do express a first way the Church is one: in doctrine. Fidelity to her teaching is a test of unity with the Church. Yet the Church is not essentially or merely a teacher (though she is that too), just as Christ is not essentially a teacher or sage or philosopher. The Church, like Christ, is essentially the agent of salvation.

The same is true of a second way the Church is one: in her moral and ethical teaching. Fidelity to this teaching is as important as fidelity to doctrine; yet the Church, like Christ, is not essentially or merely an ethical teacher.

The Church is also one, thirdly, in her authority. That is why that authority must be centralized, shared and collegial though it is. Just as in a family, however equally shared the authority may be, one must be the final arbiter and have the primary responsibility, for a body cannot have two heads. Yet papal authority is not the essence of the Church's unity. The pope is only "the servant of the servants of God".

Fourth, the Church is one visibly, as a concrete institution in the world. But the Catholic Church's visible unity surpasses that of Orthodox, Anglican, and Protestant churches only in degree. The mark is enough to identify her for any honest seeker, but it is not her very essence, and therefore it can be possessed in lesser degree by other bodies also.

The same is true, fifthly, of her historical continuity, which is based on apostolic succession. That is real and distinctive and a mark for "serious shoppers"; but it is not her essence. It is not her end but only her means.

Sixth, baptism makes us really one; we are baptized into one family. Yet baptism is not the Church's reason for being; she is baptism's reason for being. Scripture always connects baptism with faith. When Michael Corleone, in *The Godfather,* had his baby baptized at the exact moment his friends were murdering his enemies at his command, that baptism did not unite him with his baby and with God.

These are all ways in which the Church is one, but not essential ways. The essential way the Church is one has six aspects.

1. The Church's unity is most essentially Christ himself. "One Lord, one faith, one baptism"—but the first is the essential thing. Christ is not only the Church's Lord but also the Church's Head. A lord need not be part of his people, but a head must be part of its body. My body is me; so the Church is Christ. That is why the gates of hell cannot prevail against her. That is why every time she seems

to be dead she rises from the grave. That is why the world hates and fears her. That is why she is the agent of salvation.

2. The Church is one as a vine is one: the very same life courses through all its branches, namely the life of the vine itself. If this metaphor seems too bold and strong, remember it is Christ's own choice of images, not ours. The life, or soul, of the Church is Christ's Spirit, the Holy Spirit, God himself, the very spiritual life-blood of the living God, which is as present in the soul of the believer as in the Eucharist (though in a different form).

3. Christ as a human being has body and soul, visible and invisible aspects. So the Church too is both visible and invisible, both organization and organism, both historical body and mystical body.

4. The unity of a person is more than the unity of an animal. (Ants, bees, and birds almost seem to have more of a group consciousness than an individual consciousness.) And the unity of an animal is more than the unity of a plant. (Is a tree one and the orchard a group, or is the orchard one and the tree a part of it?) Finally, the unity of a plant is more than the unity of an inorganic thing, like a stone, which can be divided without killing its unity. A person is one because he or she can say "I". This is the image of God, who is I AM. Christ is one as a person is one, and because the Church is Christ's body, she is one. We are all one person. This does not mean we are not also different persons. Many human persons make up the body of one single divine person, Christ.

5. This Church, this person, cannot be split by death. That is why the Church is also one throughout time and eternity: "the Church militant" (the Church on earth), "the Church triumphant" (the Church in heaven), and "the Church suffering" (the Church in purgatory) are one Church.

6. Finally, the Church is eschatologically one. When Christ comes again at the end of history, he will not marry a harem but a bride. And that bride will be "without spot or wrinkle". He will remove all three enemies of oneness, all three separations, all three alienations from his Church then: sin, death, and suffering. Sin is alienation between soul and God; death is alienation between body

and soul; suffering is alienation between body and world. Sin was defeated on Calvary. Death was "swallowed up in victory" on Easter morning. And finally "God will wipe away every tear from their eyes" in heaven. Tears, like the water of the sea, symbolize parting and death. The Church, like Noah's ark, floats on the flood of tears. The ark sails for heaven, God's answer to the song of earth, "somebody's always saying goodbye."

39
The Four Marks of the Church:
Holiness

Holy means set apart, special, different. Every Christian is holy. If we are not holy, we are not saved. A Christian is one who belongs to Christ, one who has been taken out of the world, Satan's kingdom, and placed into the Church, Christ's kingdom, the kingdom of heaven. The Church is the kingdom of heaven.

The doctrine of holiness, the doctrine that we do not belong to this world, that we are pilgrims and strangers here, "strangers in a strange land", that "our citizenship is in heaven" not earth—this is not an outdated, culturally relative idea that is no longer necessary or binding for modern Christians. It is the consistent and constant teaching of Christ and of the entire New Testament. If it is not true, then Christianity is not true.

Catholics believe we are made holy by being incorporated into Christ's holy body, as Noah's family was set aside and saved by being put into the ark. Protestants emphasize the reverse; they believe we are saved first as individuals and then these individuals constitute the Church.

The holiness of the Church is more than the holiness of each of her members. Protestants are not necessarily less holy as individuals than Catholics are; in fact many of them put most of us to shame. Nor are their diverse churches necessarily more spotted with crimes and failings throughout their history than the leaky old ark is. The Church is holy not because she is perfect but because she is Christ's.

But there is a close connection between these two meanings of holiness, as between root and fruit. Because we are Christ's, we are called to live as Christ lived. Once we are called into God's household, we learn the ways of that household, however slowly and fitfully we learn. Once we are set apart, we learn to live in a set-apart way.

Set-apartness is especially unpopular today because it confronts a popular false religion, the modern worship of equality. Equality is good politics but bad religion. Equality of rights, equality before the law, is a fine thing, but absolute equality is simply silly. The universe is not a democracy; God is King, not partner or even chairman of the board. There is hierarchy in all of nature and no less in the supernatural order. The Church is set upon a hill, like Mount Zion, for the world to look up to it. One of the greatest pleasures in life is looking up to something or someone superior to yourself. Absolute equality makes one of the greatest virtues impossible: humility.

How is the Church superior? Catholics are often outdone in good works not only by Protestants but sometimes even by atheists. How can we claim superiority? Isn't this both arrogant and simply false? It is not arrogant for the same reason the Jews' claim to be God's chosen people is not an arrogant claim. It is God's call and God's doing, not theirs (or ours), and it is not based on our worth but on his grace and our need. Neither of those two things is anything for us to boast about. Furthermore, he calls everyone. The Church is not supposed to be the select few but the select many, in fact the select all.

The Church is holy because its Lord is holy and his call to us is holy. That call is to live a different kind of life, to be a lighthouse to the world, living epistles for the world to read. We have not always responded in a holy way to that call, but the call is holy. The call is to "be perfect even as your Father in Heaven is perfect."

Holiness is not a negative thing, as its definition might seem to imply. We are set apart from the world only to be set there for God. Holiness is positive because it is defined by the positive nature of the God who calls us, not by the negative nature of the world from which we are called. Holiness is more do's than don'ts.

But there is a negative aspect to holiness. Saint Paul uses the analogy of the athlete to explain this. The athlete says no to foods and drinks and indulgent lifestyles that would interfere with his goal because he has first said yes to the goal of winning his race. A good athlete does not use drugs, and a Christian similarly avoids the drugs of self-indulgence, which blind the soul to the infinite and overriding importance of the Christian's race, the race to heaven and the race to bring the world to heaven before it goes to hell.

Holiness is the most important of the four marks of the Church for two reasons. First, it is the Church's final end and goal. Second, holiness is the Church's crucial mark because it is her number one selling point. Mother Teresa and John Paul II have brought more people into the Church than any argument. Authentic holiness is irresistible.

No matter how cynical and dissipated a person is, the image of God is still there in the soul, like a homing beacon. Holiness attracts because it reveals the shape of God to our heart, a God-shaped hole. It attracts because it is what we were designed for.

Holiness is the most beautiful thing in the world. We have beauty detectors in our souls, and when they are in the presence of a saint, they hear the call of the beauty of sanctity like a distant horn calling to adventure. The wrinkles on Mother Teresa's face are surpassingly beautiful. They bespeak the work of Christ and the suffering of Christ. They are like valleys down which reverberate the echoes from the song we sang in Eden, when God walked with us in the cool of the evening in the garden.

If the Church's holiness were clearly visible and audible to the world, the world would soon empty out into the Church. If the song of holiness were clearly broadcast, the only people who could resist it would be the tone deaf, the most hardened and insensitive. Sanctity is a highly infectious condition. Eleven out of twelve ordinary men became saints because they were with Jesus. But as it stands now in our world there are many good and sensitive people who remain untouched by the infection of holiness and remain outside. It must be, then, that the Church's holiness is not clearly seen and heard by the world.

This situation has two possible causes. Insofar as it is the fault of the world, we must labor to change the world's perceptions of the Church. We must do all we can to heal the world's blindness and deafness, to wipe the dust of prejudice from the mirrors the media hold up. The encyclical *Inter Mirifica* speaks of the Catholic's call to infiltrate and purify the media.

But there is also a second possible cause for the world's perception of the Church: us. The world does not see the beauty of holiness because we are hiding the light under a bushelbasket. The simple solution is repentance, the one-word summary of the message of all the prophets. We must turn back to God, to the light that reflects off the mirrors of our lives and into the world's darkness. But we must first turn our mirrors to the divine sun, our faces to the face of God.

If we do not understand the way to holiness, we cannot call mankind to it. It is not hard to understand. All the saints say the same thing. The secret of sanctity is misunderstood not because it is complex but because it is too simple. We want to run away from it, so we design complexities as excuses. The secret is in a single word, Mary's word when she made the most important choice any mere human being ever made in all of history, when she said Yes to God's appeal through his angel: Will you allow the world to be saved through my Son coming into your body and your life? We all have hope of heaven only because Mary said *fiat*, "let it be done."

That is all sanctity is: willing God's will. All the methods and teachings and techniques and good works are roads to that or roads from that. "That" is simply yessing God. The alternative is noing God, or sin. There are only those two alternatives, life or death. Sanctity is to choose life. The alternative to holiness is not ordinary life but death. The alternative to heaven is not earth but hell.

And yessing God, loving God, is the only way to know God. Only when the will is aligned with God's will can the mind be aligned with God's mind. That is why Jesus said, "If your will were to do the will of my Father, you would understand my teaching, that it is from him." Our only alternatives are knowing God or noing God.

Holiness is power. It is objectively real. It is not just an ideal or intention somewhere inside our own consciousness. It is Christ's own presence. Christ does not help us to holiness; Christ is our holiness. "God has made him to be our righteousness", says Saint Paul. Therefore as long as we have Christ we have holiness. The dullest and weakest of us can still be holy because holiness is not an ideal for our energy to generate, but a gift from God for us to share. We are saved by being made a part of the Church, Christ's body, and the Church is holy and makes us holy. We do not make it holy. Every animal in the ark is holy. The very splinters of the ark are holy, for they grow from the wood of the Cross.

Holiness is ultimately identical with *agape,* for holiness is being set apart by God for God, and God is *agape. Agape* is not what the world means by "love"; it is 1 Corinthians 13 love. It is distinctive; that is why holiness is distinctive. Jesus predicts, "By this shall all men know you are my disciples, by your love for one another."

The Church turned the world upside down once by this mark. It can happen again. And the way our world is heading, teetering over a nuclear abyss and already in a moral abyss, it had better happen again. Once, the world said about Christians, "Here are those people who are turning the world upside down." It is not saying that today. That is why the world *is* upside down. We want to turn it upside down to get it right side up. We want to turn it upside down as a farmer turns a small basket of fruit upside down to empty it out into a larger basket. For the Church is much larger than the world. The world has the whole picture not only upside down but inside out.

40
The Four Marks of the Church: Catholicity

"How can you Catholics believe that the Roman Catholic Church is the one true church? Your very name gives you away. 'Catholic' means 'universal', but you contradict that by adding 'Roman'. You're only one particular church, one of many, not the universal church. Even though you're the biggest one, that doesn't make you universal, any more than being the biggest animal makes the whale the universal animal." Another way of putting this challenge is to ask, as many Catholic colleges have asked themselves, whether we are Catholic with a capital C (i.e., Roman Catholic) or catholic with a small c (i.e., universal, ecumenical). Which is it?

The answer is: both. And the answer to the first challenge—are we Roman or Catholic—is also: both. The Church is both (1) a concrete, particular church, with its center of authority at a specific place, Rome, and (2) the universal church for all people, for the whole world. Just as Jesus is one concrete individual and also the universal Savior, so his Church is one concrete and visible church, and also the universal instrument for salvation.

But, the objector will reply, if you believe that the Roman Catholic Church is the universal instrument for salvation, then you must believe that no one but Catholics can be saved, that even the most saintly Protestants are all going to hell.

No, we do not. The Church does not teach that. Vatican II expressly said that believing Protestants can be saved. They are brothers in Christ. The "separated brethren", though separated, are still brethren, members of Christ's family. They lack the fullness of the faith, but they can still have saving faith. In fact, Father Feeny in Massachusetts was excommunicated long before Vatican II for insisting that Protestants were all doomed to hell. Ironically, he found himself outside the very Church that he insisted was the only place for salvation, so that if he was right, he was wrong. Only if he was wrong could he be saved. Fortunately for him, he was wrong.

How then is the Church universal? How is the Roman Church catholic? How can one thing be all things? How can the particular be universal? We can understand this paradox better if we look at the thing closest and most familiar to us that illustrates it: ourselves. A human being is both a particular individual and also a whole universe of experience and consciousness. The whole world can re-exist in an individual's consciousness. Our minds are like mirrors. A mirror is a concrete individual thing, yet it also reflects all things, universally. That is why Aristotle says "the soul is in a way all things."

This ability to reflect all things in the mirror of our mind, to give the whole world a second life as our world, is not supernatural but natural. All humans have this ability just by being human. But there is also a second, supernatural ability: to become part of the Church, Christ's body, to be taken up into the life of God as the world is taken up into our life. And this too is universal: in Christ, "all things become new."

What does that assertion mean? It means that just as anything and everything in the material world can become a part of us, of our experience, so anything and everything in us, with the one exception of sin, can become part of Christ. In Christ God has assimilated fully "catholic", universal, total humanity, not just souls but bodies too and the whole world that goes with bodies. Everything truly human is saved and transformed. Christ doesn't take us out of the created world, but puts himself into that world. God does not fish us out of the sea as a fisherman catches a fish; he takes the whole sea with us. He promises us a resurrected body and a new earth. He does not rip up his original design for us to be embodied creatures; we do not change our species and become angels. We, the saved, the Church, are catholic (universal) because in and through us the whole material universe is transformed and saved.

This is not speculation; this is Scripture. From the beginning, God made Adam (mankind) priest of creation, and at the end he promises us a new creation. In between, Saint Paul tells us that this whole creation is now "groaning and travailing together with us". As Christ is our priest, we are nature's priest; as we are divinized by Christ, nature is humanized by us. In both cases, the whole lesser world is invited into the greater one, with catholic hospitality. And the agent of the greater transformation is the Church. That is how the Church is universal: it gives the whole universe a resurrected life in and through saved humanity. Through the Church mankind, and through mankind the universe, is in labor with a new birth.

It is a typically Protestant rather than Catholic sensibility to confine this new birth to individuals. But God did not do so; the Incarnation was out there in history, for the whole world, and the Incarnation was in the outer world what the new birth is in the inner world of the individual: Christ's coming and saving and giving a new beginning. Baptism is the Incarnation really happening again in the life of an individual as it happened in the life of the world. Just as what happened on Calvary really happens in the Mass, so what happened in Bethlehem really happens in baptism. (I mean complete baptism, baptism as Scripture and the Church mean it: "being born again by water *and* the Spirit", sacrament *and* faith; the two are always joined.) Baptism and the Incarnation are mirror images of each other. God works in both worlds, individual and universal, microcosm and macrocosm. God is catholic, complete, universal.

A second and simpler way the Church is universal is that it is hospitable. It invites in all nations, races, sexes, ages, economic or social classes, and even all levels of sanctity, from the grossest criminal (like the thief on the cross) to the purest saint. Just as the ark contained male and female of every kind of animal, the Church gathers men and women of every kind. It is the ultimate equal-opportunity employer. "In Christ there is neither Jew nor Greek."

But the Church is not a melting pot. It is more like a stew. Every ingredient is preserved, not melted down. Individuality and differences are not erased. Sexual, racial, personality, and other differences that make us *us* are transformed and perfected. In the

Church, black is beautiful and white is beautiful; men are men and women are women. "In Christ there is neither Jew nor Greek, neither male nor female" does not mean we are deracinated and neutered, but that all are equally welcome. God loves differences. That's how he created the universe, by acts of discrimination: light from darkness, waters above from waters below, land from sea, living from nonliving, birds from fish, man from animals, women from men. *Vive la différence!* The Church of this God is therefore a family, not an anthill. The life she offers us is like salt (to use Jesus' own image). Salt brings out the distinctive flavors of different foods. It makes fish fishier, eggs eggier, and steak steakier. That is why saints are all different, while sinners are drearily alike. Totalitarians and tyrants are all stereotyped; saints are unique, the quirkiest individuals this world has ever seen.

A third meaning of universality is that the Church encompasses earth, purgatory, and heaven. The "Church militant" (the Church on earth), the "Church suffering" (the Church in purgatory), and the "Church triumphant" (the Church in heaven) are all one family. It is like a very large family with members living in three different countries or going to three different schools. In fact, earth is rather like elementary school, purgatory like high school, and heaven like college.

Even hell is part of the Church's universality. Though it is not part of the Church and the Church is not part of it, it is bordered and defined by the Church as darkness is defined by light. Hell equals the absence of the Church. The outer darkness is defined as outer by the bridegroom's wedding party within. Some of the saints, in fact, say that the very fires of hell are made of the life-blood of the Church, namely the light and love of God. The damned experience this fire as torture because they hate it. That's why they're damned: because they hate what God is, light and love, truth and self-giving. Cardinal Newman, in a famous sermon, compared heaven to a church service, and said that even if God brought all the people in hell up to heaven, that would only increase their torture, like bringing someone who hated church into church.

Finally, a fourth meaning of catholicity or universality is the eschatological one. The Church is catholic in her ultimate destiny. The Church is the key actor in the story of human history, for the Church is the extension of the Incarnation, Christ's continued presence in the world, and history is "his story". The story is still unfinished, in process. The Church's universality is not yet complete. That's the only reason history is still going on: to make up the complete number of the saints. Our most important job in this world is to help the world to end, to complete the task God put us here for, which is nothing less than to make up in our own bodies and lives what still remains to be made up of Christ's work of suffering love to save the world. That is the startling doctrine Saint Paul teaches us: that we complete Christ! We bring Christ's humanity to fulfillment, we complete his body, which is the Church. The catholicity of the Church is identical with the completeness of Christ's human nature.

One day this world will be dead and the Church will be fully born. When the catholicity of the Church is perfect, the world will end, as a placenta is sloughed off after a pregnancy. The world is raw material out of which God is making the Church, his people, his masterpiece. The world is like a block of marble out of which a great sculptor makes a statue. Once the statue is finished, the unused marble is thrown away.

The ultimate point of history is the catholicity of the Church. That is "the mystery of faith" Saint Paul speaks of in Ephesians, hidden from all previous ages and now for the first time revealed in Christ: God's plan "to complete all things in Christ". The world is to be taken up into the Church, the Church into Christ, and Christ into the Father. Then God will be "all in all".

Thus we catch a glimpse of the ultimate meaning of everything that has ever happened, the very purpose of God's creating in the first place. This whole universe is here for us and we are here for Christ. The universe is only the stage set for the saints, the stuff the Church is made from. The world is there for the Church, not vice versa. In one sense, of course, the Church is there for the world: to save the world. But to save the world means to make the world the

Church. The world is there for the Church, to be made into the Church, as the block of marble is there for the statue.

Appearances are deceiving here. They produce the inside-out illusion. It looks as though the Church is in the world, but really the world is in the Church. It's like a play: it looks like the play is in the sets, but really the sets are in the play. It looks like the play takes place in its setting: the stage, the scenery, the sets. But really, the setting is in the play; it is an aspect of the play, a part of the play. Physically, the play is in the setting, but spiritually, the setting is in the play, it is part of the play's meaning. So with the Church and the world. Physically, the Church is in the world, but spiritually the world is in the Church, as its setting.

No one but a Christian knows and no one but a Catholic appreciates the ultimate meaning of all things. Science only explores the sets. Science has its proper glory, and it is a high and holy enterprise, for "the heavens declare the glory of God." But the point of this universe is not galaxies and gases, but gods and goddesses: the creatures God has designed this cosmic mother to bear, the animals into whom he breathed his own breath, the sinners he saved and sanctified, the children he will not rest until he has made perfect, the only entities in the universe that he destines to become sharers in the divine nature. All the chemistry of life and all the providences of history are only means to that end. The universe is a great saint-making machine. All the quarks and quasars are but its gears and wheels. Its product is the Church. Or to use the better metaphor, as Saint Paul does, the universe is a gigantic mother. "The whole creation is in labor", and the Church is her baby.

The Church is universal because in her everything of value in the universe is preserved and purified and perfected. The world is humanized in us and we are divinized in Christ. The humanity that Christ divinizes is a humanity in which the universe has been humanized; and the universe no more loses its nature in us than we lose our human nature in Christ. Thus the Catholic Church, the universal Church, is more universal than the universe.

41
The Four Marks of the Church:
Apostolicity

Apostolic succession dates from the very first generation of the Church. The twelve apostles not only were called to be with Christ for the three years of his public ministry but also were appointed by him to teach and rule in his name: "He who hears you, hears me." The original apostles appointed successors before they died by laying on of hands (Holy Orders). No one but an apostle could appoint another apostle. The laying on of hands was not a mere symbol of an administrative decision, but a sacred rite, a sacrament. Although the seven sacraments were not clearly defined and enumerated until much later, in the Middle Ages, they existed from the beginning, for they were all instituted by Christ himself, and the Church continued to practice them in obedience to his command. If a Protestant were to ask you how you know this, the answer is: for the same reason we both know about Christ—his apostles have told us, his Church has taught us. (One of the ways the Church has taught us is by writing and canonizing the New Testament.)

The line of apostles and their successors, called bishops (*episkopoi*, overseers), was never broken. For nearly two thousand years there have been apostles, and the Church will be apostolic until the end of time. Whatever other changes may come, apostolicity cannot change; it is a defined mark of the true Church. The pope may wander the earth barefoot, begging. The Vatican may move to Moscow. Protestants may unite with Rome. Priests may be allowed to marry. But there will always be bishops.

Paradoxically, apostolicity is the only one of the four marks of the Church not mentioned in the Apostles' Creed. The creed of the apostles could take apostolicity for granted. But by Nicaea, in the fourth century, it had to be specified. The fact that apostolic succession is defined as early as Nicaea and practiced as early as the first century is a very strong historical case against Protestantism, which does not have or even claim apostolic succession. This fourth mark of the Church distinguishes the ark from the many little lifeboats even more sharply than the other three. It is a crucially important question to know just who speaks in Christ's name, who succeeds to his commission, "He who hears you, hears me." Many claim to speak in his name, but they contradict each other, which he never does. Nor is he divided.

Protestants can make out a case for their churches having unity (spiritual, not visible) and holiness and catholicity (again, spiritual, not visible); but they do not even claim apostolic succession as Catholics do. Methodists call their church leaders "bishops", but do not claim literal apostolic succession. Anglicans claim it and may have it; theologians are divided on this question. And Eastern Orthodox churches both claim it and have it, and Rome accepts this claim. All they lack is adherence to the papacy. Because they are so close, the Holy Father has quietly resolved that reunion with the Eastern Church must be a top priority. A friend in Rome tells me that he will consider his papacy a failure if this reunion is not accomplished by the year 2000.

All Christians are apostolic in a general and spiritual sense, for an *apostle* is one who is sent (*apo-stello*), and all Christians are sent by God. They are also called out (*ek-klesia,* church). But only the specific and visible Church has the specific and visible apostolic succession in addition to the general and spiritual one.

The fourth mark of the Church, let it be admitted at once, is not as grand, as soaring, as inspiring as the other three at first sight. Apostolicity is the Church's nuts and bolts, so to speak; how it works, how it is structured. This fourth mark is earthy, human, practical, yet it is in a sense the most important mark of all. For one thing, it is the most clear and concrete and distinctive mark of the true Church, the simplest sign for "shoppers". For another thing, it is our historical connection with Christ himself. Without the apostolic *magisterium* (teaching authority) of the Church, our continuity with Christ becomes uncertain, subjective, and merely individual. The terribly important question to which apostolic succession is the answer is: How are we made contemporaries with Christ? What link spans the nineteen centuries that separate us from our Lord? How do we know what Christ really taught? How do we know what to believe?

Most of what we believe about secular as well as sacred matters we believe because we trust the authority of our teachers, formal or informal (parents, friends, books, even newscasters). Why do we believe in Christ? He no longer walks the earth in visible human form. Why do we believe he rose from the dead? Why do we believe the good news? Why do we hope for heaven? Why do we not despair on our deathbeds? The question, you see, turns out to be rather important! And the answer is: because the Church has told us about Christ through her succession of apostolic teachers (bishops). The Church's essential task is to be an eyewitness to Christ and his Resurrection. The Church is the eleventh-hour news, and the apostles are the cameramen.

An immediate corollary is that if the Church does not seem trustworthy to people, they will not trust and believe the gospel. People decide what to believe more on the basis of personal trust than reason, by determining whom to believe rather than what or why to believe. Thus holiness is necessary for apostolicity to work. If the Church is not holy and honest and trustworthy, her message will not sell, for it will not sell itself: it is "foolishness to the world". People believe this "foolishness" for the same reason they believed Christ's "foolishness", because they believed him.

There must be apostolic succession because there must be historical continuity, and there must be historical continuity because our faith is not based on ideas or ideals, abstract possibilities, but on eyewitnessed historical events. The original apostles' message (kerygma) always centered on the decisive event of Christ's Resurrection. Look at any sermon in Acts. So central, in fact, was the Resurrection to Paul's preaching that the Athenians at first thought he was preaching two new gods. Jesus and *Anastasis* (Resurrection).

It is sometimes with a wonderful shock that we realize how

earthily concrete our faith is. Visitors to the Holy Land often say
that their pilgrimage was deeply satisfying to them despite the
hustle and the hucksters because "I walked today where Jesus
walked. This very pebble that I hold in my hand may well have
touched Jesus' toes. He was here, right here, really here!" Our
faith is not like an airplane soaring off into beautiful blue emptiness
but like an earthly hand reaching out to touch a flesh and blood
man: "That which was from the beginning, which we have heard,
which we have seen with our eyes, which we have looked upon and
touched with our hands". And this touchable man appointed
twelve touchable men to tell the world what they had touched and
seen. This appointing continues. That is the essence of apostolic
succession.

The electricity of the real events of gospel history continues to
course through the wire of the Church because of its apostolicity.
That is why the Church's message can be electrifying, as was Jesus'
message that day in the synagogue when, having read an Old
Testament prophecy about himself, he closed the book and said, to
the ears and eyes that turned to him with the stock-still
anticipation that surrounds decisive moments that are about to
change lives and even worlds, "Today is this Scripture fulfilled in
your hearing." Suddenly, a book leaps out from its pages and
becomes a person. Suddenly, we realize that the word of God is not
just a what but a who.

Apostolicity is one thing with two faces. One face looks back on
history and makes our faith concretely real. The other looks
forward to our task to tell the world. Christ's last command before
his ascension was: "Go out into all the world and preach the good
news." That is the Church's "great commission", her apostolic
task. She does that not only by words but also by deeds. Even
ethics, for the Christian, is not abstract, not mere imitation of an
ideal figure or obedience to a law; it is showing forth Christ, it is
the fruit of the vine of which we are branches. It is the result of
Christ's historical invasion of our world and our lives, and the fruit
of our encounter with him through his apostles. Even ethics is
apostolic.

Both of the faces of apostolicity, what we are "sent" from and what we are sent to, are the face of Christ. An apostle is one sent by Christ to proclaim Christ, to complete his work. The church is the continuation of the Incarnation. What would Christ do in India? Look at Mother Teresa. What would Christ do in the Middle Ages? Look at Saint Francis. How would Christ theologize? Look at Saint Thomas. What would Christ be as a woman? Look at Saint Catherine, Saint Teresa.

What the Church is sent apostolically to do is to make saints, i.e., to make humans completely human. This phrase, *completely human,* is often misused today to mean its exact opposite, to reduce the Church's supernatural task to a merely natural one. But the Church betrays her mission and her Lord if she lets psychologists and sociologists who do not know Christ as her source dictate her end. We are sent to be completely human *as Christ was,* to love *as he loved,* not to be nice, not to "have a nice day", not to pitch in a little bit to help build what everyone else is building. No, we are sent with a distinctive task: to build an eternal kingdom, a different building. We live in two worlds, and we rightly cooperate in building this one too, but the Church's raison d'être is not to be one more social service agency but to be the one and only ark of eternal salvation, to be Christ to the world. This *includes* social service and liberation of the poor. Christ healed some bodies, but as a sign of his essential mission to heal all souls. Christ loved and liberated the poor, but as a sign of his love and liberation of our spiritual poverty. His work in time was a sign of his work for eternity. Even Lazarus had to die again, but "he who believes in me will never die."

The apostolic Church is sent to be Christ to the world. This is not a comfortable thought. Eleven of the first twelve apostles were martyred. That is the norm. Christ himself says so: "If they hated me, they will hate you also." We are called "not to be understood, but to understand, not to be loved, but to love". When we love as Christ loved, we will find a cross, as he did. If the world prepares no crosses for us, then we are not loving enough, not loving as he loved, not fulfilling our apostolic vocation. "Woe unto you when

all men speak well of you, for so they spoke of the false prophets."
The Church is a prophet-making organization, not a profit-making organization.

Prophet, apostle, and church are three aspects of one thing. *Prophet* means mouthpiece; *Apostle* means sent. And *Church* means called out. Our bishops are apostolically sent to speak prophetically to us about what we are called out to, what we are sent to, and what we too are called to prophesy to the world about: our faith. And our faith is: to live with Christ in love, to die with Christ in hope, and to rise with Christ in glory.

42
The Nature of the Church

I was a Protestant (Dutch Reformed) for the first twenty-one years of my life. Becoming a Catholic was one of the two best things I ever did—that, and marrying the greatest woman in the world. Yet, I have never lost my respect and affection for the faith of my Protestant friends. This part of the book is designed to help Catholics understand the most serious Protestant objections to Catholicism and to answer them.

Such a task is necessary, not optional. We have entered upon a new age of ecumenism. Battle lines are being radically clarified and redrawn. It is finally becoming clear (almost everywhere except in Northern Ireland, it seems) to both "sides" that we have misidentified our real enemies; that an orthodox Catholic and an orthodox Protestant have far more in common than either has with a Modernist in his own church. For the questions that divide Protestants from Catholics, like whether popes are infallible, are obviously less important than the questions that divide orthodox Christians from Modernists, like whether Christ really rose from the dead. If popes are not infallible, then our certainty about dogma may be in trouble, but "if Christ is not risen from the dead, your faith is vain and you are still in your sins."

More misunderstanding and hostility have been overcome in the last thirty years than in the previous three hundred, in large part because of Vatican II and the last four popes, all of whom have placed dialogue with Protestants high on their agenda. In fact, John Paul II announced that one of the three priority items for his pontificate was reunion, first with Eastern Orthodoxy. (The other

two were cleaning up the church in America and preventing a
nuclear war.)

Healing the schism of 1054 with Eastern Orthodoxy involves
overcoming far fewer obstacles than healing the division of the
Protestant Reformation, of course. Yet we may not abandon even
that harder hope, for it is clearly our Lord's will that we be "one
flock, with one shepherd". Our divisions are not necessary, not in
the nature of things. They all began in history, and they can end in
history.

One thing we can do to help is to understand our Protestant
"separated brethren". This task involves understanding how they
understand us, or misunderstand us. That is our topic here.

The umbrella issue that separates us, under which the other
issues stand, is the nature and authority of the Church, for all the
things that Catholics believe in that Protestants don't (e.g., the
seven sacraments, transubstantiation, praying to saints, Mary's
Immaculate Conception and Assumption, papal infallibility),
Catholics believe in because of the teaching authority of the
Church.

What is the Church? As Pope John XXIII put it, she is our *mater
et magistra* (mother and teacher), but she is our mother before she is
our teacher. We are born into a spiritual family, not by physical
birth but by faith and baptism. This spiritual family has various
names. The three most important ones are (1) the Church, *ek-klesia,*
literally the called-out ones, those who are called by God out of the
world to be part of his new world, new kingdom; (2) the mystical
body of Christ, Christ's own hands and feet; (3) the people of God,
the family of God.

How do Protestants understand the Church? Because everything I have just said about the Church is clearly taught in
Scripture and because orthodox Protestants believe everything in
Scripture, they believe all these things. Where, then, is the
disagreement?

For one thing, it is a difference in emphasis. Protestants are more
individualistic than Catholics. They tend to think that individuals
are saved first and then join a sort of society of the saved. Catholics

think, rather, that being saved *is* to be put into the Church, as Noah's family was saved by being put into the ark. (The Fathers of the Church often used Noah's ark as a symbol for the Church, by the way. When you compare the variety of creatures in both vessels, the comparison seems apt).

But Protestants too have to admit that the Church is not just a human social club but of divine origin because Scripture clearly teaches this. Where, then, do they differ with us? Their criticism is usually that Catholics ignore the need to make an individual, personal decision for Christ, or choice to believe; that Catholics think they can be born into the faith, inheriting salvation from their parents.

But this is not a doctrinal disagreement. It is a practical, pastoral concern. Most Protestants are willing to admit that individualism is a mistake, and most Catholics are willing to admit that being born into faith is a misunderstanding. Where, then, is the doctrinal, dogmatic disagreement about the Church?

Perhaps it concerns the authority of the Church. Let's assume that both Protestants and Catholics understand the true nature of authority: that it means right, not might, in fact, "author's rights", and that in Christ it is wielded by love and service, not by lording it over others. Once Protestants understand this definition and understand that Catholics understand it too, the fear of the authority of the Church is largely dissipated.

Because Protestants accept Scripture and because Scripture clearly teaches the authority of the Church ("He who hears you, hears me," said Christ to his apostles), Protestants admit that the Church has authority. But some of them restrict this authority to the first generation of apostles, forgetting that these apostles themselves authorized successors, bishops. If you believe in the authority of Christ and Scripture, you must believe in the authority of the apostles because according to Scripture Christ authorized them; and if you believe in the authority of the apostles, you must believe in the authority of their successors because the apostles authorized them.

Some Protestants will accept this succession in principle but say that the Catholic Church has betrayed its authority by misusing it (this argument confuses the person with the office) or that the Church claims too much authority (but how do they know what is too much?) or that the Catholic Church is not the only church with divinely commissioned authority. This last idea is quite unscriptural, for Christ never spoke of "churches", only the "Church". He is not a polygamist.

Protestants reply that these references to the one Church apply only to the "Church invisible", not to the "Church visible". But although the Church *is* invisible (mystical), it is also visible, and visibly one, in Scripture. Saint Paul was utterly scandalized at the beginnings of denominationalism in Corinth.

Some Protestants think Catholics hold that the Catholic Church is divinely inspired, like Scripture, and has the authority to invent new dogmas. This is a misunderstanding. The Church does not claim divine inspiration to add to revelation, only providential protection to safeguard it from subtraction. Even the dogmas not explicitly found in Scripture, like papal infallibility and Mary's Assumption, are not new but old. The Church merely defined the doctrines that had been believed and lived from the beginning.

Papal infallibility certainly seems to be a specifically Catholic dogma that Protestants cannot accept. But they often misunderstand it. First, they often think of the pope as an autocrat rather than as the head of a body. (A head is part of a body, not floating above it in the air.) Second, they often think of the Church along political lines and want it to be a democracy. But Scripture thinks of the Church along organic lines, and no organic body is a democracy. Third, they often misunderstand infallibility as attaching to the Pope personally. In fact, it attaches to the office, not the person, and only when defining a doctrine of faith or morals.

Perhaps in my haste I have overlooked something. But it seems that all the differences between Protestants and Catholics on this fundamental, divisive issue, the nature and authority of the Church, come down to (1) differences in emphasis, (2) practical, pastoral criticisms, (3) scripturally answerable arguments, or (4) misunderstandings. If this is so, then there is no obstacle in principle to reunion without compromise of dogma.

This morning, while receiving the Eucharist, the thought struck me: "How different we are from Protestants: they have no eucharistic Real Presence!" But then a second thought struck me: "How like them we are even while receiving the Eucharist, for the whole point of the Eucharist is that very Christ whom they too love as their whole point and end and meaning." Our signs are richer, but the one signified is the same. He comes to us down different roads (e.g., the Mass), but the one who comes to fetch and fondle his sheep is one. And he wants to fetch them all home to be one.

43
The Authority of the Bible

Protestants come in two different sizes: traditional, or orthodox, Protestants, who follow the teachings of the Protestant "Church Fathers", Luther, Calvin, Zwingli, and Knox; and Modernist, or liberal, Protestants. The clearest litmus test to distinguish the two is their attitudes toward the Bible. Modernists reduce the Bible to a human book. This low view of Scripture they (naturally) call "higher criticism". They are the "demythologizers". Because they dis-myth the Bible, let us dismiss them for now and explore the dialogue between orthodox Protestants and Catholics.

We should explore four questions, not just one: how orthodox Protestants experience the Bible, how they think Catholics experience it, what they believe about the Bible, and what they think Catholics believe about it. It is important to begin with experience, with the spirituality of the Bible, for this is the key to understanding the beliefs about it.

How, then, do Protestants experience the Bible? First of all, it is sacred. It is God's word to man, not man's words about God. In it God spoke and continues to speak, not only to humanity at large but also to the individual.

Second, it is what Catholics would call sacramental: that is, it helps to effect what it signifies. It does not do this by its own power (*ex opere operato*) but only by the power of the reader's faith; so in Catholic terms it is not a sacrament but a sacramental.

Third, it is truth—not just truth as logical correctness, but truth as food, nourishment, solid substance. Protestants echo the words of Jeremiah (15:26): "Thy words were found and I ate them, and thy words became to me a joy and the delight of my heart."

Fourth, it is certain and sure, a rock in a marshmallow world, an absolute in a relativistic age, an anchor in a stormy sea. For

Protestants, Scripture rather than Peter is the rock on which the Church is founded.

Fifth and most important of all, it is a place where we meet Christ. Christ, the word of God, comes to us through Scripture, the word of God. It is no coincidence that the same title is given to the man and the book, for the whole point of this book is this man. (See Jn 5:39.)

All this is quite Catholic, you say. How then do Protestants think we experience the Bible? The classic Protestant suspicion is that Catholics fear the Bible; that the Church forbade the laity to read it for centuries because if that had been allowed, the people would have seen how unscriptural Catholic doctrines were.

This is simply historically untrue, of course, but it is still widely believed by Protestants. The belief is dying, though, in the face of the strong encouragement by Vatican II and all recent popes to Catholic laity to read Scripture regularly. This encouragement has done more to win Protestant respect than anything that has come from Rome since the Reformation.

Protestants fear that we have feared the Bible ever since Luther discovered its dynamite. The Reformation really began when Luther experienced the liberating power of the gospel in his Bible but not in his Church; when grace replaced guilt and faith replaced legalism in Luther's life upon the occasion of his reading the New Testament, especially Romans. That is where he found his keystone doctrine, justification by faith.

We shall explore this doctrine in the next essay. Suffice it to say now that Catholicism is not legalism, though this is often news to Protestants; that we read and believe the same Bible, including its clear teaching that we are saved by God's free grace, not by working our way into heaven. Protestants often simply cannot believe their ears when we tell them this, as the pope told the German Lutheran bishops.

Orthodox Protestant belief about Scripture can be summarized in three main points: Scripture is inspired, infallible, and sufficient. First, it is inspired. Each of its books has at least two authors, one human and one divine. The primary author is God, whose Spirit inspired (in-breathed) and guided each human author as an instrument to say exactly what God wanted to reveal to the world.

Second, it is therefore free from error, or infallible, for God does not goof. Fundamentalists insist on even scientific and historical infallibility, though it seems to other Protestants unnecessary nitpicking to make the divine authority of the Bible depend on whether the soldiers in Sennacherib's army were counted accurately.

It is the third belief, the sufficiency of Scripture alone (*sola scriptura*), that separates Protestants from Catholics. Protestants do not believe any doctrine they do not clearly find in Scripture (e.g., transubstantiation, Mary's Assumption, the seven sacraments).

What do they think we believe about Scripture? That it is second to the Church and that the Church teaches things quite independent of it. They think that we, like the Pharisees condemned by Jesus, confuse human tradition with divine revelation, "teaching as doctrines the precepts of men, . . . making the word of God void through your tradition" (Mk 7:7, 13). Their information is mistaken, but their motives are high. In fact, given this mistake, their criticism is admirable. But we must now look at the mistake.

We have seen (1) the Protestant experience of Scripture, (2) the Protestant idea of the Catholic experience of Scripture, (3) the Protestant belief about Scripture, and (4) the Protestant idea of the Catholic belief about Scripture. The first and third points are largely right and admirable; but the second and fourth are mistaken. Catholics can and do agree with all the positive Protestant points about Scripture but correct the negative ones. These are the *sola scriptura* and the misunderstandings of Catholic attitudes and doctrines. Let us now summarize what such a fraternal correction should be.

There are at least four things wrong with the *sola scriptura* doctrine. First, it separates Church and Scripture. But they are one. They are not two rival horses in the authority race, but one rider (the Church) on one horse (Scripture). The Church as writer, canonizer, and interpreter of Scripture is not another source of revelation but the author and guardian and teacher of the one source, Scripture. We are not taught by a teacher without a book or by a book without a teacher, but by one teacher, the Church, with one book, Scripture.

Second, *sola scriptura* is self-contradictory, for it says we should believe only Scripture, but Scripture never says this! If we believe only what Scripture teaches, we will not believe *sola scriptura,* for Scripture does not teach *sola scriptura.*

Third, *sola scriptura* violates the principle of causality: that an effect cannot be greater than its cause. The Church (the apostles) wrote Scripture, and the successors of the apostles, the bishops of the Church, decided on the canon, the list of books to be declared scriptural and infallible. If Scripture is infallible, then its cause, the Church, must also be infallible.

Fourth, there is the practical argument that private interpretation leads to denominationalism. Let five hundred people interpret the Bible without Church authority and there will soon be five hundred denominations. But denominationalism is an intolerable scandal by scriptural standards—see John 17:20–23 and 1 Corinthians 1:10–17.

Fifth, *sola scriptura* is unhistorical, for the first generation of Christians did not have the New Testament, only the Church, to teach them.

Finally, we must clear up two misunderstandings.

First, the Catholic Church does not claim to be divinely inspired to add any new doctrines, only divinely protected to preserve and interpret the old ones, the deposit of faith. It does not affirm additions but denies subtractions.

Second, all the doctrines of the Church derive from Scripture. Saint Thomas Aquinas identifies *sacra doctrina,* sacred teaching or divine revelation, with Scripture.

Even the Marian doctrines fit these two criteria. For example, Christians believed in the Assumption from the beginning, not from 1954, when it was defined. And the Marian doctrines are based on what Scripture tells us about Mary.

Our answer to Protestant objections must come on two fronts, for the objections come on two fronts: experiential as well as doctrinal. Protestant arguments spring from Protestant loves and fears—love of Scripture and fear that Catholics miss or mitigate that love. Only by loving and living Scripture can we prove to Protestants that we are brothers and therefore should not remain separated. Ecumenism and the road to reunion begin here, with Scripture as our common road map. How dare we know and love it any less than Protestants? It's our own Book!

44
Justification by Faith

The Protestant Reformation began when a Catholic monk re-discovered a Catholic doctrine in a Catholic book. The monk, of course, was Luther; the doctrine was justification by faith; and the book was the Bible. One of the tragic ironies of Christian history is that the deepest split in the history of the Church, and the one that has occasioned the most persecution, hatred, and bloody wars on both sides, from the Peasants' War of Luther's day through the Thirty Years' War, which claimed a larger percentage of the population of many parts of central Europe than any other war in history, including the two world wars, to the present-day agony in Northern Ireland—this split between Protestant and Catholic originated in a misunderstanding. And to this day many Catholics and many Protestants still do not realize that fact.

Luther's story is well known. Passionate, impetuous, demand-ing, sensitive, and pessimistic in temperament, Luther had never been able to find inner peace. He could not overcome his sense of guilt despite all his good works, prayers, penances, and alms. His confessor advised him to read Romans. No more historically momentous advice was ever given by a confessor. In Romans Luther discovered the simple bombshell truth that God had forgiven his sins freely, not because of Luther's works in Germany but because of Christ's work on Calvary. That discovery freed Luther's spirit and ignited a fire that swept over Europe. The watchword of the Reformation became Saint Paul's summary of the gospel: "The just [justified, saved] shall live [have eternal life] by faith [in Christ]" (Rom 1:17).

Where then do good works come in? In *Christian Liberty,* Luther explains that after the great liberation about faith—that we are saved by faith in Christ's work, not by our works—comes a great liberation about works: they need not be done slavishly, to buy our way into heaven, to pile up merits or Brownie points with God, but can be done freely and spontaneously and naturally, out of gratitude to God—not to get to heaven but because heaven has already gotten to us. Thus they can be done for the sake of our neighbor, not for our own sake, to purchase salvation. And this is winsome. No one wants to be loved as someone else's good deed for the day.

The origin of the Reformation is often said to be Luther's act of nailing ninety-five theses against the sale of indulgences to the door of the church in Wittenberg. This event is celebrated as Reformation Day (October 31, 1517). Luther's decision to go public was occasioned by the scandal of Tetzel, a Dominican monk who shamelessly peddled forgiveness of sins for a fee. He even had a singing commercial: "Sobald das Geld im Kasten klingt,/Die Seele aus dem Fegfeuer springt!" ("As soon as the money clinks in the casket, the soul springs free from the fires of purgatory!") The story was told of the thief who asked Tetzel whether he could buy forgiveness for all his future sins as well as his past sins. Tetzel said yes, but it would cost him a thousand gold pieces. The thief paid the money, took the indulgence, and then stole back the money from Tetzel!

But the scandal of selling indulgences was only the catalyst, not the cause, of the Reformation. The Church soon cleaned up its act and forbade the sale of indulgences at the Council of Trent, agreeing with Luther on this point. But one does not split the Church over a practice; one splits the Church over a doctrine, for the Church can change its practice but never its doctrine. To change a practice, one stays in the Church; to change a doctrine, one must start a new Church.

Luther eventually came to reject many Catholic doctrines that he thought he could not find in Scripture. But only one justified his bold words before the Diet of Worms, which condemned him: "Here I stand. I cannot do otherwise. God help me." The doctrine was justification by faith. The justification of Luther's faith, he thought, was the doctrine of justification by faith.

For everything is at stake here. The question is nothing less than how to get to heaven. Luther thought the Catholic Church was teaching not only heresy (heretics always call orthodoxy heresy, by the way) but another religion, another way of salvation, "another gospel" (Gal 1:6). That's about as serious a charge as you can imagine. We need to examine this charge very carefully to justify the surprising claim that the fundamental dispute between Protestants and Catholics was due to a misunderstanding.

It certainly doesn't look like a misunderstanding. It looks like a flat-out contradiction: the Catholic Church taught that we are saved by faith and good works, while Luther taught that we are saved by faith alone (*sola fide*). But appearances may be deceiving.

For one thing, even if the two sides did disagree about the relationship between faith and works, they both agreed (1) that faith is absolutely necessary for salvation and (2) that we are absolutely commanded by God to do good works. Both these two points are unmistakably clear in Scripture.

For another thing, the terms of the dispute are ambiguous or used in two different senses. When terms are ambiguous, the two sides may really disagree when they seem to agree because they agree only on the word, not the concept. Or the two sides may really agree when they seem to disagree because they agree on the concept but not the word. The latter holds true here.

When Luther taught that we are saved by faith alone, he meant by *salvation* only the initial step, justification, being put right with God. But when Trent said we are saved by good works as well as faith, they meant by *salvation* the whole process by which God brings us to our eternal destiny and that process includes repentance, faith, hope, and charity, the works of love.

The word *faith* was also used in two different senses. Luther used it in the broad sense of the person's acceptance of God's offer of salvation. It included repentance, faith, hope, and charity. This is the sense Saint Paul uses in Romans. But in 1 Corinthians 13, Paul uses it in a more specific sense, as just one of the three theological virtues, with hope and charity added to it. In this narrower sense faith alone is not sufficient for salvation, for hope and charity must be present also. That is the sense used by the old Baltimore

Catechism too: faith is "an act of the intellect, prompted by the will, by which we believe what has been revealed on the grounds of the authority of God, who revealed it".

This "faith", though prompted by the will, is an act of the intellect. Though necessary for salvation, it is not sufficient. Even the devils have this faith, as Saint James writes: "Do you believe that there is only one God? Good! The demons also believe—and tremble with fear" (James 2:19). That is why James says, "It is by his actions that a person is put right with God, and not by his faith alone" (James 2:24). Luther, however, called James' epistle "an epistle of straw". He did not understand James' point (applied to Abraham's faith): "Can't you see? His faith and his action worked together; his faith was made perfect through his actions" (James 2:22).

Faith is the root, the necessary beginning. Hope is the stem, the energy that makes the plant grow. Love is the fruit, the flower, the visible product, the bottom line. The plant of our new life in Christ is one; the life of God comes into us by faith, through us by hope, and out of us by the works of love. That is clearly the biblical view, and when Protestants and Catholics who know and believe the Bible discuss the issue sincerely, it is amazing how quickly and easily they come to understand and agree with each other on this, the fundamental divisive issue. Try it some time with your Protestant friend.

But many Catholics to this day have not learned the Catholic and biblical doctrine. They think we are saved by good intentions or being nice or sincere or trying a little harder or doing a sufficient number of good deeds. Over the past twenty-five years I have asked hundreds of Catholic college students the question: If you should die tonight and God asks you why he should let you into heaven, what would you answer? The vast majority of them simply do not know the right answer to this, the most important of all questions, the very essence of Christianity. They usually do not even mention Jesus!

Until we Catholics know the foundation, Protestants are not going to listen to us when we try to teach them about the upper stories of the building. Perhaps God allows the Protestant/ Catholic division to persist not only because Protestants have abandoned many precious truths taught by the Church but also because many Catholics have never been taught the most precious truth of all, that salvation is a free gift of grace, accepted by faith. I remember vividly the thrill of discovery when, as a young Protestant at Calvin College, I read Saint Thomas Aquinas and the Council of Trent on justification. I did not find what I had been told I would find, "another gospel" of do-it-yourself salvation by works, but a clear and forceful statement that we can do nothing without God's grace, and that this grace, accepted by faith, is what saves us.

The split of the Protestant Reformation began when a Catholic discovered a Catholic doctrine in a Catholic book. It can end only when both Protestants and Catholics do the same thing today and understand what they are doing: discovering a Catholic doctrine in a Catholic book.

45
The Sacraments

Adult conversion to Catholicism involves more than adding a few new beliefs. It means a whole new world and life view. No ingredient in that new perspective was more of a shock to my old Protestant sensibilities when I became a Catholic than the idea that the God-man is really present in, and not just symbolized by, what appears to be a wafer of bread and a cup of wine. It seemed scandalous!

It has ceased to scandalize me, though it has not ceased to amaze me, that Almighty God suffers me to touch him, move him and eat him! Imagine! When I move my hand to my mouth with the Host, I move God through space. When I put him here, he is here. When I put him there, he is there. The Prime Mover lets me move him where I will. It is as amazing as the Incarnation itself, for it is the Incarnation, the continuation of the Incarnation.

I think I understand how the typical Protestant feels about sacramentalism not only because I was a Protestant but because it is a natural and universal feeling. The Catholic doctrine of the sacraments is shocking to everyone. It should be a shock to Catholics too. But familiarity breeds dullness.

To Protestants, sacraments must be one of two things: either mere symbols, reminders, like words; or else real magic. And the Catholic definition of a sacrament—a visible sign instituted by Christ to give grace, a sign that really effects what it symbolizes— sounds like magic. Catholic doctrine teaches that the sacraments work *ex opere operato,* i.e., objectively, though not impersonally and automatically like machines. They are gifts that come from without but must be freely received.

Protestants are usually much more comfortable with a merely symbolic view of sacraments, for their faith is primarily verbal, not sacramental. After all, it is the Bible that looms so large in the center of their horizon. They believe in creation and Incarnation and Resurrection only because they are in the Bible. The material events are surrounded by the holy words. The Catholic sensibility is the inside-out version of this: the words are surrounded by the holy facts. To the Catholic sensibility it is not primarily words but matter that is holy because God created it, incarnated himself in it, raised it from death, and took it to heaven with him in his ascension.

Orthodox Protestants believe these scriptural dogmas, of course, just as surely as Catholics do. But they do not, I think, feel the crude, even vulgar facticity of them as strongly. That's why they do not merely disagree with but are profoundly shocked by the real presence and transubstantiation. Luther, by the way, taught the real presence and something much closer to transubstantiation than most Protestants believe, namely consubstantiation, the belief that Christ's body and blood are really present in the Eucharist, but so are the bread and wine. Catholics believe the elements are changed; Lutherans believe they are added to.

Most Protestants believe the Eucharist only symbolizes Christ, though some, following Calvin, add that it is an occasion for special grace, a sign *and a seal.* But though I was a Calvinist for twenty one years, I do not remember any emphasis on that notion. Much more often, I heard the contrast between the Protestant "spiritual" interpretation and the Catholic "material", "magical" one.

The basic objection Protestants have to sacramentalism is this: How can divine grace depend on matter, something passive and unfree? Isn't it unfair for God's grace to depend on anything other than his will and mine? I felt that objection strongly until I realized that the sheer fact that I have a body—this body, with this heredity, which came to me and still comes to me without my choice— is also "unfair". One gets a healthy body, another does not. As one philosopher said, "Life isn't fair."

It's the very nature of the material world we live in, the very fact of a material world at all, that is so "unfair" that it moved Ivan Karamazov to rebellion against God in that profoundest and most

Christian novel, Dostoevsky's *The Brothers Karamazov*. As he explains to his believing brother Alyosha, "It's not God that I can't accept, it's this world of his"—a world in which bad things happen to good people and good things happen to bad people. But it might be better than fair rather than less, gift rather than payment, grace rather than justice, "fair" as "beautiful" rather than "fair" as "rational"—like a sacrament.

In fact, the world is a sacrament. We receive God through every material reality (though not in the same special way as in the sacraments proper). The answer to the Protestant objection to the unfairness of the sacraments is that only a world of pure spirit would be perfectly fair. Only angels get exactly what they deserve individually.

Praise God, we get infinitely more than we deserve! The sacraments remind us that the whole world is a sacrament, a sacred thing, a gift; and the sacramental character of the world reminds us of the central sacrament, the Incarnation, continued among us in the seven sacraments of the Church, especially in the Eucharist. The sacramental view of the world and the Catholic doctrine of the sacraments illuminate each other like large and small mirrors.

Both the sacrament of the world and the sacrament of Incarnation/Eucharist also remind us that we too are sacramental, matter made holy by spirit. Our bodies are not corpses moved by ghosts, or cars steered by angels, but temples of the Holy Spirit. In our bodies, especially our faces, matter is transmuted into meaning. The eyes are the windows of the soul.

Protestants sometimes object to the sacraments by asking whether a baby's eternal destiny is altered if the water of baptism does not quite reach his forehead before the church building falls on him and kills him, or whether a penitent who gets run over and killed by a truck while crossing the street on his way to a sacramental confession will suffer hell or a longer purgatory only because the truck happened to hit him before rather than after confession. The answer to such a question is: not necessarily. We do not know God's plan unless he reveals it to us, and he *has* revealed the sacraments. But not only the sacraments. The early

Church called the death of martyrs who had no opportunity for
baptism "the baptism of blood", and the intention (explicit or even
implicit) to be baptized "the baptism of desire" (thus allowing
good, God-seeking pagans into heaven). This Catholic doctrine of
"back-door grace" seems shifty verbal trickery to many
Protestants, but it is necessary to preserve two undeniable truths:
first, that we are commanded to receive the sacraments and told
that "unless you eat my body and drink my blood, you have no life
in you" and, second, that God is just and merciful and does not
deny grace to any who seek it.

Perhaps we Catholics are like the laborers who worked only an
hour, in our Lord's parable (Mt 20:1–16), and those without the
sacraments like those who worked all day. It seems unfair that both
groups got the same wages. So it seems unfair that we are given all
this extra sacramental help, easier grace, so to speak. But the Lord
of the vineyard replied to this objection: "Is it not lawful for me to
do what I wish with my own?" This reply scandalizes our sense of
political justice. But it fits the nature of the world; and it is the
world of nature, God's creation, rather than politics, man's
creation, that declares the glory of God. The sacraments declare
the same scandalous generosity.

We don't deserve to be born or to be born again or to be
baptized. We don't deserve God's sun or God's Son. We don't
deserve delicious bread and wine or the Body and Blood of Christ.
But we are given all this, and more. As Christopher Derrick put it,
in a poem entitled "The Resurrection of the Body":

> He's a terror that one:
> Turns water into wine,
> Wine into blood—
> I wonder what He turns blood into?

Catholics often have a more-than-intellectual faith in the
sacraments that Protestants do not understand. Thus they don't see
why Catholics who come to disagree with essential teachings of
the Church don't just leave. The answer is symbolized by the
sanctuary lamp. They do not leave the Church because they know

that the sacramental fire burns there on the ecclesiastical hearth. Even if they do not see by its light, they want to be warmed by its fire. The real presence of Christ in the Eucharist is a magnet drawing lost sheep home and keeping would-be strays from the deathly snows outside. The Church's biggest drawing card is not what she teaches, crucial as that is, but who is there. "He is here! Therefore I must be here."

46
Toward Reuniting the Church

Born into a strong evangelical Protestant family (Dutch Reformed), I became a Roman Catholic while studying philosophy at Yale. I did so for the only valid and honest reason anyone ever should become a Catholic or a Protestant or a Christian or an atheist: because I believe it is true.

But I also believe everything affirmed and emphasized by evangelical Protestantism is true. And since truth cannot be opposed to truth, I also believe reunion without compromise is possible. This essay investigates that reunion. First, I shall explore the major obstacles to unity; second, the way to unity, the way to overcome these obstacles; finally, the nature of unity: What would a reunified church look like?

I see six major obstacles to unity. Two are general philosophical and theological problems, two are specific doctrinal problems, and two are radical problems out of which all the other problems grow.

The first and most general problem dividing Catholics and Protestants seems to me to be the problem of nature and grace. I became a Catholic partly because I found a greater appreciation for the natural order, for human reason and human tradition, and for the sacramental power of matter in Catholicism than in the Calvinism I knew. Other converts to Catholicism have often come from the opposite branch of Protestantism, from liberalism or Modernism, and were attracted by the supernaturalism of the Catholic Church. It seems pretty clear that the solution to the problem of nature and grace is a strong affirmation of both, and that this affirmation would unite Protestants with each other as well as with Catholics.

A second, more difficult problem may be called the problem of the objective versus the subjective in religion. Protestants often see Catholics as superstitious believers in a magical religion of automatic, objective institutional and sacramental efficacy, while Catholics often see Protestants as subjectivists, individualists, sentimentalists, or humanists. The issue surfaces in the form of the institutional church, a visible and objective thing: How important is it? Is it necessary to salvation?

Any church, in fact any publicly visible, externally observable religion, has three manifestations: its theological beliefs, its ethical values, and its liturgical worship: creed, code, and cult; words, works, and worship. These fulfill the three parts of the human soul: thought, action, and feelings; mind, will, and sensibilities; the intellectual, the moral, and the aesthetic. Catholics emphasize these three aspects of religion, while Protestants deemphasize them relative to the subjective, personal core of religion, the individual's relationship with God face to face, heart to heart, center to center, unmediated by church, creed, code, or cult, mediated only by Christ.

The solution here, too, is a both/and solution. Each side sees something. Since man is both invisible and visible, religion must be both: both the internal and the external, the nut and its shell, the heart and the flesh, the meat and the sandwich, the picture and the frame, love and the expression of love.

But could this general solution apply to specific doctrinal controversies such as the real presence of Christ in the Eucharist and objectively efficacious sacraments, which work *ex opere operato*? I think so. Objectively efficacious sacraments do not exclude individual subjective freedom and responsibility, as magic does, any more than an objectively efficacious God excludes human freedom and responsibility. God works through man, not through magic. Yet it is *God* who works, and therefore with certain and objective efficacy.

These first two problems are merely cases of different emphases. The relatively simple solution was a both/and rather than an either/or. Our next two problems are more specific issues, which seem logically to demand an either/or answer and therefore the exclusion of either the Protestant or the Catholic answer as false.

The third problem is the problem of the source of authority. All the distinctively Catholic (as opposed to Protestant) teachings of the Catholic Church follow from the teaching authority of the Church. Most Catholics believe in such things as Purgatory, the Immaculate Conception, and the seven sacraments not because they have thought through each issue separately and have come to the Catholic position by theological reasoning, but because the Church teaches them and they accept the Church's authority—just as orthodox Protestants accept all the teachings of Christ simply because they accept his authority as teacher. But Catholics seem to believe in *two* sources of authority, or rather two channels of authority through which Christ reveals his mind and will to successive generations: the Bible and the Church; while Protestants believe only one as unerringly authoritative: *sola scriptura.* Are these two horses in the authority race or only one? It cannot be both. How can this disjunction be overcome?

There is only one horse, and it is the Bible. But it needs a rider, and that is the Church. From the Catholic side, Thomas Aquinas— certainly no maverick among Catholics—teaches that the Church is authoritative *as interpreter of Scripture,* that all the teachings of the Church must be based on Scripture. And more and more people from the Protestant side are coming to believe that it is the unified Christian community that gives the Holy Spirit's authoritative understanding of Scripture. The letter kills, the Spirit gives life; and the Spirit of the body of Christ lives *in* the body, the Church.

The fourth issue is the most crucial of all. It is the issue that sparked the Reformation, and it is the issue that must spark reunion too. It is, of course, the issue of faith, of faith and works, of justification by faith.

This is the root issue because the essence of the gospel is at stake here. *How do I get right with God?* This was the issue of the first-century church at Galatia, a church Protestants see as making the same essential mistake as the Catholics—preaching the gospel of good works. Protestants dare not compromise on this issue or they would be turning to what Paul calls "another gospel". Thus his harsh words to the Galatians, the only church for which he has not one word of praise:

> I am astonished that you are so quickly deserting him who called you in the grace of Christ and turning to a different gospel—not that there is another gospel, but there are some who trouble you and want to pervert the gospel of Christ. But even if we, or an angel from heaven, should preach to you a gospel contrary to that which we preached to you, let him be accursed.

How do I resolve the Reformation? Is it faith alone that justifies, or is it faith and good works? Very simple. No tricks. On this issue I believe Luther was simply right; and this issue is absolutely crucial. As a Catholic I feel guilt for the tragedy of Christian disunity because the church in the fifteenth and sixteenth centuries was failing to preach the gospel. Whatever theological mistakes Luther made, whatever indispensable truths about the Church he denied, here is an indispensable truth he affirmed—indispensable to union between all sinners and God and to union between God's separated Catholic and Protestant children.

Much of the Catholic Church has not yet caught up with Luther; and, for that matter, much of Protestantism has regressed from him. The churches are often found preaching one of two "other gospels": the gospel of old-fashioned legalism or the gospel of new-fangled humanism. The first means making points with God and earning your way into heaven, the second means being nice to everybody so that God will be nice to you. The churches, Protestant and Catholic, may also preach the true Christian gospel, but not often enough and not clearly enough and often watered down and mixed with one of these two other gospels. And the trouble with "other gospels" is simply that they are not true: they don't *work,* they don't unite man with God, they don't justify.

No failing could be more serious; but on the Catholic side, as distinct from the liberal Protestant side, it is a failing in practice, not doctrine. When this happens, the Catholic Church fails to preach *its own gospel.* It is sitting on a dynamite keg and watering the fuse; it is keeping a million dollar bank account and drawing out only pennies. Catholicism as well as Protestantism affirms the utterly free, gratuitous gift of forgiving grace in Christ, free for the taking, which taking is faith. Good works can be only the fruit of faith, flowing freely as a response to the new life within, not laboriously, to buy into heaven.

But there are two important verbal misunderstandings in the Reformation controversy over faith and works. First, when the Council of Trent affirmed, contrary to Luther, that good works contribute to salvation, it meant by *salvation* not just getting to heaven but the whole process of being transformed and becoming incorporated into the life of God. In other words, *salvation* meant not just justification but sanctification as well; and it was quite correct to say that both faith and works contribute to sanctification, thus to salvation.

Second, Catholic and Protestant theologians mean different things by the word *faith.* Protestants usually follow biblical usage: *faith* means saving faith, the heart or will accepting Christ. Catholics usually follow a more technical philosophical and theological usage: *faith* means the act of the mind, prompted by the will, which accepts Christ's teachings as true. In Protestant language, *faith* means heart faith, or whole-person faith; in Catholic language, *faith* means mind faith. Thus, Catholic theologians are right to deny justification by faith alone in that sense (which of course was not Luther's sense). For "the devils also believe, and tremble." In this narrower sense faith can exist without the works of love; as James writes, "Faith without works is dead." In the larger sense, faith cannot exist without works, for it *includes* works as a plant includes its own blossoms.

The last two problems are the deepest of all. The deepest obstacle to Christian unity is not theological but moral: the deepest obstacle is *sin.* The root of disunity is sin; the root of separation among men is separation from God, *Sünde.* The reason for the Reformation was sin. The root of theological errors, *whoever* made them, was being out of alignment with God. We know his mind and his doctrine clearly only if our will is pure: "Blessed are the pure of heart, for they shall see God." Jesus solves the hermeneutical problem, the problem of interpreting his words and his authority correctly, in one amazingly simple stroke when he says: "If any man's will is to do the will of my Father, he will know my teaching" (Jn 7:17). We will have church unity only when we have God unity. We will be one with each other only when we are one with God. And we will be one in mind with God, and thus with each other, only when we are one in heart and will with God. The opposite of that oneness is sin.

The last obstacle to unity is paradoxical: it is the illusion that unity is wholly absent. We already have unity, if we would only see it. The illusion is that unity must be visible in order to be true unity. Unity must be visible to be *complete,* for we are visible as well as invisible creatures, bodies as well as souls. But *incomplete* unity is still *real* unity, as a soul without a body is an *incomplete* human but is still a *really* human soul.

We already have Christian unity, unity in Christ, in his mystical body. The Church is always one (and is therefore one now) because the oneness of the Church is an inseparable property of her very essence as a body: a body must be one to be a body. If the gates of hell can never prevail against the Church's essence, they cannot prevail against her unity either. "We *are* one in the Spirit, we *are* one in the Lord." This Spirit is real, objective, metaphysical, and factual; it is not just a thought, belief, aspiration, or feeling, like the spirit of Socrates or the spirit of democracy. *Spiritual* does not mean subjective.

But *spiritual* does not mean visible either, and we do lack visible unity. Visible unity is not unimportant. First, it is the natural, fitting, and proper expression of invisible, spiritual unity. Second, it is a testimony to the world, which is impressed by appearances: "They'll know we are Christians by our love." Christians are not very visible in Northern Ireland. Love creates unity. Unity between individuals is certainly more important than unity between Christian institutions; but the latter is a sign and testimony to the former. Our signs are obscure today; that's one reason our gospel is not selling as well as it could.

Can unity be achieved? If and only if there is a way, a road. A dream is not enough. There must be a Jacob's ladder to connect the heavenly dream to earth. There is a ladder, and the angels continually ascend and descend on it. It is not a method or a teaching or a technique. It is a way, not a method; a truth, not a teaching; a life, not a technique. It is, of course, the one who said: "I *am* the Way, the Truth, and the Life," and then continued: "No man comes to the Father but by me." Unity is with the Father. The only way to unity is the Son.

The way *from* unity to disunity was through the loss of Christ as the center. Therefore the only way back is through Christ as the center, through letting Christ rule our churches completely. This is a guaranteed recipe for success. For we know his will is unity (reread Jn 17:20–26). Therefore if we only let him do his will in us, we *will* have unity.

The only road to unity is total openness to his will, even if it means admitting that we were wrong. We don't know in advance what letting Christ have his will completely in us will lead to, except that it will lead to truth. "Follow me." Where? "Come and see." Might it lead to an admission that we Catholics were wrong? That you Protestants were wrong? It might. I firmly believe all that the Catholic Church teaches; but if I should meet God face to face and find that I was wrong in this, I would still be his child.

Catholicism and Protestantism do not essentially define our identity, as Christ does. If I should die and find out that Christ is not my Savior, I could not be me, I could not exist in such a world. Christ is essential to my very self: "For me to live is Christ." The Church is like my family: very close to me, loyal to the death—but not my essence. Saint Paul did not say: "For me to live is Catholicism." He did not say: "I live, nevertheless not I but Protestantism lives in me." The only absolute certainty we have is Christ.

The unity we already have in Christ includes doctrinal unity, for if we accept the teacher we also accept all his teachings, at least through Scripture. None of the Catholic Church's interpretations of or additions to Scripture is as important as the scriptural agreements between Protestants and Catholics. The agreements between orthodox Protestants and orthodox Catholics are far more important than the agreements between orthodox Catholics and liberal, or Modernist, or demythologized Catholics, and far more important than the agreements between orthodox Protestants and liberal Protestants.

The following questions do not divide Protestants and Catholics—and they are the most important questions of all—but they do divide the orthodox from the Modernist in both churches:

1. Is God a transcendent, supernatural, personal, eternal, omnipotent, omniscient, providential, loving, just Creator? Or is God an immanent cosmic force evolving in nature and man?

2. Do miracles really happen? Or has science refuted them? A transcendent God can perform miracles; a merely immanent, naturalistic God cannot. The three great miracles essential to orthodox Christianity are the Incarnation, the Resurrection and the new birth.

3. Is there a heaven? Or is heaven just all the good on earth?

4. Does God really love me? Or is that just a helpful sentiment?

5. Does God forgive my sins through Christ? Or is sin an outdated concept? In other words, is Christ a mere human example or a Savior from sin?

6. Is Christ divine, eternal, from the beginning? Or is he only divine "as all men are divine"?

7. Did he physically rise from the dead? Or is the Resurrection only a myth, a beautiful symbol?

8. Must we be born again from above to be saved, to have God as our Father? Or is everyone saved automatically? Does everyone have God as Father simply by being born as a human being, or by being reasonably nice during life?

9. Is Scripture God's word to us? Or is it human words about God? Does it have divine or human authority behind it? And can an

ordinary Christian understand its true meaning without reading German theologians?

10. Most important of all, can I really meet God in Christ? If I ask him to be my Lord, the Lord of my life, will he really do it? Or is this just a "religious experience"? This question is really one with the question: Did Christ really rise from the dead? That is, is he alive now? Can I say: "You ask me how I know he lives? He lives within my heart!"?

Affirmative answers to these questions constitute the most important kind of unity already: not unity of thought but unity of being, the new being, being "in Christ".

The evangelical resurgence, the charismatic movement, and the born-again phenomenon are all indications that God is working in our time at precisely this center, this place of unity. No human can create new being, and therefore no human can create unity, for unity follows being. But although with man it is impossible, with God all things are possible. God can and does create new being in us, and therefore God can create new unity among us—*and he's doing it right now!* We are witnessing with our own eyes in this generation the definitive solution to the problem of division in the Church. God is solving the problem in exactly the same way he solves all our problems. He has one answer to all our needs, and the answer is a Person.

It's working. You can see it, surely, at charismatic prayer meetings: without compromise, indifference, or watering down their faith, Protestants and Catholics are experiencing the kind of Christian unity New Testament Christians experienced: unity in Christ. And the world is noticing: "See how they love one another!"

My last question has to do with the nature of this unity. The most important answer to that question has just been given: Christian unity is Christ. But I should like to add three lesser points about the nature of Christian unity. First, Christian unity includes plurality. The doctrine of the Trinity gives Christianity a unique concept of unity. Nothing is more *one* than God; yet God includes plurality, manyness, differences—without compromising his oneness. In fact, he is *more* one by being also many than if he were only one; for the oneness of love among the Persons of the Trinity is a greater oneness than that of sheer identity. As C. S. Lewis puts it in *The Problem of Pain:*

> Even within the Holy One himself, it is not sufficient that the word should be God, it must also be *with* God. The Father eternally begets the Son, and the Holy Ghost proceeds: deity introduces distinction within itself so that the union of reciprocal loves may transcend mere arithmetical unity or self-identity.

Christian unity, like divine unity, is the unity among lovers, not monolithic indistinguishability. When we unite, we shall remain ourselves, and even increase our distinctive selves. The three most distinctive characters in all reality are the Father, the Son, and Holy Spirit. The most distinctive human persons are the saints. God is both one and many; therefore his people are both one and many.

Second, there are three degrees or levels of unity. At the deepest level there is God himself: there is only one of him! Next to this level is that of human experience of God's presence. Since God's unity includes infinitely diverse facets, this level of experience is infinitely diverse; and this is a glory, not a scandal, just as the experience of any human being in many different facets is a glory. The third level is theological reflection about the second level and about the first as experienced in the second. On the third level we find a diversity that is not a glory but a scandal: disagreements about God. How do we solve them? By continually plunging into the deeper levels. For the closer we get to the center, the closer we get to each other. The nearer we are to God, the more our disagreements will dissolve.

Third, what will the Protestant and Catholic roles be in such a unified church? What will Catholics have to stomach from Protestantism and what will Protestants have to stomach from Catholicism?

Catholics will have to stomach the Lutheran Reformation, will have to admit that the Church needs reformation, evangelization.

The Church will have to repent. It will have to admit in practice, not just in theory, Calvin's central insight: the absolute sovereignty of God. Many Protestant churches will also have to repent and confess in this way, like the Lutheran Church of Kierkegaard's Denmark. I believe his *Attack upon Christendom* is the prophetic voice of Christ to the churches in the modern world:

> What do I want? Quite simply: I want honesty. I am not, as well-intentioned people represent, for a Christian severity as opposed to a Christian leniency. By no means, I am neither leniency nor severity. I am—a human honesty. The leniency that is the common Christianity in the land I want to place alongside of the New Testament in order to see how these two are related to one another. Then, if it appears, if I or any other can prove that it can be maintained face to face with the New Testament, then with the greatest joy I will agree to it. But one thing I will not do, not for anything in the world. I will not by suppression or by performing tricks try to produce the impression that the ordinary Christianity in the land and the Christianity of the New Testament are alike.

The Church must repent.

And what will Protestants have to repent of? Doctrinally, whatever they left behind in the Reformation that was not a perversion—like selling indulgences or ecclesiastical politicking—but part of the apostolic tradition. I believe this includes the teaching authority of the Church, the inerrancy of her creeds, sacramentalism, apostolic succession, prayers to saints, Purgatory, transubstantiation, and even a definite papal primacy—all suitably defined, suitable not first of all to Catholics but to the Spirit of Christ.

But that is too much for both sides to stomach yet. That is as it should be: too much, not too little. The objection to faith must be: that's too much to believe, that's a myth, a fairy tale, that's too good to be true. That is the natural objection to justification by faith: that it is too good to be true. And it is the natural objection to Catholic claims: too much. But a unified Church cannot be achieved by watering down, by lessening, by a political compromise of God's word and God's will for us. A unified

Christian Church would be fully Catholic and fully Reformed, fully authoritative and fully free, fully sacramental and fully evangelical, fully institutional and fully charismatic and missionary and eschatological: the Evangelical Catholic Church, the one holy, catholic, apostolic body of our common Lord Jesus Christ. His be the glory now and forever.

Conclusion

"And with all this, what have I said, my God and my Life and my sacred Delight? What can anyone say when he speaks of thee? Yet woe to them that speak not of thee at all" (Saint Augustine, *Confessions*).

If I am honest, I must end this book of "God-talk" by admitting the radical inadequacy of all words about God and at the same time the necessity of this radically inadequate thing, just as Augustine did. After all, even Scripture does it. Christianity, unlike Zen, is not an esoteric, nonverbal mysticism, but "in the beginning was the Word." Our words aspire to be the prismatic, broken, colored refractions of *the* Word.

One very modest but very practical compensation for this inadequacy is the traditional device that I have used throughout the book of outlining, numbering, dividing the one into the many: the three aspects of religion (creed, code, and cult), the four last things, the three theological virtues, the four marks of the Church, et cetera. The Church gives us these traditional divisions for the same reason Mommy cuts up baby's food. In fact, it is Mommy cutting up baby's food.

But I must not leave the impression that Christianity is served to us like a bag of separate jellybeans. Repeatedly throughout this book I have tried to return our focus to the single point of it all, "the one thing necessary", what everything else in our religion and, indeed, everything in the universe is there for—everything from the Bible to doorknobs on cathedrals and from the Big Bang to the human brain. The Alpha is also the Omega; the Creator is also the End of all things, and *our* end is to be married spiritually to *the* End.

All words and all metaphors limp, including this one, though it is a favorite of saints, mystics, and Scripture itself. For a human husband is not his wife's lord. He is her head, but not her God, and

she is his heart. He dare not play God. But God dare play God. Our
ultimate destiny is not just to love God in any old way, not just to
marry God as we would marry a creature, but to adore and
worship. "God is not an uncle. God is an earthquake", says Rabbi
Abraham Heschel. "I fell down at his feet as one dead"—that is the
language of one who has seen God. It is not the language of
modern-day Eliphazes, Bildads, and Zophars, the "experts" in
theology and religion.

The last impression I ever want to leave in this book is that it is
the "wisdom" of an "expert". There are no experts on God except
Jesus Christ. And in every field, but much more here, the test of
real wisdom is the realization that we are not wise. The wisdom of
Socrates is indispensable at the beginning and also at the end.
Unless it surrounds our "God-talk" as a bird surrounds her egg,
our talk will be stillborn, dead words, chattering and nattering,
"expert opinions". The poem I have chosen from C. S. Lewis to
end this book by making that point merits as much meditation as
anything else in the book. I hope you can pray "The Apologist's
Evening Prayer" with your heart, as he did.

> From all my lame defeats, and oh! much more,
> From all the victories that I seemed to score;
> From cleverness shot forth on Thy behalf,
> At which, while angels weep, the audience laugh;
> From all my proofs of Thy divinity,
> Thou, Who wouldst give no sign, deliver me.
>
> Thoughts are but coins. Let me not trust, instead
> Of Thee, their thin-worn image of Thy head.
> From all my thoughts, even from thoughts of Thee,
> O Thou fair Silence, fall, and set me free.
> Lord of the narrow gate and needle's eye,
> Take from me all my trumpery, lest I die.